Exploring Twentieth-Century Vocal Music

Exploring Twentieth-Century Vocal Music

A Practical Guide to Innovations in Performance and Repertoire

SHARON MABRY

3 1336 06585 9259

OXFORD

UNIVERSITY PRESS

2002

OXFORD
UNIVERSITY PRESS

Oxford   New York
Auckland   Bangkok   Buenos Aires   Cape Town   Chennai
Dar es Salaam   Delhi   Hong Kong   Istanbul   Karachi   Kolkata
Kuala Lumpur   Madrid   Melbourne   Mexico City   Mumbai   Nairobi
São Paulo   Shanghai   Singapore   Taipei   Tokyo   Toronto

and an associated company in Berlin

Published by Oxford University Press, Inc.
198 Madison Avenue, New York, New York 10016

www.oup.com

Oxford is a registered trademark of Oxford University Press

Library of Congress Cataloging-in-Publication Data

Mabry, Sharon.
Exploring twentieth-century vocal music : a practical guide to innovations in
performance and repertoire / Sharon Mabry.
p.   cm.
Includes bibliographical references (p.) and index.
ISBN 0-19-514198-9
1. Singing—Instruction and study.   2. Vocal music—20th century—Instruction and study.
3. Vocal music—20th century—Bibliography.   I. Title: Exploring 20th-century vocal
music.   II. Title.

MT820 .M129   2002
782'.009'04—dc21   2001052354

1   3   5   7   9   8   6   4   2

Printed in the United States of America
on acid-free paper

AUTHOR'S PERSPECTIVE

My undergraduate days as a voice student were steeped in repertoire from standard, traditional vocal literature. However, I was fascinated with new music and would often search the music library for anything that looked remotely *modern*. I delighted in perusing the unique scores and trying out all of the unusual notations and vocal directions found in them. Occasionally, I would bring the new works to the attention of my voice teacher. She had a marvelous voice rooted in the traditional repertoire of both the concert and opera worlds and was not known for singing contemporary, experimental music. So it was not surprising to find that she was less than enthusiastic about the pieces I wanted to study. Her advice was to stick with tried-and-true repertoire and forget about this "bizarre" music. I stopped taking the "strange" pieces to voice lessons, but they became even more interesting because they were forbidden. I continued to sing a wide variety of traditional repertoire during my studies. But over time, I discovered that when I sang certain pieces, my voice became freer, my mind more imaginative, my interpretation more natural, and my vocal self-confidence more bold. At some point, I realized that most of the pieces that brought out those positive effects were pieces written since 1900. They were not always in English and they did not always contain experimental vocal techniques, but they contained a spontaneity that eluded me in much of the traditional repertoire I had been singing. So my interest grew.

It is almost universally accepted that there has been a wealth of fine vocal repertoire written since 1900 in several languages, especially in English. Much of that music is traditional in its use of the voice, though the harmonies may be unlike Schubert and the text settings quite unlike Debussy. There is also a considerable body of repertoire, mostly written since 1950, that uses what are called "extended vocal techniques." These pieces present new possibilities for vocal sounds and colorations, while generally using the voice in a traditional, functional manner. Some of these experimental qualities and articulations could be considered *vocal effects*.

Twentieth-century composers have asked the singer to produce a plethora of vocal sounds. A few of these, known as "extended techniques," are vocal muting, nontextual sonic vocabularies built on IPA symbols, *sprechstimme*, cluck tongue, whistling, use of falsetto, whispering, and tongue trills. Composers such as Crumb, Boulez, Vercoe, Berio, Rochberg, Schoenberg, Stockhausen, and others have used these novel ideas.

A singer faces many obstacles when reading some of these musical scores. Occasionally, the process can be likened to reading elaborate directions for assembling a complex machine. Ideally, a page of instructions is included at the beginning of a piece to aid the performer. The instructions are often explicit and give specific directions for interpreting the notation. Unfortunately, some composers provide little information and leave the interpretation of the new music notation to the discretion and imagination of the performer. If the performer is well informed and experienced in this kind of repertoire, this may not present a problem. However, even seasoned performers of contemporary works occasionally encounter new kinds of notation or a novel use for a rather well-known symbol. Imagine the frustration for a performer who is new to the genre. Inaccurate presentations of the material are more likely to occur.

It is the composer's duty to develop and construct notation and individual symbols in such a way as to give a visual likeness that can be understood by the performer. If there are no written descriptions or clues to what the composer had in mind, then the singer is often at a loss, not knowing where or how to begin. Composers who wish for multiple performances of their works must be aware that if no clear indications are given in the score for the desired realization of unusual notational devices (including those familiar ones that may be used in a unique manner), the performer will most likely be overwhelmed by visual strangeness. That will frequently lead to a "fright and flight" reaction. The score will simply be closed, put aside, and never performed. As Gardner Read (1979, p. 453) puts it,

> Scores prefaced by esoteric essays on temporal and spatial phenomena do not, unfortunately, significantly aid the performer in decoding new and confusing notational symbols. Before the philosophy of the new music can make sense, its format on the printed page must be clearly understood. . . . If the composer says in effect to the performer: "I do not care whether you perform my music or not," we cannot argue the matter. But if he indicates: "I want you to perform and respond to this music," then his fundamental duty is to write his music so that it is accessible to interpretation. When the performer cannot approach the composer's meaning because of capri-

ciously obscure notation, he may in effect say to the composer: "Why should I bother to puzzle out your music?"

Twentieth-century repertoire using extended vocal techniques requires good tonal memory, a flexible voice, and the ability to use the imagination effectively. Studying this repertoire can also *promote* just those qualities in the young singer. Repertoire from this genre comes in varying levels of difficulty, with pieces available for every level of vocal expertise. In all cases, it should be assumed that its performance is based on a good foundation in traditional repertoire and a confident, flexible vocal technique. Since today's voice students will spend their singing careers in the twenty-first century, it is time they experience all styles of music from the twentieth century.

It has been my experience as a teacher that some students feel liberated by this repertoire. They find twentieth-century music vocally and mentally freeing and begin to sing other vocal styles better after having sung some of this literature. I am not suggesting that one should sing *only* music of the twentieth century. Having come from a traditional background of study that relied primarily on songs by major composers of the eighteenth and nineteenth centuries, I feel it is important to present a variety of musical styles to students, eventually finding a core of repertoire that agrees with their particular technique and the size of their vocal instrument. In order to feel comfortable with one's repertoire, a singer must have examined many different works from various historical style periods and composers to determine those areas where his or her voice is most adept at vocalism and interpretation. The inclusion of twentieth-century music—of any genre or compositional trend—in the vocal studio has often been sorely lacking. Incorporating it into the young singer's course of study can play a major role in the journey toward artistic development.

My purpose in writing this book is not only to bring organization and clarity to the deciphering of twentieth-century solo vocal repertoire that uses nontraditional notation or novel interpretative markings, but also to present practical ideas concerning the selection, preparation, interpretation, and programming of these works. My intent is not to write a complete history of twentieth-century compositional trends. Other valuable sources have that objective. Rather, all information presented here, concerning aspects of musical notation, is written from a pedagogical point of view. Particular choices for discussion were made based on their relationship to vocal technique, not necessarily their compositional prominence during the century.

As one traces the output of composers during the century, it is evident that they had to make critical choices about whether to rely on well-established compositional techniques from the past or to experiment with new ways of organizing sound. Writers and scholars on this subject have used varied terms to describe the music. Terms such as *new, contemporary, avant-garde,* and *modern* appear regularly in books and articles. I use all of these terms interchangeably when referring to twentieth-century vocal music that is not considered traditional in its use of the voice.

MISSION OF THE TEXT

This book ventures to aid the modern performer and/or voice teacher in finding and deciphering appropriate repertoire for all major voice types. Discussion includes a description of commonly used notational devices developed by composers in the twentieth century; rehearsal techniques useful for mastery of the individual symbols or overall organizational method; a description of one or more ways in which the symbols can be interpreted; vocal problems likely to be encountered during rehearsal; discussion of some compositions in which the device can be found; the relationship of the information given to vocal pedagogy in general; and vocal exercises that will be useful for incorporating the devices into the singer's daily practice routine. Only frequently used notational gestures are presented and related to compositions in which they appear. Again, this is not an exhaustive list of modern musical notation, nor does it represent every possibility for interpretation. Teachers may find it helpful to use some of these gestures as warm-up exercises whether or not the student is preparing a piece that includes them. Once familiar with this distinct vocalization, the singer will be able to transfer the gestures to a given musical score more easily. In addition, sample repertoire listings are given for each major voice category with a designation for difficulty. Sources for the acquisition of scores are also listed.

Many of the topics discussed in this book are interrelated, and an occasional repetition of pedagogical concepts and rehearsal suggestions may occur. Since the book may be used as a reference source, it is necessary to give the reader sufficient information on each topic at the point of discussion. This will eliminate the need to search the entire book for a solution to a particular problem or a practice routine for a difficult vocalization or notation.

Probably the most important function of this book is to encourage singers at all levels of study to investigate the wealth of fine vocal repertoire from the twentieth century. With a deciphering plan in mind, singers are more likely to feel unfettered and ready to experiment with some new ideas for the recital hall, a performance genre that has lost much of its audience in recent years. Up-to-date creative ideas for performance venues, unexplored aesthetics for the listener, and fresh challenges for the performers may help invigorate this ailing format and get the attention of a new audience.

Resources include published books and articles concerning notation and its modern usage; composer-generated information printed in musical scores; personal interviews with composers and performers; recorded examples of major works by well-respected artists; personal vocal experimentation; personal collaboration with approximately thirty composers in the preparation of new works; and the opinions of vocal pedagogues on the subject of vocal technique and its application to new music notation.

FEATURES OF THE BOOK

The book is divided into three sections. Part I discusses positive aspects of singing twentieth-century repertoire and describes common characteristics of vocal writing from the period. Part II focuses on the description and performance of novel notational gestures and extended vocal techniques found in the repertoire. These two sections offer numerous relevant vocal exercises, step-by-step practice routines, and suggestions for the development of spontaneity and confidence in performing the material. Many of the exercises, though designed for a particular vocal gesture being discussed, have been adapted from standard exercises traditionally used for vocal warm-ups and general technique development. Part III provides sample recital programs and repertoire lists for various voice types. The selection of repertoire is not comprehensive. It is a personal preference list, intended to encourage the reader to seek out contemporary repertoire in all of its stylistic manifestations. The list includes well-known and lesser-known composers and compositions, both published and unpublished. Many other choices exist, giving individual readers room to discover other fine examples of twentieth-century music. This section also contains a list of suggested sources for contacting living composers or finding and acquiring musical scores.

It has been a pleasure to become acquainted with many composers during my thirty-year teaching and singing career. During that time, I have been privileged to perform, premiere, or record dozens of works by over thirty contemporary British, American, Belgian, Canadian, German, and Australian composers. In addition, as founder and coordinator of the Dimensions New Music Series at Austin Peay State University, I have been inspired to perform new music by the more than forty composers who have come to the campus since 1980 to lecture and have their works performed as part of the series. Several have become close friends and have given excellent advice during the writing of this book. In particular, I must thank Frederick Goossen, Persis Vehar, Elizabeth Vercoe, and Rhian Samuel for information regarding composer contacts and score location.

I wish to thank all of the composers I have worked with for their patience, interpretational insight, rehearsal advice, encouragement, and, most of all, contributions to the vocal art. I am indebted to Elizabeth Vercoe, Kenton Coe, Rhian Samuel, Frederic Goossen, Persis Vehar, Jeffrey Wood, Michael Rose, Christina Kuzmych, George Rochberg, Thomas Pasatieri, and Seymour Barab for allowing me to premiere and/or record some of their most memorable and significant works. What a joy for a performer!

I greatly appreciate the encouragement and support of the National Association of Teachers of Singing and their members who have read my column, "New Directions," in the *Journal of Singing* since 1985. In response to the column, I have received a multitude of thought-provoking questions and suggestions concerning the performance of contemporary music. Many readers have personally encouraged the writing of this book.

I deeply appreciate the help of several professional singers who gave excellent advice and support to this project, in particular Dorothy Crum, D'Anna Fortunato,

Neva Pilgrim, and Christine Schadeberg. Each drew from her extensive knowledge of this repertoire and suggested several works listed in appendix B.

Two major influences in my musical life occurred during doctoral studies at George Peabody College for Teachers in Nashville. Though I had been intrigued by twentieth-century music since my undergraduate days, it was not until Gilbert Thrythall, my major professor, asked me to perform some works at his annual Electronic Music Symposium that I realized just how important this new and experimental music would become for me. My early success there was encouraged by my mentor and voice teacher, Louis Nicholas, who saw where my creative abilities needed to be channeled. He has remained a stalwart supporter of my efforts in performance and writing. For that, I am most appreciative.

Many thanks to Edward E. Irwin, professor emeritus of languages and literature, colleague and friend, who gave valuable advice regarding grammatical and syntactical issues during the editing of this book.

I am most grateful to three people who contributed mightily to the writing of this book:

First, to Sally Ahner; singer, voice teacher, Alexander Technique specialist, colleague, and friend. She dutifully read every word I wrote and made helpful comments concerning everything—grammar, form, content, and methods used in the text. What a friend!

Second, to Jeffrey Wood; composer, pianist, professor, colleague, and friend. He beautifully translated musical examples into the proper versions you see in the book and had great patience for this singer/writer who would rather write a million words than learn the meaning and workings of EPS files. I am grateful!

Finally, to my husband, George Mabry; conductor, professor, composer, singer, and colleague. He read every chapter of this book with a keen eye for understandability and content, using his extensive knowledge and expertise as a musician and teacher. But on a larger scale, since the days when we were undergraduates, he has made every day special, supported my musical endeavors, given a sympathetic ear to all kinds of complaints, and been part of every triumph. It's been lovely to have such a wonderful relationship for so many years. I am blessed!

Part I
New Directions   I

1   The Art of Singing Twentieth-Century Music   5

2   Choosing Appropriate Repertoire   14

3   Vocal Requirements of Twentieth-Century
Music: Common Characteristics   28

4   Vocal Coloration   39

Part II
Nontraditional Notation and Extended Vocal Techniques   53

5   The New Language of Notation   59

6   Vocal Hybrids: *Sprechstimme* and Recitation   77

7   Nontextual Sonic Vocabularies   105

8   Vocal Effects   122

Part III
Repertoire Choices   141

Appendix A   SAMPLE PROGRAMS   143

Appendix B   SUGGESTED REPERTOIRE   154

Appendix C   SOURCES FOR COMPOSER AND SCORE LOCATION   181

Bibliography   187

Index   189

The music of the twentieth century fluctuated between periods of extreme experimentation and periods of conservatism. At the turn of the twentieth century the major issue seemed to be *what to do with tonality*. Some composers chose a neoclassical approach, a few adopted the twelve-tone organization, and others delved into atonality, expressionism, or quarter tones as the modern aesthetic. A fringe group of composers were considered eccentrics by many as they chose to invent novel musical instruments. Leon Theremin's "ether-machine" is one example. Composers in this group also incorporated elements of the world around them, adding sounds from nature or street noises to the musical mixture, and a few simply abandoned all past musical concepts and invented new ones, producing what some critics of the era called "noise."

Between 1900 and 1935 numerous changes occurred in the organization, texture, timbre, instrumentation, and visual appearance of musical composition. As a result of this experimentation and search for a new aesthetic, the human voice was asked to produce sounds, colors, vocal effects, and other vocal techniques previously unused in Western culture. All of these changes must have been a shock to singers of the time. A few singers, such as contralto Radiana Pazmor, seemed to delight in this new interpretative challenge, premiering numerous works by Ruth Crawford Seeger, Henry Cowell, Charles Ives, Marc Blitzstein, and others. These com-

posers relied on her to present accurate, well-prepared, and imaginative performances of their innovative musical ideas to a public that consisted of other enthusiastic experimentalists, intellectuals devoted to keeping the artistic mind open,
critics rooted in the nineteenth-century aesthetic, and casual concertgoers who
often rejected anything that was in the least unfamiliar. But most singers of the
time reacted with dismay or disinterest, choosing to disregard these modernistic
ideas as *passing phases*, unworthy of study, perhaps even detrimental to vocal health.
Most felt that singing this repertoire would certainly be a career-ending decision.

In the second half of the century, there was an explosion of ideas. Myriad
exploratory developments surfaced, such as multiserialism, electronic music, musical graphics, multimedia works, and indeterminacy. Composers such as George
Crumb, Luciano Berio, John Cage, Luigi Dallapiccola, George Rochberg, and
many others continued to experiment with the human voice as it relates to the
interpretation of musical notation. There was a proliferation of new notational
symbols. Though there was an increased interest among singers to investigate the
latest repertoire, the deciphering process became more difficult since no practical
guide was available for interpreting many of the new notational gestures found
in the scores. In addition, only a few singers, such as Jan DeGaetani and Cathy
Berberian, contributed fine recorded examples of the music, generally limiting
themselves to major works.

New designations and treatments of the voice as a producer of color and
texture within the overall fabric of a composition were also explored. This change
of attitude by composers toward the use of the voice and its utterances may have
been the single most challenging element the modern singer faced when deciphering some twentieth-century scores. Once a composer determined that the
traditional use of the voice could be expanded, the creation of new visual representations for the desired vocal production became a source of experimentation
and innovation. New ways of visually expressing the composer's musical ideas
had to be found. After all, the visual effect of the score relates to the sound and
shape of all elements of the vocal performance: tone quality, vocal registration
and its usage, voice placement, phrase shape, spacing of tones in pitch and length,
declamation, coordination with other instruments, use of improvisatory elements,
and the interpretation of an overmarked and interpretatively controlled score.

This lack of information, a proliferation of individual compositional styles, and
singers' reluctance to seek out modern music and its creators resulted in a general
fear of the unknown that prevented vocalists from delving into this vast repertoire.
Many singers are still rather nervous about tackling some of this music, which
can no longer be called "new" or "modern"—much of it is half a century old.
However, since modern audiences seem to require variety, a quick pace, and
anything avant-garde, contemporary singers need to be prepared to provide diverse repertoire that explores a wide emotional range through the use of adventurous vocalizations.

Since the twentieth century is now history, the psychological distance from
the music of the period has affected how seriously it is taken. Contemporary

music is reaching a greater audience and receiving keener, more refined and accurate realizations than ever before. New works are being performed more often by opera companies, symphony orchestras, and solo artists. In addition, composers such as Libby Larsen and Ellen Taaffe Zwilich continue to be employed as composers-in-residence for major symphony orchestras, opera companies, and chamber ensembles. Solo artists regularly commission new works for performance and recording purposes. This growing communication between artists and composers is a positive element for the future of musical collaboration. Definitive performances of works using novel, complex, or representational notation are much more likely to occur if all involved parties have an opportunity to articulate their ideas and intentions through a workable partnership.

chapter 1

The Art of Singing
Twentieth-Century Music

WHY SING TWENTIETH-CENTURY MUSIC?

This question has haunted singers for decades. Let's investigate some answers. In pedagogical terms, it seems absurd to summarily banish one hundred years of vocal music from a singer's programmable repertoire, whether it be the twentieth century or the eighteenth century, without giving the music a thorough reading over a considerable period of study. The musical offerings of the twentieth century are so diverse in style, mood, interpretation, and genre that any voice type should be able to find pieces suitable for study or performance. Much of the music has qualities that relate to the modern singer's experience living in a world that is increasingly bombarded by gadgets, media sound bites, computer technology, and constant sensory stimulation. In such a society, anachronisms have a place, but often an uncertain one, catching the attention of only a few devotees. The traditional solo recital, which typically presents one singer and a pianist on a rather bare stage and includes vocal standards by composers such as Schubert, Fauré, Handel, and Brahms, is considered anachronistic by many potential audience members. It has fallen victim to a society more inclined to buy the latest CDs of famous singers than to attend live concerts, an electronics oriented society that clamors for the latest video and audio equipment and prefers to sit at home channel surfing on large-screen TVs.

How does the modern vocal soloist fit into this landscape? Some would say he or she doesn't. Others believe that as our society changes, musical offerings by working artists must adapt in order to attract a new audience while reviving the enthusiasm of faithful, dedicated, and educated fans. There will always be followers of anachronistic endeavors, but musical performance in general cannot survive by relying only on those kinds of patrons. We must capture the attention of a larger pool of listeners by offering a gourmet's delight in musical style, mood, and vocalism, and by giving the audience more choices and new alternatives to the standard concert fare. Change is not necessarily negative. It can be exciting, positive, and inspiring for performers and listeners alike. Singers who are the most imaginative will come through this musical evolution with renewed enthusiasm and larger, enlightened audiences.

Music of the twentieth century is well suited for today's society because it speaks the language of the present. It uses instruments, technology, and sentiments that are familiar to the contemporary listener. Additionally, the century's philosophical, political, and social upheavals were often chronicled through its musical works.

Having said this, we must establish diverse means of attracting the attention of the modern listener. The education of young people should always be a priority for the performer. There lies the future audience. Those of us who teach and/or perform can positively affect students by presenting current and experimental ideas to young people in our schools. They are often more receptive to change and new ideas than older, more established concertgoers who hold preconceived notions about the content of traditional programming. Children can be encouraged to interact with performers, compose pieces of their own, or shed inhibitions through exposure to the improvisatory elements in contemporary music. Their successes are easily recorded with in-school video, computer, or audio equipment. An experience of this kind, with documented evidence, is a valuable tool for imprinting positive reactions to contemporary music.

Engaging an uninitiated adult audience requires some inventive changes in the traditional concert venue. In a time when people are often juggling enormous family responsibilities with full-time jobs, performers can no longer rely on the public to come to an established concert setting to hear music of any kind. When they do come, it may be due primarily to innovative, inspirational, high-tech, casual, or unconventional ideas that have been used to create interest in the performance. Aggressive ideas for presentation of both traditional and twentieth-century song literature need to be investigated and tried. The following suggestions for solo singers may serve to trigger some creative thinking along these lines:

1. Collaborate with other musicians to present lunch time concerts at an indoor or outdoor venue, such as the lobby or courtyard of a bank, corporate building, church, or art gallery. The concert should be quite short, perhaps fifteen to twenty minutes, and could be repeated in segments to suit shift changes or a quick lunch break.

2. Use a popular outdoor community setting, such as a town square, riverfront park, band shell, or amphitheater, and invite attendees to bring a picnic and relax. These short concerts could be given during the lunch hour or on a weekend afternoon when people have time to enjoy a day of leisure outside.

3. Establish a corporate collaboration, performing for workers at their place of employment. This could take place in a large meeting space or a centrally

located walkway or lobby. Talk with the company's public relations or human relations director for promotion of this idea. Many companies already provide events of this kind for their employees, while others have never considered it. Prepare a clear-cut proposal showing benefits to workers for such an event. These concerts should be short—fifteen to twenty minutes—and mobile, able to be done at almost any location in the corporation.

4. Collaborate with a composer in a more traditional concert setting. He or she could briefly discuss salient characteristics of the work to be performed, using short excerpts for demonstration before performing the piece in its entirety. Encourage the audience to ask questions and to look at the musical scores or any unfamiliar instruments involved. If equipment is available, use audiovisual aids to project texts and music onto a large screen for viewing by a larger audience.

5. Create a new relationship between the performer and the audience. A normal fixed-seating format could be changed to one that brings the performers closer to the audience or puts them in the midst of the audience. This format works well if chairs are movable and can be placed in any imaginable fashion. The performers should decide on the stage setting in advance, placing audience members in strategic sections of the performance arena. This will allow the performers to move to different parts of the room or disperse among the audience according to the design of the music being performed. Some contemporary works contain prescribed movement during the work, requiring walking space to be arranged among the audience. Seating flexibility allows for experimentation in spacing the instruments, creates greater possibilities for acoustical diversity, and gives the audience a feeling of being an integral part of the performance.

6. Create variety within the traditional concert-hall setting. Slides might be shown between or during vocal selections to give presence to a character, an author, or a scene, or to enhance a particular poetic idea. Always rehearse this effect to make certain that stage lighting is at an effective level for viewing the slides or reading scores. Also be aware of any extraneous and distracting sounds that might be created by the operation of a slide projector; this problem would need to be resolved before performance. Special lighting effects are often requested by composers of contemporary music. But effects may also be added when the score makes no indication for special lighting. Subtle theatrical elements such as these will enhance the uniqueness of a particular text or musical style. Colors can be projected onto a scrim or blank wall behind the performers and used as a backdrop for poetic or dramatic ideas expressed in the text. The colors could change as the mood changes within the music or text. If basic lighting equipment is available, subtle color washes or *gobos* (metal cutouts that can be used with lights to project images onto a surface) would be an effective way to create an exotic atmosphere. Dramatic lighting (a strong down light, up light, or silhouette light) is another spectacular effect for an individual performer who wishes to be set apart from the rest of the ensemble. Get to know a lighting designer in your area, and don't be afraid to let that person experiment and be

creative with special effects. Have several meetings with him or her where you can see the lighting possibilities for the performance space. Bring someone with you to sit in the audience and give an opinion while you are on stage experimenting with the possibilities. Always make sure that you have enough light to see if you are using a musical score for the performance.

7. Join with visual artists, dancers, or actors to bring contrast to a performance. For instance, a dancer might be engaged to choreograph a group of songs or a chamber work. Invite an actor to recite the English translations of foreign-language songs instead of using printed translations. He or she might read other related material by a poet being featured.

8. A theme could be established for the concert and implemented through collaborative efforts with someone who is not ordinarily involved in musical offerings. For example, a humorous lunchtime concert could involve a short program of songs about food in collaboration with visual artists who provide edible art to be eaten at the concert's end. The same idea could involve music about animals or birds, with live examples on the premises, or the combination of music about flowers and a flower show. The appropriate setting for these concerts would necessarily be a factor in their success. For instance, a botanic hall, arboretum, or aviary would be an excellent venue for a concert about birds, flowers, or nature. Many such establishments have small lecture halls, courtyard areas, or gallery spaces where a performance could be scheduled. Contact the events coordinator to set up such an event.

9. Select a twentieth-century work that employs interesting and unusual extended vocal techniques, electronic tape accompaniment, or other theatrical elements as a *centerpiece* for an otherwise traditional program, providing a stimulating contrast in the middle of the program. Either include program notes that clearly describe the novelty of the work or talk to the audience, giving your own ideas about the special character of the piece and what they might expect to hear in the performance.

10. Finally, the recital format might need to be shortened to accommodate the venue in which it is performed and to retain the attention of those whose interest wanes easily. A thirty-to-fifty-minute program without an intermission may fit current lifestyles better than the traditional one-and-a-half to two-hour recital that includes a lengthy intermission.

Most important, it is the performer's responsibility to be the link between recent trends in music and the appreciation of those trends by the listening public. Performers need to acknowledge an obligation to those composers who contribute to the repertoire and give their music a fair and thorough reading. Appreciation of their creativity can best come through promotion of their works in a public performance. Only through performance, perhaps numerous performances, can the truly outstanding works of the century become standards in the twenty-first century.

THE STUDIO APPROACH

For most singers, the voice teacher is a central figure in their musical lives. They rely on voice teachers for musical direction in repertoire, vocal technique, and development of performance skills in general. For some, the voice studio may be the primary domain for the development of the student's musical aesthetics. This places an enormous responsibility on the teacher to have an expansive knowledge of repertoire appropriate for any voice type at any level of study. Also, flexibility in studio teaching techniques is necessary in order to accommodate inherent differences in the students' musical background, foreign-language comprehension, personality traits, and acting skills. A zeal for knowledge and a desire to remain connected to music of the past and present are characteristics of teachers who successfully assume this important role.

Since more singers are finding their niche in twentieth-century music, a pedagogical plan and programming strategy is needed to provide musical enlightenment in this compositional realm. The voice teacher may be the sole source for the student's knowledge of recent compositional trends in vocal music. Consequently, introducing twentieth-century music in a positive and enlightening way is a serious responsibility. Singers at all levels rely on information gathered in the vocal studio that pertains to the study of new works. The performance outcome significantly depends on it.

The inclusion of a variety of twentieth-century musical styles should be considered an enhancement rather than a replacement of traditional vocal studio goals and used to broaden the aesthetic sensitivities of singers. In the future, those vocalists who have been exposed to a plethora of styles will be better prepared to make decisions concerning their own performance goals and the repertoire that most keenly displays their vocal talents. By the time they have reached an advanced technical status, most singers have gradually narrowed their repertoire to favorites anyway.

The uses of twentieth-century music in the voice studio are numerous, the most obvious being the expansion of vocal technique and the development of musical and textual interpretation. Beyond these considerations are those that involve career development and the use of this repertoire for the twenty-first century. It is often difficult to convince students that they need a broad knowledge of repertoire to be successful, especially when they see well-known performers who have achieved renown through a rather limited scope of works. As communication arts change, so does the musical society and its requirements of performers. It is becoming less likely that singers will find eminence and prosperity through narrow endeavors. Versatility seems to be the prevailing goal, and it shows no signs of decline. In addition, many young singers are gaining recognition for their willingness to experiment, making a name for themselves in premieres of new works. Today, twentieth-century repertoire is commonly required for major vocal competitions (both concert and opera), university scholarship auditions, and other types of auditions necessary for career advancement.

The music created in the twentieth century is here to stay, and through an increasing number of performances it is becoming more familiar to audiences. Teachers, performers, and listeners face new pedagogical, performance, and response challenges, requiring a sincere effort to close the gaps between composers, performers, and their audiences.

At first hearing, some contemporary pieces display an alarming or disconcerting lack of organization. They may contain essentially no obvious design, the composer having felt no need or obligation to provide the listener with a noticeable scheme or logical development of ideas. Charles Ives, for example, questioned whether a song should be required to have a particular structure or, for that matter, whether it should even be singable in the traditional sense. In the epilogue to his 114 *Songs*, Ives states, "Some of the songs in this book, particularly among the later ones, cannot be sung,—and if they could perhaps might prefer, if they had a say, to remain as they are,—that is, "in the leaf,"—and that they will remain in this peaceful state is more than presumable . . . —In short, must a song always be a song!"

Occasionally, a casual or frivolous atmosphere prevails in some of this repertoire. The composer may have incorporated popular, folk, or jazz features into the musical texture, making it seem unsuited to the traditional concert hall. Perhaps we feel uncomfortable with this because we are still listening with nineteenth-century ears, minds, and expectations. The performer must take the music for what it is and move on intellectually, emotionally, and musically. Ultimately, each performer chooses repertoire that fits his or her personality and vocal capabilities. There is nothing new in that concept, since it applies to music from every period of music history and ethnicity. So if the casual style of some works fits, then sing it; if not, there are numerous other musical avenues to pursue with contemporary repertoire.

Should we poise our intellect, musicianship, voices, and careers between safety and danger? If the answer is yes and we are to prosper as functioning and literate musicians in the twenty-first century, then we must devise ways of continuing to promote functional vocal technique, a thorough understanding of the musical and textual ideas, and inventive performance venues for the public, while performing twentieth-century music.

DEVELOPING SKILLS

Twentieth-century composers such as John Alden Carpenter, John Duke, and Charles Griffes, who chose to adhere to musical ideas from the nineteenth century, wrote beautiful, interesting, and sometimes technically difficult songs. However, their works present no extraordinary aesthetic or technical difficulties for the modern singer since they used the voice in a traditional manner. Other composers like Benjamin Britten, Francis Poulenc, or Aaron Copland took traditional harmonic ideas and changed the musical context through innovative rhythmic structures, coloristic devices, and melodic intricacies. With these changes came new and daunting vocal and interpretative challenges for singers. Pitches were slightly more difficult to locate, large leaps became the norm, and clarity of diction became a cause for concern as the singer's attention was drawn to technical demands rather than clear declamation of the text.

Numerous composers, such as Charles Ives, Igor Stravinsky, Arnold Schoenberg, Anton Webern, George Crumb, George Rochberg, John Cage, Luigi Dallapiccola, and Ruth Crawford Seeger, pioneered in musical and aesthetic directions. Historically, their inventions and those of other innovators have given twentieth-century music a reputation as a musical language that is difficult to fathom. Their musical ideas were often steeped in mathematical concepts, wide vocal ranges, unfamiliar notational devices, International Phonetic Alphabet or syllabic declamation, angular melodic lines, grinding dissonance, and the use of theatrical elements involving stage movement or special lighting techniques. Faced with these added musical, vocal, and theatrical elements, singers often felt as if roadblocks had been placed in their way to a successful performance, rather than as creative and intellectual challenges ripe for investigation. Also, singers did not consider the numerous aural, vocal-technical, and interpretative skills that could be developed through this unique repertoire.

Given these new creative stimuli, the possibilities for educational enhancement are only limited by the singer's imagination. Since the dramatic and emotional response to this music is sometimes different from that of earlier periods, it also presents an opportunity to release innate emotional and aesthetic ideas that traditional works do not expose. This element of psychic freedom is important to the expansion of the singer's knowledge of his or her intellectual and emotional expression through the voice. When encouraged to experiment with these new responses, singers may achieve levels of musical and textual understanding previously closed to them.

At first, the fear of failure to correctly produce an accurate realization of the score may be overwhelming. For this reason, it is wise to start the foray into this foreign musical landscape with short pieces that have only a few nontraditional ideas, increasing the difficulty as technical and musical demands are accomplished. Once success has occurred, the singer's confidence in singing other experimental works will increase, heightening performance accuracy.

For study purposes, the following concepts can be addressed individually or collectively through the use of twentieth-century repertoire. These concepts, inherent in the study of music from any era, take on special significance when applied to modern works. They relate to a singer's overall improvement in vocal technique, musicianship, intellectual understanding, and interpretation of musical material.

1. *Vocal maturity*

A singer's vocal response to nontraditional score indications can be gradually strengthened by carefully selecting repertoire that suits his or her performance level. It is important that inherent difficulties of all kinds (vocal, musical, and intellectual) indicated in the score not exceed the limits of the singer's present vocal technique. Yet there should be enough challenging material to achieve a positive progression in technical execution. As technique develops, gradually add works that offer more complex or experimental uses of the voice.

2. *Diction practice*

Numerous contemporary works incorporate the use of International Phonetic Alphabet (IPA) phonemes, repeated syllables, gradually morphing vowel changes, vocal muting, or nonsense syllabic repetition. These works provide a wealth of delightful challenges and opportunities for enjoyable diction practice. The texts, sometimes quite intricate, offer excellent substitutes for the "tongue twisters" regularly used for developing diction accuracy and flexibility. Small sections may be extracted from these works and used as diction exercises to develop vowel and consonant clarity or precision of articulation.

3. *Vocal range, stamina, and flexibility*

Given the variety of musical styles available from which to choose study pieces, it is possible to exercise the voice in a myriad of ways. Some pieces cover a wide vocal range, contain angular vocal lines with large skips, or require a command of extreme vocal dynamics from *ppp to fff*. Others are built on vocal flourishes, roulades, extravagant glissandos, or vocal effects, such as laughing, whispering, or intoning. Pieces may be selected that gradually strengthen the range, stamina, and flexibility of the voice without putting too many demands on its current abilities.

4. *Intellect and imagination*

Several unique qualities of twentieth-century music offer tremendous opportunities for developing spontaneity, imagination, intellectual alertness, and sensitivity to abrupt changes within a musical score. To promote these skills, choose repertoire that requires a variety of vocal colors, spoken interjections, extended vocal techniques such as *sprechstimme*, the playing of musical instruments while singing, or designated stage movement. These unfamiliar elements will need to be incorporated one or two at a time in order to be accomplished successfully. For the uninitiated, many unusual demands occurring simultaneously can be difficult to fathom.

5. *Ear training*

Modern repertoire is ideal for developing the singer's ability to locate pitches. Begin by using works that only slightly stretch present capabilities and progress by small incremental steps to pieces that have few pitch references or require self-reliance and independence from accompanying instruments.

6. *Mental and vocal freedom*

Contemporary pieces often incorporate improvisatory elements such as ad lib sections or ambiguous synchronization of the voice with other instruments. Some works even allow the performers to become composers by choosing their own organization of pitches and rhythms given in the score. All of these devices are useful in promoting mental and vocal freedom. They can easily be dissected from the score and rehearsed individually.

7. *Musical discipline*

A plan for the analysis and realization of all musical gestures, unifying compositional tools, innate rhythmic structure, and text setting is necessary for a successful performance of any work, traditional or contemporary. Devising such a plan can be part of the learning process. The plan can be quite formal, involving a detailed notebook of daily tasks for analysis, or it can be broader in scope, setting general goals to be reached by a given time. Participation in such an endeavor will strengthen the singer's resolve to prepare music thoroughly, so that the intended performance will be of the highest quality possible.

8. *Independence, individualism, and self-confidence*

As singers become increasingly involved with twentieth-century repertoire, they will be more inclined to try new ways of interpreting diverse musical styles. This process can be aided by working with composers, listening to recorded examples of relevant repertoire, scheduling regular performances of contemporary works, and developing an extensive repertoire of new works in different compositional styles.

chapter 2

Choosing Appropriate Repertoire

*H*istorically, contemporary music has been considered by many singers to have a musical language that is difficult to fathom and places unrealistic demands on the voice. Music of the period has been lumped together into one impenetrable category. This may have occurred because singers are generally unfamiliar with the repertoire, having heard only a few pieces that seemed to bear out their worst fears. Some of this literature certainly contains dissonance, angular melodic lines, and mathematical concepts of construction. But for every piece that involves those concepts, dozens do not. Singers must have a higher vocal/technical or musical/intellectual achievement level for some works than for others in order to perform them well, a concept that also applies to vocal music from other historical periods.

The performance outcome must appear natural, unpretentious, and spontaneous. Listeners should not be made to feel that the performance is causing undue stress upon the performers. Therefore, careful consideration should be given to the repertoire's vocal difficulty and musical complexity, with a special focus on the realistic outcome given the performers involved. These are subjective decisions, but they must be made in relation to the experience and innate technical ability of the musicians, as well as the amount of rehearsal time required to satisfactorily prepare the piece for public performance.

Singers who fare well in this repertoire exhibit a keen sense of organization in their practice routine, a zeal for knowledge, strong musicianship, and a willingness to experiment with new musical and vocal/technical ideas. These characteristics of work habits, native ability, and psyche are desirable for serious performers of any musical genre or stylistic period. But they are crucial, primary features for singers dealing with complicated new music that involves numerous aural, visual, and kinesthetic adventures not found in traditional repertoire. The nimble coordination of vocal and musical skills is necessary to project a satisfying interpretation of works that may be deemed *inaccessible* upon first hearing.

Since the early part of the twentieth century, the term *inaccessible*, when applied to modern music, has often been considered a death sentence by many composers, arts presenters, and performers. If the music seemed "good" or "serious," it was treated like bad medicine that had to be taken for a short time and then put away with the hope that one would not have to experience it again. As a result many fine vocal works have had limited performances and have all but disappeared from the concert repertoire. Other works considered more accessible have been heard with more regularity. That accessibility most often meant that the music was easy to listen to, memorable, or likable, or that it had a tune easily whistled.

Random House Webster's College Dictionary includes the following definition for *accessible*: "Easy to approach, reach, . . . or use, . . . readily understandable." The same source gives the following definition for *inaccessible*: "not accessible; unapproachable." Given the relationship of these two often-used terms to the performance of twentieth-century vocal music, it seems obvious that neither gives an adequate picture of much of the music of the period. Rather than debating the value of accessible or inaccessible music, singers should be delighted that they have available a legion of ideas, musical styles, intellectual approaches, and experimental theories that can be used to establish a contemporary repertoire that displays a multitude of diversity. A varied repertoire is the key to keeping the audience fascinated, stimulating them with new ideas. This has been the case with some well-known performers, such as the Kronos Quartet, Nexus, and Jan DeGaetani. They and others have boldly brought contemporary music to a large audience. Doing so requires knowledge of the repertoire and of one's ability to present it with excitement and without apology. Only then can the so-called inaccessible be reversed. With understanding comes access to any new idea, musical organization, or textual setting.

VOCAL CONSIDERATIONS

Singers must consider numerous details when choosing repertoire, whether the music was composed in 1875 or 1975. Experience has taught us that not all voices are suited to all musical style periods, composers, or compositional mediums. Individual voices are endowed with diverse abilities, even within each general vocal category. For instance, not every lyric soprano is capable of spinning out sustained tones in the upper range of the voice, though it may be a desirable characteristic of that particular voice type. Albeit a lofty goal, not every lyric tenor has exactly the same ability to sustain a high B natural or C. Each singer must give careful thought to the establishment of a core repertoire that suits his or her particular voice, not just the voice type.

Theoretically, in order to accomplish this goal, a singer must seriously consider the strengths and weaknesses apparent in his or her voice. Showing off the strong points, while trying to minimize faults through the chosen repertoire, is one way of achieving vocal security. However, those faults—and every young voice has them—must be addressed and eliminated as soon as possible. This can be done through a combination of technical exercises and the establishment of correct vocal habits through repertoire choices. Voice teachers vary in their emphasis on either technical studies or the use of repertoire for solving vocal problems. Whatever the emphasis, the singer must eventually be able to successfully negotiate a large amount of repertoire in varying styles. Initially, it is the teacher's responsibility to analyze each student's vocal development, maturity level, and intellectual prowess in order to select pieces that are effective vehicles for vocal progress and performance security.

Establishment of a "comfort zone" in the repertoire one sings is important. Young performers need to have a wide range of pieces that they can rely on for immediate use, pieces that allow them to perform without undue vocal stress while developing musicianship, language proficiency, and acting skills. However, they also need to have a small number of works that challenge their vocal technique, musical expressiveness, and intellect. If all the repertoire is too easy, too accessible, or too similar in style, mood, or declamation, then the performer may not develop the broad technical and musical skills needed to reach professional levels of performance.

The incorporation of diverse styles of twentieth-century music into the normal study routine of a young singer is valuable in priming that singer's vocal, aesthetic, and physical responses to the organization of musical materials. As one becomes more familiar with the wide choice of twentieth-century repertoire, it becomes clear that a workable plan is essential for the selection of individual pieces for study. One must determine exactly how and for what technical purpose each piece can be used effectively for a given learning situation relating to vocal development. The following categories should be assessed when choosing twentieth-century repertoire.

Vocal range

Determine the singer's range, from the lowest easily singable note to the highest, through vocalises and previously performed repertoire. As Clifton Ware maintains (1998, pp. 186–187), "Although well-trained singers may be able to vocalize a three-octave range, it does not necessarily follow that their effective singing range will encompass such wide parameters of pitch." Most of the pitches in the chosen new work should lie within that comfortable range, with only a few pitches appearing outside it. This will put less stress on the voice yet allow for range development.

Tessitura and passaggio events

The demands an individual piece places on a voice may relate directly to whether the voice is technically proficient when negotiating register changes. The term *vocal registers* refers to a series of pitches that can be sung with the same resonance and mechanical/muscular action. Register transitions or passaggio events are the connectors between vocal registers. These transitions are often the weakest areas of the voice and become stressed when the singer is required to sustain tones for an extended period on pitches within that passaggio. Finding the voice's easily singable and comfortable pitch level for sustained vocalization is important. As the singer matures vocally and physically, the optimum singable tessitura (the comfortable, freely produced pitch level in which the voice can sing for an extended period without vocal stress or fatigue) can change considerably. If the tessitura of a chosen piece lies in a weak area of the singer's voice, it may produce undue stress, causing physical and psychological tension. This is a good reason not to choose the piece for study. Young voices are best strengthened through repertoire that makes few demands in tessitura and passaggio coordination.

Vocal difficulties

Vocal/technical requirements are the most critical aspects of consideration in choosing repertoire from this period. Given the fact that the music varies widely as to organizational and compositional models, an individual selection may contain a minimum or superabundance of vocal difficulties and novel vocal techniques to be mastered. Each new piece should be assessed carefully for cumulative technical demands so that the inexperienced singer is not overloaded with obstacles. However, normal caution needs to be balanced with intellectual curiosity. Some pieces may give the visual impression that they are extremely complex and vocally taxing. In reality, the opposite may be true. Only careful analysis of the work will determine the correct judgment.

The kinds of vocal demands that need to be monitored are tessitura, overall vocal range, flexibility requirements, rhythmic and tonal complications, range of dynamics, presence of unusual vocal effects or extended techniques, and phrase lengths that will affect breath management. This process may sound daunting, but it is not much different than deliberations for choosing traditional repertoire. The primary difference involves the use of vocal effects or extended techniques and the context in which each item appears.

It is best to begin with short pieces resembling works with which the singer is familiar, gradually developing expertise by adding pieces with only a few new technical demands. This will allow for an increase in vocal stamina and flexibility as the music becomes more demanding.

Diction

Singers talk to an audience every time they perform. Stories, characters, emotional contrasts, abstract pictures, and dialogue are presented through song. Most singers flinch at the thought of speaking to an audience, but that is, in fact, what is happening each time we declaim a text. The text may be a traditional love poem or individual phonemes strung across the score in an elaborate, decorative arc. Determining the essence of the text is crucial to deciphering it, culminating in an appropriate declamation.

Some contemporary text settings are conversational, eliciting a more direct response from the audience than traditional recital fare. This can be unnerving if the singer is used to a one-sided conversation. Numerous pieces in the contemporary idiom are either built on a form of *recitation* or are what could be called "personality pieces." Charles Ives's "Charlie Rutlage" and "The Greatest Man" are early examples of this kind of art song literature. But there are dozens of examples of this conversational writing in the repertoire as a whole.

When selecting new pieces, the style of the text setting must be contemplated. It is a major factor in the ease or difficulty of the learning process. A singer who has only sung lyrical vocal lines containing traditional syllabic or melismatic text settings will need to consider the elements of articulation, enunciation, and pronunciation when faced with contemporary recitation, IPA vowel designations, nonsense syllabic articulation, and myriad other vocal effects, such as *laughing on pitch* or *intoning* vowels and vocalized consonants. Each sound will have to be dissected and practiced individually before a consistent flow in the vocal line can be attained. Starting with pieces using only a few new diction ideas, followed by more complex texts, will be more effective and satisfying for developing a continuous growth of diction technique.

USES FOR THE MUSIC

One of the voice teacher or performer's most important activities is to select appropriate repertoire for study and performance. It is time-consuming to go through unfamiliar song materials in search of exactly the right piece—one that fits the singer's achievement level and personality yet is an effective tool for attaining vocal progress. When all of those criteria are met, everyone knows it— the teacher, the performer, and the audience. A sense of buoyancy about the final product propels a singer to the next level of accomplishment.

Singers at all levels need specific repertoire for many purposes: technical/vocal development, performance engagements, auditions, recital development, studies in musical/historical perspective, development of variety in emotional expression, vocal competitions, development of self-confidence, and to have a few pieces that are simply fun to sing.

The inclusion of twentieth-century repertoire in the vocal studio can help the student fulfill the aforementioned teaching goals. Its uses for the development of vocal technique and musical responsiveness are numerous, as we will see in later chapters. It is also of critical importance in establishing a recital repertoire that reflects trends in composition and musical/theatrical presentation. Technical skills such as ear training can be honed through specific contemporary repertoire that requires vocal independence from accompanying instrumental lines. Self-discovery can be heightened by experiencing the creative process while performing music that incorporates ad lib, aleatoric, improvisatory, or theatrical elements. See appendix B for these repertoire suggestions, which range from "moderately easy" to "moderately difficult."

There are numerous ways to involve students in the process of learning about this music, depending on their attitude or level of self-confidence. Many voice teachers use recital-class performances as a forum where new repertoire can be tried somewhat informally. Some of these classes could showcase songs, arias, or short theatrical pieces written since 1950 by composers from several countries. This would create an opportunity for discussion and comparison of contrasting compositional styles of the period.

Students spend much of their academic lives studying music by composers who are no longer living. As a consequence, many of them have the impression that all composers must be dead. It may seem obvious or naive to point out that a composer may be your next-door neighbor, but in fact that is often the case. There may be several working composers in your geographical area. However, many singers are shy and fearful about making contact with a composer, assuming that he or she does not want to be bothered. This fear is unfounded, as is the notion that all composers who write music of worth reside in large metropolitan areas or work at major universities.

Meeting a composer and becoming familiar with his or her music is an easy process. It does, however, require action, initiative, and the assumption that a collaboration between composer and performer is not only possible but desirable and workable. Bring a composer to a studio class to work with students, to participate in a reading session of his or her works, or simply to have an informal chat with students after a performance. These experiences will reap rewards on several levels. Performers may feel freer to choose new music for themselves, to contact young composers on their own, or to investigate unfamiliar compositional ideas; they may also be more willing to listen with an open mind to experimental musical materials. Another composer-related activity might include scheduling a premiere performance of a work by a local or regional composer. A relatively simple piece or one that is complex and elaborate could be tailored to the singer's capabilities and rehearsal time. The excitement of a premiere can create lasting interest among those participating in the event.

For an advanced singer, the overriding uses for twentieth-century repertoire include performance repertoire expansion, intellectual curiosity, and the desire to specialize in this genre. Vocal technique and performance skills may already be at a high level, allowing the singer to pursue some of the more esoteric pieces of the period. Several important works for professional level singers are listed in appendix B. They are marked as "difficult" and "very difficult." The ability to present unique material, in addition to traditional fare, in an audition or performance venue will gain the attention of those interested in hiring singers with unabashed versatility, an asset in today's musical/theatrical scene.

DEVELOPING VERSATILITY

What does it mean to be a versatile singer? The term versatility is used often today by critics, concert goers, and arts managers when referring to those who can perform well in several musical styles. These performers are also capable of easily and spontaneously shifting through a wide range of emotions, vocalizations, and theatrical elements, presenting each with satisfying artistic expression. The versatile performer has the ability to cope with complex ideas while displaying creative responses to those ideas through mental imagery and an enhanced perception of the external world. This kind of performer exhibits keenly developed aural, kinesthetic, and perceptual skills. He or she can incorporate popular styles, serious art music, and musical theater pieces into their repertoire and sing them convincingly.

The versatile singer can also do more than one thing at a time. The days are numbered for the singer who merely stands, staring forward, with no particular facial expression while performing a complete recital or operatic role. Intuitive acting, natural and facile stage movement, appropriate facial expressions, and sympathetic text interpretation are now required. In addition, some contemporary scores request specific physical gestures, the playing of musical instruments while singing, and coordinated stage movements (walking from one part of the stage to another, sometimes while singing).

Today's media-addicted, channel-surfing audiences will no longer sit for long periods through a passive performance. They crave variety, excitement, and passion in short doses. This societal change has many negative implications for the vocalist. Keeping the audience interested is sometimes a challenge. Beautiful vocal tones are still desirable, but they are not the only goal in performance. Sincerity of sentiment and the ability to shift that sentiment when called for is more important than in the past.

Some singers resist becoming psychologically involved in the drama of the performance. They feel it is somehow an intrusion on their inner self. This is perhaps more a fault of their training than of any perceptual inadequacy. When encouraged to project physical, sensory, or perceptual ideas through mental imagery and physical movement, these singers find avenues for expression of which they were previously unaware. As Wesley Balk (1978, pp. 85–86) states:

> The most important use of the imagining powers is that which enables the performer to make the connection between an external requirement and its internal validation. For example, it takes an act of imagination to incorporate and make sense of a series of arbitrarily assigned emotional attitudes; it takes an act of imagination to incorporate and make sense of the accidents of performance, or an assigned gesture, or a costume, or a prop, or a physical movement, or of the musical score itself. The translation of the technical intricacies of a musical score into stylized but seemingly natural expression by a human being is an incredible act of the imagination.

Mental imagery is an invaluable tool in learning to be a versatile performer and has been well documented in the vocal pedagogy literature. Mental imagery involves the use of an inner visualization of events, moods, characterizations, and physical space while singing. When singing modern music, the use of mental imagery is quite effective in developing a large spectrum of vocal colors needed for text expression. As the singer captures an image, in the mind's eye, of the vocal sound to be rendered, it is more likely to come to fruition than if the imagination is dormant. These inner visual images can also be applied to the interpretation of notational devices in modern scores, especially those that give creative freedom to the performer. Pacing and real-time musical expression as it relates to tempo, the spacing of barless phrases, the coordination of the voice with a prepared electronic tape, or notation that uses approximate timings in seconds all rely on this inner visual image to direct the physical properties of singing while coordinating pitches, rhythms, tone production, and emotional expression. Short segments that are built on these principles should be dissected from the larger work and rehearsed separately, and should be gradually incorporated into ever larger segments of the piece until there is a natural flow from one section to the next.

A complicating factor in some contemporary music is the need for the singer to vocalize while doing something quite different. Frequently, the singer is asked to play an unfamiliar instrument, such as wind chimes, finger cymbals, gongs, claves; strum the strings of the piano; or sing through a speaking tube. These requests require separate practice, especially if the singer feels awkward or is fearful of failure. In the case of playing a percussion instrument, the singer should always seek the advice of a qualified percussionist to determine the proper playing technique and to secure the best available instrument for the performance. Singers often treat these requests to do extraneous things as nuisances and leave the details until the last minute. This is a mistake. These requests are an important part of the work's musical organization and contribute to the overall color and musical aesthetic. It is best to tackle all unfamiliar requirements at the outset, locate the necessary instruments, talk with experts who can offer advice, and rehearse with an adviser from the beginning. Then it will be a simple matter to combine the newfound instrumental technique with the vocalization.

Another important part of developing vocal versatility involves text declamation. The analysis of a text and its musical setting is integral to the study of any new piece. Many composers of the era continued to set poetry or prose in a rather traditional manner, pairing a familiar mode of text declamation with neoromantic, melody-oriented writing. Composers such as Theodore Chanler, Richard Hundley, and Samuel Barber fit nicely into that category. Elizabeth Vercoe, George Rochberg, Arnold Schoenberg, and Charles Ives are among a large group of composers who chose to use alternative forms of text projection, such as word painting through recitation or spoken vocal inflection on indeterminate pitches, incorporating both the chest and head vocal registers for declamation. Techniques such as intoning or chanting in a monotonelike voice within a limited pitch range or a gradual gliding between designated IPA vowel and consonant indications have been used by George Crumb, Ramon Zupko, Thomas Albert, Milton Babbitt, and Ennio Morricone, among others (see part II). Still other composers, such as John Cage, Luciano Berio, Philip Glass, and Pauline Oliveros, treated the voice as an equal partner with other instruments. In works of this kind, the voice merely projects colors within a large spectrum of sound, adding to the overall texture. These pieces are generally quite free in rhythm and organization. The specific text may not be important; rather, the linking of the vocal color at a given moment with other sounds being produced provides the essence of the composition.

Since contemporary composers have approached the use of a text in such extreme manners, the singer's priority is to determine exactly what part the text setting plays in the piece. Analysis must come early in the preparation stage. Questions to consider include the following:

1. Is the text set with normal word stresses, or has normal inflection been disguised in some artificial way? If so, how has it been clouded and for what purpose?

2. How has the text influenced the musical setting? Is word painting or vocal-speech inflection a part of the piece's construction?

3. Is a recurring form used in either the text or the setting of the text?

4. Has the text been chosen merely for the sound of the words or for a deeper psychological/emotional response?

5. Does the text meaning and innate construction affect the musical tempo or rhythmic structure, use of particular vocal registers or tessitura, melodic or harmonic organization, or style of vocal declamation?

6. Has the composer treated the voice in a traditional manner when projecting the text, or are there numerous extended techniques such as intoning, *sprechstimme*, spoken interjections, vocal effects (i.e., sighs, laughs, whistling, tongue clicks), fragmented words on indeterminate pitches, or coloristic devices (breathy sounds, straight tones, glissandos)?

7. Does the text flow in a logically connected pattern, or has it been truncated and separated by rests, musical interludes, nonsense syllables, unrelated words or sounds, or simply soundless space?

8. Does the text contain a specific emotional expression that should be projected in this particular setting or has the composer presented the voice as an instrument equal to others, sublimating the words, nuance, and "interpretation" of the text?

9. Can the text be easily understood in its setting, or has comprehension been complicated by rhythmic, melodic, tessitura, or ensemble complexities?

10. What is the impact of the text as it relates to the overall construction of the piece? Are there points of great drama or perhaps musical repose that relate to textual content?

Once these questions have been answered, the singer will have a clearer picture of how to proceed with the realization of the score and how to plan a practice scenario for the development of spontaneity in the text declamation. Spontaneity comes through mental, physical, and emotional gearing of reactions to creative ideas. The mind is always collecting and retaining information at some level. That information may not always be at the immediate recall level, but it is lying in wait, so to speak, for the moment when it can be applied to a given situation. Spontaneity relies on preparation and a store of knowledge and experience that can be drawn to the surface in response to trigger stimuli. That stimuli can be aural, visual, kinesthetic, or perceptual and can occur simultaneously or separately. For the seasoned performer of contemporary music, the act of opening the score and looking at the graphic designs sometimes found there is stimulus enough to bring about spontaneity of interpretation and declamation. However, for singers who have not investigated much of this music, it will require consistent analysis and rehearsal of all elements involved: (1) sounds, colors, and articulations; (2) score notations and textual meaning; (3) coordination of ensemble or electronic tape synchronization; and (4) coordination of extraneous phenomena, such as multimedia effects, stage movement, or the need to play musical instruments or use props. Careful deciphering and systematic rehearsal of all of these elements will elicit a more satisfactory, spontaneous, and versatile response to the musical score.

One of the most creative ways to develop versatility of performance through twentieth-century music is to select a piece that requires or would fit into a nontraditional performance setting. The terms mixed media and multi media refer to contemporary works that combine theatrical elements, electronic media, or aspects of several art forms. This movement toward musical "events" or "happenings," as they have been called, began in the 1960s with composers like John Cage and Luciano Berio and continue in the works of Philip Glass, Robert Ashley, Laurie Anderson, and others. These composers and experimentalists like them have evolved the traditional concert venue into what is sometimes called "performance art." Numerous composers have stepped lightly into this milieu, only slightly broadening the traditional format with pieces that add relatively few theatrical elements to the normal performance expectations. Elizabeth Vercoe, Richard Rodney Bennett, Jean Eichelberger Ivey, Thomas Schudel, and Victoria Bond could be placed in this middle category, having one foot in tradition and the other in experimentation. Representative works by these composers are listed and discussed in appendix B.

Choosing a piece of this type necessarily means a larger number of distractions for the singer. However, it can be looked upon as an opportunity to build on the versatility that was begun in more straightforward, less complex works. One can encounter diverse requirements with each individual piece. No two are exactly the same in construction, ensemble, physical space requirements, or the use of the voice. Again, it is best to start with works that contain only a few new organizational ideas, progressing to the more complex.

A good starting place would be to investigate works that combine traditional singing techniques with theatrical lighting and simple staging. In these works, the composer usually draws a diagram of the stage setup, using designated letters or numbers for the performers' stage positions, specifying movement at certain points throughout the score. Occasionally, pacing of physical movement is indicated in the score by tempo markings or descriptive adjectives, such as slowly glide, step lightly, and move unobtrusively to stage left. If there are no such indications, only a direction to move from one position to another, then the performer must be careful to stylize the movement to coincide with accompanying music or events so as not to draw unnecessary or unwanted attention to that movement. In a piece that requires movement of any kind, the movement must be rehearsed separately in order to develop an appropriate walking tempo and a pattern for the movement from one stage position to the next. Then the movement can be combined with other elements, whether they involve singing, speaking, instrumental interludes, or silence. If special lighting is required (and especially if intricate lighting changes occur during the work), these must be thoroughly rehearsed to ensure that participants can still see musical scores, if needed, or see adequately if making a stage movement. Nothing is more alarming than suddenly finding the stage too dark to move safely or see clearly.

If a work incorporates electronic media of any kind, qualified personnel must be found to furnish needed equipment, to rehearse extensively with the equipment, and to be certain that the performance space is satisfactory for the equipment needed. More elaborate pieces sometimes utilize complex electronic setups and may not be feasible in certain locations. When selecting a piece of this type for the first time, choose one that can be rehearsed simply, perhaps involving only one solo voice and a two-channel electronic tape. Tape cues are usually explained and clearly marked in the score. But there is generally a great deal of freedom in the synchronization of the voice and the tape, allowing the singer to be somewhat free in declamation between large points of voice and tape convergence. These pieces are quite satisfying when working on spontaneity and flexibility in the spacing of pitches while singing. Regimentation and metronomic movement have little to do with this kind of music. Rather, the singer's inner breath rhythm and its application to tonal attacks, pacing of text, and syllabic inflection are more important to the final product.

As the singer gains confidence in this mixed-media genre, more elaborate pieces can be found that add elements such as the use of slides, dancers, audience participation, spoken narrative, instrumental sound effects, or musical ideas and instruments taken from ethnic sources. The ability to feel at home within a multitude of distractions takes time and preparation. But these "happenings" may bring out previously untapped emotional, psychological, perceptual, or technical creativity.

DEVELOPING A PERFORMANCE PERSONALITY

A judge of a national vocal competition was overheard making this statement about the tenor who won. "He sings all of his repertoire well, but the contemporary English group allowed his unique personality to emerge." Since the singer was American born and trained, it is only natural that songs in his native language were his strongest suit. Although American singers are well-trained in the interpretation of the German, French, Italian, and Spanish repertoire, it is difficult to feel comfortable with this music until they have considerable study and numerous performances under their belts. Some singers continue to feel uneasy singing in a foreign language, unable to get past the mental process of translating as they sing, rather than intuitively expressing the foreign text.

This complication should not be taken as an excuse or a reason to sing only in one's native language. Rather, it merely shows that a singer can begin with native language pieces, particularly from the twentieth-century repertoire, to develop an individualized, well-projected stage personality and move with confidence to foreign-language repertoire from any era.

What is meant by a "performer's personality"? A number of characteristics come to mind. The performer's personality is an attitude that the singer must project and communicate to the listener. This attitude, though developed through repetitive practice, must appear spontaneous, changing at will. It must come from a thorough understanding of the composer's design and the interpretative practices of the musical style. The singer's years of study and practice must ultimately result in a musically sensitive, versatile performer who can cope with the repertoire's multiplicity of technical, musical, and expressive demands. The highly skilled interpreter has the ability to magically transport the audience to an imaginary place without the aid of paraphernalia such as sets, costumes, props, or special lighting. When those extramusical elements are added to a performance, the mastery of personality projection becomes even more fascinating within a musical/theatrical context.

It is no easy task to appear spontaneous when performing a series of works, each requiring different attitudes, changes in declamation, and frequent modification of tone color while singing in several foreign languages. But the most persuasive performers are able to achieve this as if merely turning on and off a mental switch. The ability to become a chameleon on stage is essential when one is faced with a high degree of difficulty in the presentation of widely ranging moods, characterizations, and musical styles.

The desired characteristics of the well-projected performer's personality can be significantly enhanced through the use of contemporary literature for the voice. Imagination and insight, essential to the fulfillment of this goal, must be cultivated early in a singer's study, before emotional and imaginative inflexibility is set. Balk (1978, pp. 87–88) provides valuable insight into the process and technique required to connect with and incorporate imagination into performance practice:

> These kinds of skills require technique, practice, and control: in short, an intense awareness of means. One must move from an unconscious, unselfconscious use of natural technique to an equally free, but increasingly aware use of more formalized techniques. In a Jungian interpretation one might say that the goal of singer-actors is to make more and more of their unconscious artistic life available to conscious control. . . . At the same time, this conscious manipulation of physical, vocal, and emotional language must *seem* to be unconscious and natural, which is not an insoluble paradox but a matter of exercise. . . . Adults who wish to become singer-actors must again become as children, trying on sounds and movements and feelings which are not immediately comfortable.

Attention to acting skills and stage presence in general, as well as to vocal technique, will allow the voice and psyche to grow in tandem, creating the singer's true performer's personality as he or she matures physically. As with traditional vocal music, the contemporary repertoire is replete with pieces for all levels of vocal study. Many are useful for focusing on specific practice skills needed to acquire a confident stage personality. To increase musical and theatrical development, pieces should be selected that focus on the following areas for personality development.

1. *Sensitivity to diversity of musical styles*

Choose a variety of twentieth-century song types in contrasting compositional styles (i.e., neoromantic, neoclassical, improvisational, aleatoric or chance, twelve-tone).

2. *Sensitivity to differences in text setting*

Choose works that set texts in varying ways (i.e., syllabically, melismatically, nonsensically, and phonetically) or select a variety of poetic subjects (i.e., humor, sadness, anger, pictorialization, or fear).

3. *Relaxation of body and mind*

Begin with works that do not contain an abundance of novel notational gestures, stage movement, multimedia effects, or extended vocal techniques. When confidence is secure with these pieces, move on to works requiring more complex rehearsals and technical facility. This natural progression from simple to difficult repertoire will prevent physical and mental tension overload during practice periods. Use exercises for development of physical freedom, taking ideas from various visualization/meditation or body alignment approaches, such as the Alexander Technique, visual imaging, or relaxation-response while intoning or casually singing short phrases taken from the repertoire.

4. *Development of stage presence*

Choose pieces that require strong, specific moods that can be conveyed by the eyes and face, practicing the alternation of moods by changing eye positions abruptly or the range of eye focus from near to far, or select pieces that require a more direct audience response to the text and rehearse physical gestures that are geared to elicit that response.

5. *Development of appropriate body language*

Find works requiring subtle body movement or transfer of body weight at significant points in the score. This could involve more elaborate stage movement or merely shifting body language without moving the feet, using equal and unequal body weight, leaning on the piano, or changing from a formal to a casual pose. All of these body responses would necessarily be directed by the mood and meaning of the text being performed.

The vocal artist has a responsibility to communicate both intellectual and emotional ideas while interpreting the composer's intentions. He or she must be committed to the projection of an internal intent, vocalizing and physically representing that which lies in the mind and emotions. If the vocal artist is successful, a memorable performance will result. The translation of complex ideas into un-

derstandable and meaningful declamation requires research, coordination and habituation of physical and psychological responses to musical and textual stimuli,
and careful attention to detail. From these practiced beginnings, a distinctive
performer's personality is born.

In summary, the selection of appropriate twentieth-century repertoire for vocal
study involves numerous elements. A satisfying and economical plan would involve choosing a body of new works that addresses several vocal, dramatic, and
musical issues. Considerations should include range and tessitura, text (suitable
for stated performance purposes), vocal/technical difficulties, and additional performance requirements (i.e., electronic media or stage movement). Choose repertoire with the development of large concepts in mind. Some of these are sensitivity to diverse musical styles found in twentieth-century literature; a means
for mood and character portrayal; a desire to elicit audience response through
humor or overt expression of dramatic ideas; a need to improve aural skills, or
emotional and vocal flexibility within a performance environment. All are valid
reasons to choose certain repertoire to establish a confident performer's personality, one that is unique, mesmerizing and captures the listener's attention.

chapter 3

Vocal Requirements of
Twentieth-Century Music:
Common Characteristics

NONTRADITIONAL VOCAL LINES

One of the singer's most important goals should be the development of a smooth legato connection between pitches, enabling the vocal tone to flow from one register of the voice to the next without undue stress on the musculature controlling the action of the vocal cords. Pedagogues disagree when establishing a practice routine for the development of this essential vocal technique. Some concentrate on elongating the sung vowels while making the intermittent consonants short and crisp. Others talk about achieving a consistency in vocal placement or resonance as the magic recipe for developing a seamless legato. Whatever the technical approach, most pedagogues agree that it is considerably easier to effect a beautiful legato when singing a cantabile or traditional melody, one that is lyrical and contains unifying elements such as stepwise intervalic motion; moderate dynamic levels; a consistent tempo; simple, syllabic declamation; and few, if any, difficulties of range or tessitura.

As the young voice learns to habituate a clean legato through repertoire built on these characteristics from music of the twentieth century and earlier periods, a solid, usable technique will emerge, enabling the singer to begin investigating more adventurous literature. A dependable vocal technique free from physical tension and capable of expressive interpretation through clear, precise diction and appropriate tone color is necessary in order to move to the next level of repertoire difficulty. This concept applies to music selected from any historical period. However, among the varied repertoire of the twentieth century are numerous works that present unique uses of the voice, stretching the singer's vocal/technical skills, interpretative expectations, and musical preparedness to new levels.

The term *nontraditional vocal lines* has been used by numerous writers and performers to describe innovative, noncantabile uses of the voice. This all-inclusive term can manifest itself in numerous ways. The following compositional characteristics are prevalent in some of the music of the past one hundred years. Occasionally, a piece may contain only one of these items, but some works are overflowing with nontraditional elements.

1. *Complex intervalic movement*

Vocal lines containing large skips, very little stepwise motion, angular movement (sudden shifts in direction up or down), the combination of specific and indeterminate pitches, and purposeful dissonance with accompanying voices or instruments.

2. *Experimental declamation*

Text projected through recitation, *sprechstimme*, declamatory-recitative parlando style, a sudden switch from cantabile to experimental effects, or the use of IPA phonemes and repeated syllables (see part II).

3. *Vocal effects*

Imitative or improvised vocal sounds largely expressed through imagery concepts. These include laughing on indeterminate pitches; whistling; falsetto tones on indeterminate pitches; vowel morphing (gradually changing the original vowel to another indicated vowel while moving through several pitches); vocal muting (gradually opening and closing the mouth to form a particular vowel); tongue trills or lip buzzes; exaggerated glissandos; exaggerated inhalation and exhalation; tremolo muting, in which the hand is placed over the mouth and then removed to create a tonal color change; whispering; and shouting on indeterminate pitches (see part II).

In choosing repertoire from works that are built on these concepts, the present level of the singer's vocal ability must be considered. Performance results depend heavily on vocal, psychological, musical, and intellectual flexibility and preparedness for any given piece. Does the work have too few or too many new ideas for pedagogical objectives to be met? Since repertoire choices are vast among this period's output, finding appropriate music is not the issue; rather, knowing one's vocal limits, motivation level, and basic musicianship are the crucial elements.

EXTENDED RANGES

Singers have been aided by tradition and the *Fach* system (developed in Germany to categorize singers into specific voice and character types) in determining the voice type and timbre best suited for a particular work. Vocal pedagogy texts often give diagrams of expected vocal ranges for every voice category from contrabass to coloratura soprano. Many of them also specify the location of vocal register changes (passaggio events) that occur within each voice type.

To accommodate vocal range and tessitura comfort differences among voices, traditional art song literature has often been transposed to various keys according to singers' needs. This approach has worked well with selections by Schubert, Schumann, Fauré, and many others. However, as with much of the operatic repertoire of the past and present, oratorio and mass solos of various periods, and other works with specific original key performance requirements, twentieth-century composers (especially those who write music using extended techniques) would not normally allow a piece to be transposed to accommodate the singer. The composer probably had an overall sound quality and color in mind for the piece and the voice for which it was intended. As with operatic arias from any stylistic period that belong to a certain *Fach*, the singer must choose twentieth-century works of all kinds that suit the color and overall range of his or her voice without putting undue stress on the vocal stamina to perform the music.

Some contemporary works require careful score study to determine what voice type and timbre the composer had in mind. One should not assume the piece is suited to his or her voice simply because of the composer's voice type indication on the score. The repertoire contains many examples that show the confusion some singers encounter. For instance, in George Crumb's *Ancient Voices of Children*, one of the major works of the second half of the century, there is a designation that it should be sung by a soprano. The vocal range is G#3 to C6 with an approximate tessitura of G4 to F5. The voice moves freely throughout that extensive range. In Ramon Zupko's *Voices* (for soprano and electronic tape), the soprano sings from G#3 to B5, staying within a lower tessitura of F4 to C5. The soprano who could easily vocalize the Crumb piece might tire quickly in the Zupko because of the dramatic intensity required in the middle voice. Also, due to the color range required for each piece, it might be more successfully sung by a lyric mezzo-soprano with a wide vocal range, as has occurred frequently with the Crumb work.

The overall range and tessitura of any piece has a direct effect on several vocal/technical issues relating to score interpretation and realization. Some areas to consider are:

1. *Can register transitions be negotiated easily?*

In order to satisfy this requirement, the piece's major dramatic and musical stress points must be evaluated to determine if they fall within the singer's weakest vocal register or passaggio event. If so, this may place an undue burden on the voice, causing fatigue.

2. *Does the dynamic range of the piece, coupled with pitch range and tessitura, pose problems for certain passaggio events or registers of the voice?*

For instance, if there are a large number of FF pitches indicated on extremely high or low notes that are normally difficult for the singer, then there is a likelihood for the development of physical tension while the singer is trying to accommodate these requirements.

3. *Does the piece contain extended techniques such as shouts, sprechstimme, or breathy singing in extreme ranges of the voice?*

Taken alone, these do not necessarily fatigue the voice, but if combined with other range and tessitura difficulties they could compound the stress issue.

4. *Are the vocal colors required by the piece easily accommodated within the overall range and tessitura indicated?*

Many pieces contain a multiplicity of explicit instructions for vocal color changes. Sometimes each note has a different designation. The ability to easily shift from one vocal color to another directly affects the significance of range and tessitura to vocal fatigue. If extreme color changes are required in extreme vocal ranges or within weak passaggio events, psychological and physical tension is more likely to occur.

5. *In what context are the extremely low or high pitches found?*

If accompanying instruments or electronic tape are producing high volumes and/or pitch levels, surrounding the voice with numerous kinds of sonic complexities, then it will be difficult for the singer to sustain pitches at the upper and lower ends of the voice. It will also require more efficient resonation in the tone and perhaps a larger vocal instrument to easily project through the sound density.

In the final analysis, no vocal category indication can be taken at face value in some of this repertoire. As with music from other eras, singers must weigh personality, vocal technique and maturity, intellectual interest, and motivational energy when choosing repertoire. That applies when looking at the range and tessitura requirements of any piece. Some composers may be quite familiar with the salient characteristics of each voice type and may know how to use it to its optimum level, but others may not know which pitfalls to avoid when writing for that voice type, not understanding the vocal/technical problems every vocal category is likely to encounter in certain areas of the voice. In the latter case, the composer may write a piece in which he or she would like to use the range of a lyric soprano but is really looking for the darker vocal color of a mezzo. That may make the piece difficult for either voice type to realize successfully. In cases such as this, the singer must simply decide whether the piece works for his or her voice and disregard the voice category designation altogether.

AD LIB AND IMPROVISATION

One of the elements found in the structure of some contemporary pieces is a seeming lack of organization. The score may look like a graphic pictorialization of space and time, having no bar lines, meter signatures, or staff lines. It may contain notes inside boxes or notes scattered across the page in patterns to show a density or leanness of activity. These kinds of scores are representational of imaginary ideas, not outlines of specific time, space, and timbre. There may be no preconceived scheme or expectation, therefore each performance can be vastly different from all the others. Since there has been no attempt to dictate a frame or specific notation for indeterminateness, composers have been free to organize sound in quite varied and picturesque ways.

The sheer novelty of the notation and its layout on the page may cause confusion because learned mental patterns, formed through years of reading traditional notation, are turned upside down. In this context, the concepts of ad lib and improvisation thrive. These concepts have been used by numerous composers from the period. Some were seeking a randomness of sound through *aleatory* (chance elements) or indefiniteness. In this case, the piece is allowed to find its own flow, texture, and aesthetic meaning by purposely giving general outlines rather than specific directions for melody, pitches, rhythm, tempo, dynamics, and coordination of events or musical lines. Even the length of the work may differ each time it is performed. Others use these terms more conservatively, perhaps incorporating only a few improvisatory or ad lib elements into an otherwise traditional work.

Improvisation can take numerous forms and involve all aspects of a composition. The performer should look for the following types of usage as the piece is being analyzed and prepared for practice. Specific information concerning some commonly found notational devices for improvisation can be found in part II.

1. Indeterminate pitches may be indicated by using more or less than the usual five staff lines or no lines at all. The important concept to remember is that the pattern of the notes (up and down) should be followed, allowing the voice to rise and fall through both chest and head registers if indicated by the notation.

2. Rhythmic structure is often expressed by nonsynchronization of the voice with accompanying instruments. There should be no attempt to link the voice and instruments at precise points of reference unless otherwise indicated. Notational devices for this purpose can include rapidly changing meter patterns, with different metric patterns indicated for each simultaneously sounding musical line; proportional notation with graduated note beams showing accelerando and ritardando; + and − signs signifying speed; a diagrammatic spacing of the tones that shows speed deviations or duration of space between the tones; or simply a stated desire that one line should move faster or slower than others accompanying it.

3. Rhythmic and pitch organization is occasionally left completely to the performer's discretion. Specific pitches may be written and placed within a frame or box with a direction to perform them in any order and at any speed, as long as all the notes are repeated a designated number of times. The singer's imagination and will to experiment are the only guides here.

4. Improvisatory factors may include the subjective lengthening or shortening of specific tones. Some of these examples may be timed sequences indicated in seconds or held by fermati. The singer's interpretation of these notations should rely heavily on an imaginary feeling for elapsed time rather than on stopwatch accuracy.

5. Improvisation of textual materials are common. Uses may include random repetition of a sung or spoken phrase; ad lib scat singing on nonsense syllables devised by the singer; a reversal of the normal left-to-right reading of the text; or the dissection of individual consonant or vowel sounds from a text, repeated at will or outside the context of the original phrase from which it was taken.

6. Dynamics, vocal colors, and vocal articulation may be indicated by a creative use of original visual shapes rather than normal notation. These devices are

often invented by individual composers and should come with thorough descriptions of how they are to be employed, though the interpretation will necessarily be different with each performer. These artistic, pictorial representations can take different forms and have numerous realizations due to the lack of uniform use by composers. The singer's ability to free his or her inner visual concepts of sound is important. Allow for spontaneity and experimentation in vocalization. It is essential to finding a satisfying result with this kind of notation.

These improvisational possibilities should be thought of as opportunities for honing interpretive skills. Each establishes a fresh context for developing flexibility in vocal coloration, structure analysis, and rhythm expression. It also provides a frame for the synthesis of creative imagination through visualization, the stylization of vocal declamation, and coordination of external visual stimuli with an internal psychic response. A performance of this type of repertoire can be mentally and physically freeing since the parameters of allowable interpretation are extremely wide and the performer is not weighed down by traditional expectations for their realization.

WHERE'S THE PITCH?

We have already established that nontraditional vocal lines are a common occurrence in twentieth-century music. Complicated harmonies and the absence of a harmonic underpinning for the voice are also frequent compositional traits. Additionally, large vocal skips and angular vocal lines appear with regularity. Finally, pitch references may be difficult to find. Some of the immediate reactions to these pitch reference complications may be (1) Where's the melody? (2) How do I find my first pitch? and (3) How do I organize practice time to better prepare my aural/vocal response to music that seems almost random in its organization?

The idea of melody is illusory. The pitch-deciphering process does not depend on it. The term *melody* does not necessarily signify linear movement, a recognizable tune, or symmetrical phrasing. Since childhood, we have been programmed with these traditional concepts of melody, and it is difficult to think of it as something more abstract. Melodies can be mere suggestions of musical patterns, colors, or sound qualities that come into the foreground of a musical work. Therefore, a Crumb melody may be nothing like that written by Schumann or Fauré, who used mostly stepwise motion with a moderate number of large skips in the vocal line, allowed minimal interruption in the declamation of text, relied on a vocal legato, and provided a harmonic base that anchored the vocal pitch, allowing the singer to find his or her own pitches without undue effort.

Some modern works are abstract, built on random pitches that make up an overall musical pattern. This nonspecific design may be distributed among the voice and other instruments involved. Developing pitch security in pieces of this kind is a challenging musical experience, but not an impossibility in most cases. The repertoire may be "ear stretching," requiring a fine-tuning of the aural sense. It is true that some pieces in the repertoire have so few pitch references and so many musical complexities that perfect pitch is a requirement for their realization. But that scenario does not apply to the great majority of works available for all voice types.

If a piece contains numerous complexities, the singer may become distracted and find it more difficult than usual to find pitches. Those distractions could involve rhythmic structure, use of extended vocal techniques—a requirement for stage movement while singing, use of unfamiliar accompanying instrumental sounds or electronic tape, or playing instruments while singing. Any or all of these can be enough to turn one's attention from the location of an essential pitch reference. But this does not mean that the piece is beyond the singer's performance capabilities. Rather, the singer must look for new ways of rehearsing and new strategies for finding pitches, and must focus on one requirement at a time before combining all elements occurring simultaneously.

Some useful ideas for the development of confidence in securing pitches are:

1. *Analyze the notation and its structure*

Diagram the general outline of any melody present and determine if all sung notes apply to it. This can be done by taking individual sections of the work apart from the whole, drawing a pictorial diagram of the musical flow, and practicing only that section before going to the next. This will help to assimilate the vocal technique needed to achieve the coordination of text declamation, pitch, and any other extraneous requirements.

2. *Mark tape cues*

If the piece uses an electronic tape, look for visual tape cues marked in the score. Listen for the specific sounds occurring on the tape at the point of the marked cues. Practice those sections until the pitches are easy to find before rehearsing the piece from beginning to end.

Occasionally there are few visible cues marked in the score. In this case, start the tape and listen to it alone several times while looking at the score, without singing. This will allow the ear to become accustomed to sounds on the tape, the pace of the taped sounds, and to find the points of reference where large segments are to be connected to the voice. By working backward in small increments from those large connecting points, adjusting the pace at which the voice moves, you can locate references on the tape for difficult-to-find pitches. It can be time-consuming in the initial stage, but it will prevent panic later when the piece must be run from start to finish.

3. *Develop a kinesthetic response*

Play as much of the score as possible on the piano, establishing a physical, muscular response to the music. Concentrate on difficult entrances, hard-to-find pitches, angular melodic lines, and general direction of vocal movement. Exact tempo is not necessary at this stage. Instead, locate chords, tone clusters, or intervals in the accompaniment that precede a vocally difficult entrance and play them slowly, many times, getting used to the sound quality and listening for pitches that will enable you to access your beginning note. It could be the same note found in another octave or several beats prior to your entrance. It could also be another note from which you can reference your pitch by singing up or down by a small interval. Rehearse these sections in isolation, gradually assimilating them into larger sections.

4. Pay attention to voice placement

Analyze the vocal line in relation to the use of vocal registration. Most singers develop a kinesthetic feeling for certain pitches according to the singer's register events, resonance qualities, and breath energy requirements to produce those notes. When the singer does not have perfect pitch, a good relative pitch sense combined with a vocal kinesthetic feeling for pitch is key to quickly finding and retaining abstract tones.

The identification of musical stresses and releases within the construction of the vocal line is also helpful in finding pitches. The first few notes of a phrase may need to be thought of as leading tones to a stronger pitch occurring later. That later pitch may be easier to locate than the beginning one. So by changing one's aural focus, preliminary pitches may more easily be found within their new context.

5. Learn exact pitches

Never rely on native instinct or guesswork to assume that an interval is correct. Check it thoroughly against accompanying figures. If still unsure, tape a difficult segment, rehearsing with the tape until the pitch is secure. Only when notation signifies that pitches are indeterminate should a mere generalization of the vocal line shape be satisfactory. This rule applies to sprechstimme, as well. If the sprechstimme contains notated intervalic changes, then exact pitches should be learned at the outset, followed by vocal inflection of the tones. This procedure is discussed in detail in part II.

6. Excise difficult-to-hear passages

Short, difficult-to-hear sections can be taken apart and used during vocal warm-ups. Making an unfamiliar or awkward interval seem normal to the ear is the goal. If it is incorporated into a daily vocalization routine, it will soon present fewer problems when encountered in the music.

Trial and error and experimentation are needed to develop a satisfactory practice scheme for locating hard-to-hear pitches. No one plan will succeed with every person. Each singer must employ all avenues of aural, kinesthetic, and vocal response when working out a practice strategy. Persistence is also important. Aural skills cannot be magically improved in a few short sessions. But over several days or a few weeks, dramatic improvement can occur. With this improvement comes more security and self-confidence in all areas of vocal performance.

A QUESTION OF INTERPRETATION

The concept of appropriate vocal interpretation of twentieth-century music includes numerous subtopics for discussion among composers, critics, vocal coaches, concertgoers, and performers. Vocal interpretation involves such elementary components as establishment of natural breathing places within a phrase; execution of precise tonal attacks (i.e., legato, staccato, marcato); proper enunciation, pronunciation, and articulation of the text; and the projection of a clearly defined vocal tone color that expresses the basic mood or moods of the text. However, in order to fully capture the composer's intent, vocal interpretation must go beyond these basics of song interpretation.

Since this century has produced everything from twelve-tone compositions to electronic music, with a lot of neoclassicism, neoromanticism, indeterminacy, mixed media, general experimentation, and anti-anything-traditional in between, the singer must do some investigation concerning the historical or genre placement of chosen repertoire within all of these possibilities. Establishing a historical perspective is crucial in determining the particular type of vocal approach one should take when outlining a satisfactory interpretation. Once the genre and general compositional approach has been determined, a more specific examination of the composition's organization and fundamental design should be the focus. Some areas that relate directly to the vocal interpretation are:

What kind of text has been selected?

The text could be built on traditional rhyme schemes or descriptive prose. It may contain strings of words selected just for their phonemic sounds. Onomatopoeia or nonsense sounds may be present. In some cases, there may be no words at all, merely vowel and consonant sounds strung out to follow tonal graphics.

How has the composer treated the text?

There are numerous examples of diverse text treatments during this period. Many composers continue to set text in a traditional cantabile, syllabic, recitative, or melismatic fashion. These ideas reach as far back as the Baroque period for their origins. Those modern composers who have made a more personal stamp on text declamation have tried myriad experimentations with text settings. Some common devices include:

1. *Truncated textual material*

The composer may choose to set only a portion of the original poem or prose, leaving out large segments or simply omitting a few words here and there.

2. *Textual separation*

Lines or words from a chosen text have been selected for a specific emphasis and repeated several times. These repeated utterances may have appeared only once in the original text. At times a word or phrase may be taken out of its original context or may be used as a catalyst for the musical setting as a whole, appearing randomly throughout the work.

3. *Textual dissection*

Individual consonants, vowels, or phonemes from words within the original text have been extracted and employed as phrase generators for the musical development. These incomplete words might make up the textual usage throughout a work or could be combined with a more traditional text setting and used for contrast.

4. Text improvisation

In some works, the performer is directed to take a given text and repeat all or part of it in an ad lib fashion. Here the singer has total control of pacing, the number of repetitions, and, occasionally, the amount of text chosen for repetition.

There are also instances in which the sounds, syllables, or complete words used in the text are totally at the singer's discretion, with only a general direction, such as "ad lib," "scat sing," or "improvise syllabically," given over the musical tones.

5. Textual flow

Some compositions show a complete disregard in their text setting for the original flow of the text. The individual words within poetic phrases are sometimes separated by rests, small or large musical fragments containing no text, or the insertion of words or sounds totally unrelated to the original text. These extraneous insertions might include vocal sound effects such as laughing on an exact or indeterminate pitch, whistling, tongue clicks, sighs, heavy breathing, humming, or lip buzzes and tongue trills.

The performer's first task is to determine whether the text has been used to influence the musical setting or whether it is basically irrelevant to the organization of musical details. Both scenarios can occur. If the text has an influence on the setting, it may be manifested through tone painting, synchronization of musical and syllabic stress, and the coordination of text meaning with tessitura, tempo, dynamics, or vocal coloration markings. A textual influence on the musical structure can also become evident through the establishment of structural segments within the piece. These segments may be defined by key changes, a change in the type of vocal declamation, or abrupt rhythmic pattern changes that coincide with contrasts in the text. In addition, sudden shifts in tessitura or instrumental and vocal timbres can accentuate or subdue a particular textual passage.

If a composer chooses to use the voice as merely another texture within the larger coloristic context of the work, the declamation of text, as to literal meaning and projection, becomes a nonissue. Here the issue is one of creating qualities of sound. The text merely becomes a tool for the creation of timbre within the overall musical framework. This type of vocal setting presents some obvious vocal and intellectual problems for the singer-interpreter: (1) *Should the singer try to interpret the text at all, whether it consists of words, syllables, nonsense sounds, or vocal effects?* Perhaps merely developing a somewhat limited color palette for the voice, trying to blend within the ensemble surrounding it, would be more appropriate in this instance. (2) *Should the voice express emotion or mood contrasts in this context?* Perhaps not. Avoid an inclination toward natural word inflection and dramatic vocal color changes unless directed otherwise in the score. Rather, an attempt to remain emotionally and imaginatively uninvolved in the text expression is desirable.

These ideas go against most of what singers have been taught concerning the interpretation of traditional art song and operatic repertoire, but they more closely resemble performance practices frequently discussed by music historians when describing the music of the Renaissance. Consequently, it is not surprising that many singers of the contemporary avant garde also feel quite comfortable performing music from the Renaissance, showing less interest in the more overtly expressive genres from the eighteenth and nineteenth centuries.

A singer's intellectual, emotional, and vocal response to this type of contemporary writing is important. This particular style of contemporary music, used by only a segment of the composers working during the period, may not be right for the singer who requires a larger spectrum of expressive possibilities. In that case, repertoire choices can easily be taken from the other realms of available twentieth-century compositional techniques.

chapter 4

Vocal Coloration

*W*hen contemplating the musical output of the last one hundred years, no issue is more compelling than that of the composer's aesthetic intent. This aesthetic intent, as it relates to vocal interpretation, involves the coloristic expression of pitches and any text applied to them. Paramount in this relationship of the voice to interpretation is the establishment of a vocal tone color appropriate for the projection of any dramatic import inherent in the text and its setting. Since the music varies considerably in construction, aesthetic ideals, and use of the voice, no single interpretative approach can or should be used when considering how to realize individual works from the period.

WHO IS IN CONTROL: THE SINGER OR THE COMPOSER?

This question does not have a simple answer that applies to all contemporary music. As with other philosophical questions relating to twentieth-century composition, one can take numerous approaches to arrive at a reasonable clarification of this question as it relates to vocal color changes within individual works.

We have already established that the singer must do responsible research to determine the general historical, organizational, and aesthetic ideology to which each piece belongs. An inherently imposed control of vocal tone color, designed by the composer, will differ greatly from one kind of musical framework to another. For instance, in a work such as George Rochberg's *Eleven Songs for Mezzo Soprano*, the singer encounters numerous coloristic adjectives printed above the vocal line. At times, there is a different color designation for each note to be sung. For example, in song 9, "So Late!" within a span of ten consecutively notated pitches for the voice, all of the following color markings are indicated: *covered sound, dream-like, very warm, liquid, smooth throat to floating head, quasi spoken, sung (covered),* and *chest.* A singer's first assessment of this proliferation of color directions may be that the outcome has been totally dictated, giving the singer no choice in the matter. However, as we know, no two voices are exactly alike. Each has unique qualities of timbre, resonance, placement, and strength within its vocal registers. Also, each is housed in a body and coordinated by an intellect and a range of emotional experience unique to that individual. Given all of these differences among singers, an exact, preconceived interpretation of such detailed color indications could never be achieved by every singer who attempted them.

Many composers, like Rochberg, have been prolific in their use of color suggestions in the score and probably had a particular vocal color in mind when writing the piece. The composer may have even related the desired color to a particular voice for whom the piece was written. But that has nothing to do with the realization of the score by a singer totally unfamiliar with the origins of the composer's color ideas. Instead, it has everything to do with the basic vocal technique each singer brings to the realization of those color indications, how flexibly the singer can maneuver through quickly changing colors, and how imaginative he or she is when experimenting with colors that lie outside those normally used in traditional repertoire. Therefore, a work with composer-generated color designations is not necessarily more restrictive for the singer than one containing few or no directions. The singer still has the freedom to be creative and imaginative within his or her own realm of color possibilities. No particular timbre should be considered a universal requirement for any designation in the score. Each must be adapted to the singer's own voice and produced with careful attention to detail, contrast, and the use of correct, comfortable vocal declamation.

MUSCULAR COORDINATION

One of the psychological effects of looking at a score filled with specific color designations, perhaps changing on each pitch, is the danger of becoming physically tense while trying to concentrate on those fast-paced changes within the vocal line. Physical tension can be caused by several factors involved in vocalization, and it is not exclusive to the performance of contemporary music. Pedagogues who approach the teaching of singing from both the psychological and scientific points of view relate physical tension and its effect on vocalization to the concepts of muscular coordination, visualization of technical concepts, mind-body integration, and habituation of efficient technical skills. All of these are relevant to the discussion of interpretative control within contemporary music.

Quickly changing vocal colors, angular melodies, and sudden successive and cumulative shifts in dynamics present challenges to an elementary vocal technique. If the composer has indicated numerous quick changes of any kind in the score, the singer can dissect short segments from the work for slow, methodical practice, rather than merely launching into a read-through approach. As each color, vocal effect, large leap, or shift from ppp to fff is rehearsed separately, with vocal and mental rest in between, the muscle structure quickly adapts to the new demands of the score. Continue this type of rehearsal, slowly expanding the span of pitches and scope of the score until a fairly large section of the work can be sung in a relaxed manner. At the first sign of physical tension, stop the rehearsal or change the rehearsal content to another kind of musical composition with a different use of the voice. Variety in the practice session is always desirable, giving the musculature that controls the voice a chance to rest and to build stamina in its proficiency of coordination.

These psychological and technical concepts apply to contemporary works that have numerous controls imposed by the composer, as well as chance or aleatoric pieces that allow the singer almost total interpretative freedom. In either case, the muscle structure must learn to respond to novel ideas that the singer may not have previously encountered. If the singer is placed in an uncertain creative situation, physical tension can be generated as the muscles respond to nervous energy, mental confusion, or unfamiliar and unrehearsed vocal patterns.

VISUALIZATION OF TECHNICAL CONCEPTS

Singers learn to negotiate contradictions throughout their study of vocal technique. They are often confronted by opposite, perhaps widely contrasting ideas about how to perform the most elementary tasks, such as breathing. At some point in each singer's career, he or she must come to a physical and mental comfort zone in the ability to cope with all of the complexities involved in the singing process. Repertoire and technical ideas that seem to produce, rather than alleviate, physical and mental stress are discarded.

Part of this process of adapting to complex ideas in vocal technique or in score realization is the psychological approach one takes. The development of one's imagination is a primary skill needed to reach a high level of sophistication in interpretation. Again, this applies to music of all periods and genres. However, contemporary repertoire frequently inspires the singer to expand what may have been usable, interpretative skills in the traditional sense into far-reaching, exaggerated dexterity. These new, score-generated skills may require active mental imagery skills in order to activate or *imagine* novel ways of perceiving vocal tone color interpretation. According to Emmons and Thomas (1998, p. 170), mental imagery is of paramount importance in accelerating the learning process: "Any form of imagery will supplement your physical practice of a new vocal skill, will improve it, will increase your learning speed, and will aid your consistency. All imagery work can enhance your performance in some way, if only by developing a higher level of self-confidence."

MIND-BODY COORDINATION

When discussing the projection of vocal tone color, we must consider two views. Some singers have focused on the physical elements that contribute to free, balanced, and pliable tone production, such as efficient muscle function and coordination, optimum health and fitness, effective stress management, and proper body alignment. Others have emphasized psychological factors centering on the development of a positive self-image, the projection of a singer's personality, and the honing of perceptual and conceptual skills through mental imagery.

In order to reach a skillful level of tone color projection, especially when numerous colors are desired, the singer should consider all of these elements. The physical attributes help the body to function properly and efficiently when producing vocal tone. Good physical health, proper body alignment, and a release of physical tension caused by stress are necessary for development of smooth muscle coordination. However, these positive physical factors alone are not enough to bring about beautiful, memorable, expressive singing. They may produce a well-focused vocal tone that is delivered with ease throughout a wide range of pitch and dynamics. But the tone will remain neutral in color and project a sameness of expression, no matter what text or musical style is being sung, unless the psychological/imagery part of the singer's being is invoked. Emmons and Thomas (1998, p. 162) point out that "without an ability to image, expression in performance can be extremely limited."

Mental imagery is a recall of sensory perceptions as they relate to touch, taste, smell, hearing, and sight. Pictures of scenes, events, places, textures, moods, interactions, sounds, and colors are valuable references when establishing concepts of tone color, whether for a particular pitch or for an entire vocal work. A singer's skill level at sensory recall is all-important to the outcome of any score realization. Vocal tone is as dramatically affected by thoughts as it is by physical events. If we think sad thoughts while singing a cheery text, the vocal tone will not conform to that text and vice versa, because the mental imagery is contrary to that desired by the text. Our thoughts affect every physical aspect of singing, including breath management, mouth space, facial expression, physical stance, placement of tone, size and shape of vowels used, and speed of articulation. Visualization of inner thoughts is a key element in the eloquent projection of vocal tone color.

HABITUATION OF VOCAL COLOR SKILLS

The establishment of a consistent, systematic, workable practice plan is essential for the development of vocal technique, no matter what repertoire is being studied. The habituation of individual vocal skills, such as the ability to quickly manipulate vocal tone color indications prevalent in twentieth-century music, is crucial since a large number of unfamiliar notational gestures may also occur in those works, considerably complicating matters.

Analysis of the musical score is necessary to reach a high level of performance and understanding of a work exhibiting complicated vocal declamation. It is very beneficial to dissect and practice individual sections that are unusual or particularly difficult, in order to establish a vocally comfortable declamation before trying to incorporate these sections into the whole. This can be tedious work, but time will be saved later and so will the voice if the singer learns to gradually cope with a large number of new vocal, intellectual, and musical requirements, such as atypical, quickly changing vocal colors.

As the singer habituates individual vocal demands in color, he or she will more easily develop flow from one to the other and from one work to another, since devices of this type are likely to be encountered in other pieces from the period. Therefore, each singer must develop a practice scheme that will provide for the establishment of a relaxed yet stimulating process for learning each piece as quickly as possible. This kind of repertoire does not lend itself well to the "general overview" type of rehearsal, which can often be done with simple through-composed or strophic song material. That cursory approach is much more likely to build frustration, mental or vocal stress and fatigue, and a dislike for the music, leading to a failure to perform the work.

Trial and error, experimentation, and imagery must be employed when practicing and habituating the production of individual tone colors. Once a vocal placement, vowel shape, timbre, and intensity have been decided on for a particular tone or section of a work, that color can then be rehearsed repeatedly until ingrained, enabling the singer to recall it at will. When this color becomes part of the singer's usable palette of colors, it can be easily transferred to other works.

DELETION OF VIBRATO (A CONTEMPORARY COLOR VARIATION)

This element of vocal technique has been the subject of much controversy among singers. The controversy has primarily related to the use of vibratoless or straight tones when singing choral music of the Renaissance, as has been the tradition in some schools of choral singing, such as the English School or the style of singing advocated by F. Melius Christiansen at St. Olaf College in St. Olaf, Minnesota. Some choral directors and voice teachers believe that vibrato *was* used in the Renaissance. However, since there is no definitive answer to that question, the solution remains a matter of opinion and acquired taste. If one listens carefully to well-respected interpreters of songs by composers such as Poulenc, Strauss, Schubert, Duparc, and Debussy, to name a few, straight tones are a common occurrence. In this case, straight tone is used for expressive purposes, to bring out subtle emotional contrasts by means of a vocal color change. The vibratoless tone is quite useful for delineating specific or subtle characteristics of individual words in a text. For example, the word *mournful* can be made to sound as such by deleting the vibrato, giving the voice a more plaintive, sympathetic quality. Singers of folk music, multiethnic music, jazz, and other popular styles have also used straight tones to express their particular aesthetic.

Some voice teachers and vocal pedagogy texts have promoted the idea that a vocal tone should always include vibrato no matter what style or historical period of music is being sung. In general, it has been suggested that the health of the voice is somehow related to the use of vibrato, though no relevant studies have shown that using a vibratoless tone will damage the voice. As Robert Sataloff (1998, p. 21) states, "Vibrato is a rhythmic variation in frequency and intensity. Its exact source remains uncertain, and its desirable characteristics depend on voice range and the type of music sung."

Indeed, if the use of straight tones summarily destroyed voices, thousands of singers would have lost their voices by now, since the use of nonvibrato is prevalent in some musical styles and cultures. When listening to a well-known, vocally trained group such as The King's Singers, who have had a long, illustrious career, it is obvious that straight-tone singing is a staple in their repertoire of vocal colors and has not impaired their singing voices. They are able to switch at will between a normal vibrato and a straight tone according to the style of music or the interpretation of a particular text. The same could be said of highly effective interpreters of the German Lied and French mélodie, such as Dietrich Fischer-Dieskau, Janet Baker, Brigitte Fassbaender, and Gerard Souzay. Finally, acclaimed interpreters of twentieth-century music, such as Jan DeGaetani and Cathy Berberian, were facile in their use of straight tones and retained healthy voices through long careers.

Since all of these singers and many others have employed vibratoless tones and continued to sing well for decades without obvious vocal problems, it can be assumed that their use of straight tones did no fatal damage to the voice. Rather, with proper vocal technique and a relaxed, physically balanced approach to tone production, straight tones can be safely employed as a color contrast within a larger context of vocal declamation built on the use of normal vibrato.

Another curious opinion, occasionally encountered, maintains that straight tones sound flat in pitch to people used to hearing vibrato. The logic needed to support such a concept is hard to find. Since children normally have no vibrato in their tone, neither do excellent children's choirs, though they sing freely, beautifully, and on pitch. Some symphonic wind instruments play without vibrato as a matter of style, and various folk and multiethnic music types do not regularly use vibrato. Vibratoless tones are all around us. We hear these kinds of sounds daily and do not think of them as sounding flat unless they *are* in actuality, flat. If the performers are producing the tones correctly and accurately in pitch, they will sound so, whether there is vibrato or not. A healthy, well-coordinated, resonant voice, supported by efficient breath control, should be able to vary vocal tone color in numerous ways. The use of straight tones is just one of many colors available within a complete palette of interpretative expression.

Many twentieth-century composers have desired that singers produce vibratoless tones and have placed indications in their scores for this technique. However, it is not stylistically valid to state that all twentieth-century music should be performed without vibrato, as some have assumed. Not all twentieth-century music is alike in construction or aesthetic intent; and it should not be lumped together into one genre or style.

Though the incorporation of straight tones is more prevalent in contemporary music than in the Romantic period, for example, the aesthetic purpose of its use by interpreters of vocal music from both eras is similar: a desire to set apart specific words or sections of a text. The result is the emergence of vocal contrast that becomes an aesthetic aid to overall interpretation. In both historical periods, a vibratoless tone is often employed to produce a solemn, stark, unemotional, detached vocal quality. When applied sparely or continuously throughout a work, this quality can be used for dramatic projection of either textual or musical ideas, according to the composer's indication or the singer's interpretative realization of the score.

Contemporary composers often give explicit directions for the use of straight tones. A few, such as John Cage, asked for vibratoless tones to be employed throughout a work, as in *Forever and Sunsmell* for voice and percussion duo. Indications of a general use of the technique are most often found in the preface to a work or at the beginning of the vocal line, above or below the first pitch. In contrast to this general application of the technique, most pieces from the period include only a few vibratoless tones or none at all. When they are a part of the work, the composer will normally write words such as *nonvibrato, straight tone, hollow tone, white tone,* or *stark* over the pitches in question. In addition, a special footnote may be given for the production of the required sound. Composers such as George Crumb and George Rochberg have been meticulous in providing helpful interpretative remarks in the preface to works. However, other composers are not as clear or give no input whatsoever to aid the singer with realization. From the performer's standpoint, it would be wise for composers to supply a page of directions for the interpretation of any unusual requests.

Straight or vibratoless tones may be inserted by the singer even when the composer has not requested them in the score. Again, this device is generally employed for color contrast within a text or for vocal coloration of specific words or vocal lines as they relate to accompanying instruments. For instance, the last two notes of Ned Rorem's song "Look Down Fair Moon" might be sung with a straight tone to enhance the starkness of the text and music. Rorem has placed the marking *molto espressivo* over the last two words, "sacred moon," with a dynamic marking from p to pp. This comes at the end of the Walt Whitman text that describes a scene of death under the moon's light. The same effect could be used successfully for the final section of Aaron Copland's "Going to Heaven!" The Emily Dickinson poem, which contemplates the possibility of the existence of a heaven, ends with a description of seeing a loved one for the last time: "I left them in the ground." Since the piano part has been brought to a minimum and used only to suggest color under the voice, a sudden hollow, straight tone in the voice would be an effective way to interpret the bareness of the musical context and bleakness of the text.

If not requested in the score, these kinds of techniques should be used sparingly and only for a special effect. It would not be desirable for the singer to use straight tones merely as a way of stylizing all modern music, in order to set it apart from previous historical periods, since much of the music written between 1900 and 2000 was composed with traditional vocalization concepts in mind.

When rehearsing the application of straight tones to a musical context, one must consider several practical ideas. These considerations relate not only to the appropriateness of using nonvibrato, but also to the correct projection of its use for the continued health of the voice.

Interpretative considerations

The volume and color of straight tones should match musical and dramatic indications. Take cues from composer indications or from textual intent for their application. Straight tones should never bring attention to themselves in a haphazard or purposeless fashion or become an affectation of the singer's technique.

Straight tones should be used judiciously in music with no such composer indications. They must relate to a specific textual or musical nuance that would be more effectively expressed by the use of nonvibrato. A thorough text analysis is a necessity in determining where the addition of nonvibrato would be effective.

Individually rehearse all notes or sections of works that delete vibrato, gradually alternating this technique with a normal vibrato used on all other pitches. This allows the mental and physical aspects of interpretation to flow more easily between the two styles.

Technical considerations

Sing straight tones in a normal, well-supported, subtle, floating manner, never yelled or harsh. Mental and physical relaxation are essential to the production of this technique. Occasionally, a vocal score will indicate that a loud, driven, harshly projected tone is required. In such cases, the performer must approach this particular usage of straight tone with care and never force the voice to produce the sound through physical tension. As with normal vibrato production, the volume of nonvibrato singing should never exceed that which can be comfortably attained through natural resonance and coordinated, balanced breath support. Any attempt to physically force the voice to project beyond its natural limits can result in vocal fatigue. Repetitive attempts to sing in a tense, forced manner can be detrimental to vocal technique and health, whether one is using vibrato or nonvibrato. Composers need to be aware of physical demands placed on the voice by writing music that calls for harsh, forced singing. Even a short overexertion of the voice can do damage to some voices. So a composer must become familiar with the voice type for whom he or she is writing and take care not to ask that voice to produce uncharacteristic, vibratoless sounds in a vocal range or sustained volume level that is impossible to achieve.

When producing a vibratoless tone, focus the voice efficiently, support it well with air, and color it through the careful formation of vowels being projected. At no time should the tone be held in the throat, pushed forward by pressing the nostrils down, or manipulated by stiffening the tongue. Rather, the singer's normal ease of vocal production should be the goal, and he or she should merely turn the vibrato on and off by a mental imagery process rather than a physical manipulation. Concentrate on relaxation of the articulators (tongue and lips) and all muscles in the throat involved in phonation. Allow the breath to flow easily, gently, and naturally as in normal, coordinated phonation. Use the mind to delete the vibrato without added physical help. There should be no gripping or glottal onsets. Continue to use a normal legato attack that relies on a balanced coordination of airflow and vocal fold adduction (closure). It will be helpful to ingrain a feeling of inhaling while producing the vibratoless tones. Vocal pedagogues have traditionally used this technique for normal articulation and vocal production. It will be useful here, as well. It has been called "singing on the breath" or "floating on the breath." Using the mental image of air surrounding the vocal folds, with the folds slightly apart as one breathes, and continuing to phonate helps to relax the larynx and allow the tone to begin smoothly. This image also helps to keep the diaphragm in a poised position in order to give continuous support to the tone. If the breath system is balanced and there is no restriction in the throat, palate, or articulators, the vibratoless tone should float as easily as one containing normal vibrato.

Simple exercises can be used for the development of a flexible, free fluctuation between vibrato and nonvibrato.

EXERCISE 4a

Mental imagery is useful in practicing the alternation of vibrato and nonvibrato. Close your eyes. Picture a *horizontal wavy line* as you sing a sustained tone with vibrato for four counts, on a pitch somewhere in the middle of the voice. Use any well-focused vowel and precede it with a vocalized consonant such as m or n. Breathe. Now change the mental picture to a *perfectly straight horizontal line* and sing the same consonant and vowel on the same pitch for four counts with no vibrato. Once you have accomplished this variation, try to move from the four-count vibrato tone to the four-count straight tone without stopping for a breath between the two. Continue to practice only in an easily singable vocal range and gradually increase the length of counts held from four to twelve.

EXERCISE 4b

The basis for this exercise is a five-note pattern on syllables, such as "me," "ma," or "mo" (from *sol* down to *do*) in a comfortable vocal range. First, sing the scale with vibrato on each note using either syllable. Then sing each note without vibrato. Next, alternate between vibrato and nonvibrato on each note, holding the note just long enough to make the color change and then moving on to the next pitch and repeating the process. Finally, start the five-note pattern with vibrato; then alternate between straight tone and vibrato for the remaining pitches (*sol*-vibrato, *fa*-straight, *mi*-vibrato, *re*-straight, *do*-vibrato).

EXERCISE 4c

Begin on a note in the lower part of the voice. Sing the pitch lightly on "ma," using normal vibrato. Slide or glide slowly up to the next octave, using no vibrato between tones and ending with a light straight tone. When this can be done easily, extend the exercise by sliding back down to the original note and return to a normal vibrato on the final pitch. Once this exercise can be easily produced in the middle of the voice, it can be gradually expanded to the entire vocal range.

TONE COLOR: IMAGERY AND VISUALIZATION

Imagery is a necessary and valuable asset for the performer who wishes to get beyond a routine, ordinary realization of any musical score. But it is particularly crucial in the development of tone color as applied to composer indications written in the musical score. It is also a great deal of fun. It can be relaxing, mind expanding, and enables the performer to get in touch with all of the senses. Using imagery in its fullest sense involves a conscious effort to bring sound, taste, smell, touch, and kinesthetics into the mental and vocal interpretation of subtle emotional, picturesque, or dramatic texts.

For centuries, singers have employed coloristic techniques when interpreting large mood changes within a given piece. However, prior to this century, most of these mood/color changes were invented by individual singers in response to a text, musical, or general stylistic demand. In order to provide color contrast, each singer merely chose a vowel formation or focus of vocal placement that projected a darker or brighter color than their normal or medium color. Numerous pedagogical ideas have been applied to this color manipulation. Devices such as *vocal cover*, the use of mixed vowels, straight tones, vowel shortening or lengthening, and the manipulation of the soft palate and tongue have been used to describe ways of attaining vocal color changes. It has become common for singers to use these devices, as well as a speechlike approach to the declamation of text, to bring out subtle shadings of emotion or pictorial description found there. So the expansion of a traditional use of coloristic techniques into experimental, contemporary repertoire is not a far-reaching or unknown device for most trained singers. Rather, it may simply be an extension of a technique with which the singer is already familiar.

FREEDOM OF CHOICE, FREEDOM OF VOICE

Vocal and interpretative maturity affects any singer's ability to express subtle shadings of tone color. However, even relative beginners are able to achieve some measure of success at tone color variation. The mere determination to develop this important aspect of interpretation will spark intellectual and emotional energy, promote mental and vocal flexibility in the singer, and create an atmosphere of excitement during rehearsals.

For most, this kind of expressive work is a welcome relief from the drudgery of learning pitches and rhythms in an isolated setting. The practice of systematically changing vocal color develops creativity, imagination, versatility, and freedom in vocal production and can be done while preparing a piece in traditional, technical ways. The two do not have to be mutually exclusive. A portion of each practice session can be devoted to these two aspects of score realization with a meshing of the two at some appropriate moment before the session ends. The only requirement is a determination to engage the emotions in a positive way through imagery. Two or three five-minute segments devoted to this technique

during each practice session will be sufficient to significantly increase one's imagery skills. Imaging can also be done outside the rehearsal time, while performing daily tasks, sitting in traffic, or riding in a car. Allow the mind to recall
sensory memories that relate to vocal lines or texts taken from music being studied. Spend a few minutes imaging those ideas, feelings, or scenes. Making this
kind of mind play a part of the normal activities is the ultimate goal.

Once the ability to express vocal color differences is achieved, a higher level
of text interpretation and sophistication of declamation is possible, giving the
audience a clearer view of the composer's intent. The singer's overall confidence,
enjoyment of the performance, and the process required to achieve it will be
enhanced. The ultimate aesthetic effect will be different and more engaging than
if all tones were sung in exactly the same color, vocal weight, and declamation.

There is a significant psychological impact on the singer when he or she is
faced with the prospect of unlimited freedom to create. It is a liberating experience when all preconceived notions of sound, attempts at imitation of traditional
interpretations, and the influence of well-known renditions by famous singers
are eliminated from the creative process. There may not be any recorded examples
from which to pattern the vocal nuance. There may be no expert close at hand to
coax the voice, the muscle memory, and the thought processes into a particular
pattern. There may not have been enough performances of the work in question
to have developed a tradition of any kind in its overall interpretation. What then?

Now we get to the most enjoyable and most exciting part of this journey:
freedom of choice to create sounds and colors without being fettered by convention. If one chooses
to exploit this newfound freedom, it can bring out one's innermost native instincts through the use of imagery and experimentation. The process can free the
voice and mind in general. Rehearsals, voice lessons, and performances will be
less stressful due to an increased trust in one's innate ability to make interpretative
choices, without fear of comparison with preconceived ideas about the piece.

The singer's first priority is to get to know his or her voice and its capabilities
with respect to tone color. Voice classification and vocal registration events must
be carefully taken into consideration when deciding on color shadings. This will
help to prevent the overtaking of sensible technique by passionate declamation.
No voice should ever attempt to produce sounds or colors that are totally foreign
to its innate color spectrum. It would be disastrous for a light soprano to attempt
to sustain a very dark, somber, heavy declamation in the low part of her voice,
a technique that would be better suited to a mezzo-soprano. This extra weight
placed on a light voice in its weakest register would tire the voice quickly, causing
undue stress on the entire vocal production.

Dissect and practice each color indication separately. Imagery can then be
applied to relate the desired color to sensory perceptions. These sensory perceptions can be visualized, as well, and related to remembered mental pictures of
events, places, textures, smells, and tastes. It is important to create a sensory
picture of the desired sound or color in order to alert the body to the physical

requirements needed for the production of that tone color. Once the muscles and breath are responding appropriately, an emotional response can be triggered by this sensory picture, adding a final layer to the construction of the desired color.

When composers use adjectives to indicate color, those adjectives must be assumed to apply to a unique color scheme for each individual voice. Words such as *dark*, *stark*, *white*, or *muddy* have no absolute meaning. Each singer must find an easily produced tone quality for these terms within his or her vocal color spectrum. Composers such as Aaron Copland often indicate a general color designation for all or part of a song. In his "The World Feels Dusty" from *Twelve Poems of Emily Dickinson*, he gives one marking, *darkly colored*, for the entire song. This song is part of a song cycle that has other coloristic markings. The somber poem reflects on personal feelings about one's passing away. Its quiet yet passionate musical setting sets the mood for a doleful, dark sensory image. Both the text and its setting give the singer ample opportunity for vocal color experimentation through sensory imagery.

Some suggestions follow for the development of sensory imagery. Keep a small notebook nearby to write down ideas. It will save rehearsal time, give you a reference for successive practice periods, and help to build confidence in the process. The steps outlined below do not have to be accomplished in one practice period. They can be done one at a time and on different days until the process becomes natural.

1. Begin by choosing only one color on which to focus. Sit in a quiet place. Close your eyes. Allow the body to relax into a comfortable (not slouched) position. Check to see if there are tense muscles anywhere in the body. If so, concentrate for a moment on loosening those areas and letting the tension evaporate.

2. Think of the vocal sound you wish to create, mentally saying the word or words on which the color appears. Allow the mind to freely associate this color with descriptive adjectives that randomly come into your consciousness. Check each one briefly to see if it has a good fit for the color. Take your time. Eliminate those that seem too remote. Settle on two or three that feel right. Write these in your notebook so that you can refer to them later, checking to see if they still seem appropriate.

3. Draw your attention to events, places, or scenes invoked by this color. It could be something personal from your past or something quite outside your realm, such as a scene from a movie, a view from a bridge, or the bright lights of an oncoming car. Try to get a mental picture that seems to fit the color indicated within the context of the song. Write a description of this picture in your notebook. Be very detailed but curt. No complete sentences are needed.

4. Return to a concentration on physical relaxation for a moment and allow the mind to rest, picturing nothing. Then focus your attention on textures that seem appropriate to the color needed. These could include the feel of a fabric, the sensation of certain foods on your tongue, the hardness of the pavement

under your foot, or the delicate, wispy feel of a child's hair. Select those that fit your color, checking mentally to see if they work. Write them in your notebook.

5. Relax. Do not try to visualize anything for a moment. Sit quietly. Next, engage your sense of taste, recalling flavors of foods that may have a relationship to the color desired. For instance, if the indication is *brittle*, you might recall the sharp taste of something acidic, like grapefruit juice. Or, if the score says *dark and mellow*, you could relate that to the rich taste of chocolate mousse. Allow the imagination to explore all possibilities until one or two seem right. Write them down.

6. Just relax for a moment. Turn your attention to the sense of smell and try to associate familiar odors to the color needed. For example, if the marking says *ghostlike*, perhaps recalling the dank odor of an old, long abandoned house or a damp basement would be a good match. Try to recall one odor that reminds you of the color. Write it down.

7. After a moment of mental blankness, think of sounds you have heard that have a quality similar to the vocal coloration desired. Those sounds could be natural or artificial ones, sounds of other human voices, animal or bird utterances, the sound of air moving through the trees or through your home air-conditioning system, the racket of traffic or machine noise. Find two or more sounds that seem to fit. Write them in your notebook.

8. Take each of the sensory images you have chosen and review them slowly, allowing time to let each one settle in before moving on to the next. As you become more proficient and more accustomed to this process, it will take less time to select appropriate images.

9. The final step and the ultimate goal in this process is to ingrain these images so that they can be called up spontaneously and systematically. Then, through suggestion, the body's response to orders from the brain will be influenced, creating vocal color shadings and variations in declamation without unneeded, conscious physical manipulation. Once you have been successful at producing a color change designated for a large section of a piece, then experimentation can progress to situations requiring a sudden color change on each note or a quick change within sections of a piece.

The traditional idea of tonal beauty (in Western musical tradition) is not always the goal. Listening to singers from other cultures may provide a new aesthetic for vocal sound and help to glean a different mental image of the tone to be sung.

Always be careful, but be imaginative. The human voice is capable of making countless colors and sounds. The voice need not be stressed by producing them. Vocal distress is generally caused by forcing the voice; singing too loudly, too high, or too low for our natural range; or creating physical tension in the vocal apparatus itself. It is possible to have vocal freedom and color the voice in a multitude of ways. Experiment and enjoy. Remember, there is not an ideal color that must be copied. Find your own sound and relish it.

Part II Nontraditional Notation and Extended Vocal Techniques

Music notation was devised to present a visual replica of sound and its properties of intensity, duration, articulation, timbre, and pitch within an established unit of organization. Karkoschka (1972, p. 1) states that its main purpose is to "make possible the construction, preservation and communication of more complex kinds of music. The technical possibilities of a notation system also influence the act of composing—the entire musical way of thinking of all musicians—so that the aural image of a musical work in every epoch is characteristically related to its visual configuration."

Experimentation has taken place since the earliest forms of notation some 3,000 years ago with the *letter notation* of ancient Greece (Read 1969, p. 3). By the seventeenth century, the look of musical scores and the realization of notation found there had reached a point of stability and remained so until the twentieth century. Several sources are available for the serious scholar who wishes to have a more thorough understanding of the history of notation. Four that are most useful are *Handbuch der Notationskunde 1* by J. Wolf; *Notation in New Music* by Erhard Karkoschka; *New Music Notation* by David Cope; and *Music Notation, A Manual of Modern Practice* by Gardner Read. Both Karkoschka and Read relate modern notational developments to a historical perspective, describing in detail numerous kinds of *musical graphics* found in today's works and how they may refer to notational function found in music of earlier eras.

Since the twentieth century boasted a wide array of compositional styles, more than any previous century, it is not surprising that some composers felt at home with traditional notation while others were confined by it. Many retained a conventional approach to the look of the musical score, using a centuries-old notational scheme developed by the Western musical establishment. It is a system of notational symbols that requires no unique or extraordinary knowledge to be realized correctly, being universally understood by all musicians familiar with Western culture and its music.

Composers who felt restricted by traditional notation were compelled to create new ways of expressing their music on the printed score. Some combined traditional and nontraditional notation within a given work, creating novel notational "pictures" for the presentation of their musical ideas. Each composer made notational choices according to his or her individual organizational-compositional style; the subtleties or intricacies of the text being set; the desire to fully control the interpretative aspects of the performance; or the desire for spontaneity, randomness, and independence by performers, in effect making each performance a totally unique aesthetic experience. Other influences upon notational choices include the interest in music of other cultures, such as Asia or Africa; innate, tactile/kinesthetic responses to movement; the overall mood scheme decided upon during the course of the composition process; the coloristic setting of words or sound effects; and the selective use of only portions of a text or individual syllables, vowels, or consonant sounds found in a single word.

Attempts were made to improve notation by changing its representational qualities. Most of the experimentation took place in the 1950s and 1960s. Two stylistic developments evolved. One concentrated on notating with precision every possible element of the music. The other style sought freedom of expression and rejected precision of notation, resulting in indeterminacy, improvisation, and other ambiguities. Both styles developed numerous new notational symbols to express their musical ideas. The new symbols encompassed all areas of composition: pitch, tempo, meter, duration, intensity, articulation, and organization. There were added symbols for special effects and physical actions, previously unknown in classical repertoire. Three excellent sources for comprehensive information about the multitude of individual composer-generated notations are *Notation in New Music* by Erhard Karkoschka; *New Music Vocabulary* by Howard Risatti; and *Music Notation in the Twentieth Century* by Kurt Stone. The Karkoschka and Risatti books classify new signs, listing composers, single usages, and specific works in which they appear.

These notational "improvements" did not always succeed. Often, they were unclear and difficult to fathom. A few seemed impossible to perform. Some notations were used by only one or two composers, while others became commonplace to signify particular ideas. The novel notations were invented to create clear and specific representational possibilities of the composers' innermost musical intentions. Abstract symbols were occasionally combined with traditional musical notation. Karkoschka (1972, p. 5) reports that in such a case, unfamiliar or novel musical symbols should fit agreeably and understandably with traditional ones and must be different enough in character not to cause confusion. As the composers' intentions became more abstract, so did the new notational symbols.

Though some of these symbols appear to be ambiguous, in essence they express the composer's wishes more clearly than traditional notation. If notated in a traditional manner, the sheer complexity of the notation would be too overwhelming and cause a rigid, metronomic, cold, calculated performance, disappointing and perhaps mentally and physically taxing for the performers.

The intent of some composers was to create a work with multiple control factors: rhythm; tone color; pitch; dramatics; extramusical events; timed, taped interludes; or lighting effects that all occur at prescribed, specific times. Other composers gave the performers a great deal of freedom in determining pacing, pitch, tone color, overall length of the work, and improvisatory elements for vocal utterances and physical movement. The latter allows the performer to loosen all bonds of traditional musical expectation and spontaneously discover elements of sound and musical organization never heard before. The notation composers devised for these two scenarios will likely be quite dissimilar.

Depicting approximate time values or improvisatory pitch relationships required a fresh and unorthodox approach to the design of the musical score. By midcentury, *musical graphics*, similar to modern art, were invented to stimulate the imagination, spontaneity, and creativity of individual performers with the intent to discover individual, unique qualities of sound not produced by other performers.

Some composers devised their own notational systems, which necessitated many pages of complex performance instructions. There were instances in which composers were not consistent in their use of a particular symbol. Also, there have been various usages of similar symbols by different composers, as well as varying symbols printed for a particular usage. In this respect, the performer must consider the context in which the notation appears and try to make its realization fit into the overall plan for the interpretation of the work. It is more important to consider a composer's notational usage with a given composition and compare it to his or her other works than to assume its usage as being the same as that of a different composer. If there is still a question about usage, the performer should consult respected sources on modern notation. If the work is by a living composer, contact that person immediately. Composers, their works, and information about them are not always easy to find. Some suggestions for locating works and composers are listed in appendix C.

Complications arose with the new notation when uninitiated performers tried to translate these symbols into real sound and actions. The foreign language of the notation was often overwhelming, and composers did not always take the time to carefully explain their inventions or describe how they were to be realized. Some composers seemed unconcerned with how or if the music would be performed, leaving performers at a great disadvantage and without enthusiasm for the performance. This nonchalant attitude on the part of some composers may have contributed to the schism between themselves and performers. The latter felt abandoned and confused by the musical/notational uncertainty. This situation led to a fear of experimental music and a pattern of careless preparation on the part of some performers. In essence, there was a feeling that if the composer cared very little about the performance outcome, then why should the performer?

As a result of this lack of respect for the process of musical preparation and the deciphering of new compositional techniques, some concerts and festivals showcasing new music became nothing more than cursory read-throughs. These lackluster performances were caused by too few rehearsals, scant preparation, and little consideration of the composer's true intentions for the work.

If possible, the composer should be invited to a rehearsal of any new work. This will give all parties involved an opportunity to clear up any questions concerning the performance. Hopefully, dismissive attitudes by composers and performers are now history and can be avoided in the future. Communication of musical ideas is complicated enough when all concerned work toward clarity. But when indifference becomes the norm, the final outcome suffers greatly.

Unfortunately for the performer, no pedagogical uniformity or stylistic consensus has been developed as a starting point for the vocal interpretation of many of these unique schemes for musical notation. Texts such as *Music Notation: A Manual of Modern Practice* by Gardner Read and *New Music Notation* by David Cope are valuable resources for the development of an intellectual approach to the process of composition in the twentieth century. Each gives examples of some notational devices created by modern composers. However, neither addresses the use of the voice as it is applied to the individual notation symbols.

When faced with a number of alternatives to traditional notation, the singer must initially understand what each symbol signifies. In essence, it is similar to learning a foreign language. In that instance, one first becomes familiar with how new words look to the eye. Second, individual spellings are ingrained. Third, the context in which the words appear is assessed. Finally, vocal sound is applied and practiced in order to present the words in a logical manner that can be understood by listeners.

Deciphering modern notation can be likened to puzzle solving. One must assume that each notational symbol makes a contribution to the whole work. Each small part must be analyzed for characteristics that help it fill out, or make apparent, the larger musical picture. It is not merely an individual bit or hurdle to overcome on the way to the finale. Therefore, individual notation gestures must be deciphered and mastered for the performer to appreciate the composer's larger aesthetic intent. If the analysis and eventual comprehension of those gestures is not achieved, the singer will never truly feel at ease with the performance outcome. There will always be a shyness or insecurity in the vocalism, due to an intellectual uncertainty about how each gesture should be sung or, in some cases, *uttered*.

For the singer, the initial phase of dissection and analysis of musical gestures must be followed by rehearsing with a positive psychological attitude. The mastery of any unfamiliar notational devices is best achieved through curiosity, determination, and professionalism. Too often, composers have rightly complained that singers do not take unusual notation seriously and merely use a haphazard, nonintellectual approach to the rehearsal and performance, assuming that no one would know or care if the notation was realized according to the composer's intent. Singers have long shunned a careless approach to the preparation of traditional repertoire, but that has not always been true for the performance of contemporary music. An unprofessional rehearsal method is no real method at all and is discouraged by voice teachers and coaches at all levels of study. However, still more work needs to be done in this realm.

The following chapters do not attempt to outline the history of notation or to delve into the psychological, social, or practical reasons for the development of experimental notational devices. The reference books mentioned here will be valuable assets for that information. Other useful sources are listed in the bibliography.

HOW TO USE PART II

Dozens of new musical/notational symbols have been created for instruments and the voice. Some relate only to instrumental performance, some only to vocal performance, while others are used for both. Those with dual usage are mostly in the realm of rhythm and spacing, or pitch designation. A few notational devices or organizational scenarios were proposed by only one composer and never adopted for general use, while others have become more standard, being frequently used by numerous composers.

The chapters in part II present the most commonly encountered examples of twentieth-century notational innovations that apply to the voice and should not be considered exhaustive. The following five objectives are contained in each.

1. *What does it look like?*
Each unusual notation is printed in its generic form. No examples are taken directly from printed scores.

2. *What does it mean?*
A definition is given for the intent of each symbol.

3. *Who used it?*
Representative composers who used the symbol are cited.

4. *What should it sound like?*
An explanation of the vocal/technical realization of each symbol is described.

5. *How do I do it?*
Rehearsal techniques, vocal exercises, and performance difficulties are addressed.

The major premise for the organization of part II is that each singer is ultimately responsible for his or her own achievements in vocal technique and, given enough information, can set a course of action for the preparation of music of any era. It is hoped that with the following information a singer can begin the notational deciphering process without fear and apply suggested principles for musical/vocal rehearsal to various kinds of notational gestures.

chapter 5

The New Language
of Notation

Notation, whether traditional or modern in concept, is full of variables. When it is translated into sound it is not possible to have an exact replica of that notation with each performance. The performers' musical finesse and sensitivity, and their intellectual understanding of the musical symbols and their ramifications, contribute to the final interpretation of the simplest musical notations. When the notations are more complex and less well understood, these factors have a greater effect on the outcome.

This chapter presents several standard notations for indeterminacy of rhythm and pitch. Numerous other subgroups exist, making indeterminacy a complex and diverse process. Consult Stone (1980) or Cope (1997) for further enumeration of distinct systems. Also, Risatti (1975) is an excellent source for dozens of rhythm and pitch notational inventions by individual composers. The categories of rhythmic notation presented here overlap the concepts of tempo, meter, duration, silence, density, compositional organization, and improvisation.

The final part of the chapter examines the use of *microtones*, intervals smaller than a semitone. This compositional device is a major departure from the traditional manipulation of the diatonic scale. Other kinds of experimentation took the form of inexact, indeterminate, or approximate pitch. Due to their unique use of the voice and their relationship to *sprechstimme* and recitation, those inventions are discussed in chapter 6.

RHYTHM AND SPACING

Composers who were struggling with the problems of notating musical flow began to discard familiar metric indicators for new ways of sensing space and time. The gradations of musical pacing also received a new look. Writers on this subject and composers often categorize notation into descending levels of precision, such as exact notation, frame notation, proportional/spatial notation, indicative notation, indeterminacy, and musical graphics. The lines between these levels are quite blurred and become meaningless when a composer chooses to use elements of each in one composition. From the performer's point of view, the placement of a notation into a structural category is not as important as understanding a symbol's intent and how it fits within the context in which it is found. For example, some symbols, such as those for *sprechstimme*, fall into two categories of notation. They could be considered exact notation in their rhythmic indication, yet they would also be indicative notation since the pitches are approximated. The same could be said for some forms of recitation (see chapter 6).

NOTATIONAL SYSTEMS AND IMPROVISATION

Improvisation has been with us as long as music itself. Prior to the establishment of set rules for the interpretation of Western notational symbols, improvisation was the norm. It remains so in many kinds of ethnic or folk music and is one of the central characteristics of jazz. Even after the Western notational system became standardized in the seventeenth century, improvisation continued to flourish in classical vocal music. Composers such as Mozart, Donizetti, and Bellini wrote only skeleton shapes for operatic cadenzas. Singers were encouraged to improvise elaborate alternatives to the suggested outline and were thought to be dull, uninventive performers unless they took liberties with the designated melodic or rhythmic contour. In performance, the cadenzas were intricately decorated to show off the singer's particular vocal prowess and to enhance a desired dramatic effect. This traditional realization of that type of operatic display is still in use today.

Knowing that improvisation is inherent in the presentation of some classical styles of past centuries should calm any fears of improvising in twentieth-century music. The modern kind of improvisation may be quite unlike that of Donizetti or Bellini, and the look of the score may have little in common with the past. But the composer's assumption that the singer has the freedom, imagination, and capability to contribute creatively to the shape of the composition is similar. When improvisation is engaged, exactness and sameness must be abandoned. If a composer has included improvisatory elements of any kind (rhythm, pitch, pacing, organization, actions), then the singer has been given license to experiment to the fullest extent of his or her vocal and interpretative capabilities.

Twentieth-century composers incorporated improvisation into their music by various means. Some devised notational systems that they hoped would pictorially or verbally create an image or impression of what they desired.

The notational means by which some twentieth-century composers depicted interpretational freedom and improvisation include:

1. *Indicative notation*

A style that includes elements of both exact and free notation. It does not limit the singer to a strict or traditional interpretation. It usually does not contain meters and relies more on a "felt sense" of rhythm and pacing. Notational symbols for the indication of pitch, rhythm, dynamics, tempo, or special effects often look like a cross between artwork and traditional Western notation. Indicative improvisation can be drawn in numerous inventive ways. The types most commonly seen in vocal music are a frame or box (for organization); wavy lines (for pitch); arrows (for tempo change); large and small type (indicating dynamic contrasts); x's on noteheads or stems (approximating pitch); beaming variations (indicating tempo, accelerando, or ritard); and staff line variations, using from one to eight or ten (indicating vocal registers or pitch range). *Proportional notation,* a kind of indicative notation, is given special emphasis in this chapter. It is a system in which horizontal space and time are related. It is a flexible system built on approximate length of tones rather than the rigidity of the traditional metric system. Due to its improvisatory elements, it can be called both indeterminate and indicative. Writers on music notation have stated that proportional notation is one of the most significant contributions of new music to notation and to the temporal concept of music in general (Cope 1976, p. 11).

2. *Verbal cues*

Adjectives, verbs, poetic phrases, or commands for action and sound quality written in the score. Directions such as *ad lib, begin anywhere, as fast as possible, suddenly impetuous,* or *choose any notes within the line or box* are examples of this language approach to improvisation.

3. *Indeterminacy*

A notation devised for indefiniteness in music. It is also called "chance" or "aleatoric" music. All music has some inherent elements of chance due to differences in the interpretation by various performers, the quality of instruments or voices involved, and the acoustical properties of the performing space. But in a twentieth-century context, indeterminacy means much more. According to Ralph Turek (1988, p. 377):

> Within the general category of aleatoric music, there is considerable latitude. For example:
>   1. Indeterminacy may mean that *every element* of the music is subject to aleatoric procedures, or it may mean that *only one or two* musical elements are left to chance.
>   2. Indeterminacy may be *partial* (chance procedures characterizing only portions of the composition) or it may be *total* (the entire composition characterized by chance procedures).
>   3. Indeterminacy may be applied in the *compositional stage* or in the *performance stage.* In the compositional stage, the composer uses chance procedures to determine certain aspects of the music—the pitch content, the dynamic level, and so on. Once completed, however, the composition is performed the same way each time. In the performance stage, on the other hand, the composer provides one or more options

for the performer(s), usually assuring a somewhat different realization of the piece each time it is performed.

4. Musical graphics

Also called *augenmusik* (eye music).There is not a clear demarcation between indicative notation and musical graphics. However, some scores by composers such as Stockhausen, Cage, Berio, Berberian, and Crumb use an artist's approach to the depiction of events. Some pieces are merely a succession of controlled events. The events are determined by successive pictures that include skewed or circular staff lines to show pitch options and direction; circles, dots, rectangles, or squares to indicate pitch or density of sound; and abstract shapes to show pitch range or dynamics. As Cope remarks (1976, p. 11) "these graphic scores are not in their own reality attempting so much at communication as incitation." Cope's commentary alludes to the provocative and goading elements present in musical graphics. Performers react to this notation in quite dissimilar ways: some are encouraged by the vague look of the score to be more open and creative, while others feel paralyzed by strangeness.

This type of notation is especially useful for the coordination of multimedia pieces. The outlining of changing musical textures, coordination of physical movement and musical articulation, depiction of dramatic attitudes or theatrics, and simulation of activity and silence are just a few of the applications for musical graphics.

Some of these pictorially designed "art scores" (as they have become known) would confuse even the most seasoned performer of contemporary music. There is no consistency with which they are used by various composers. Since they have been created according to the individual composer's personal goals and philosophy, the range of possibilities is limitless. For this reason, they will not be dealt with here. If confronted with a work of this type, try to glean all that is available from the directions printed in the score. Call the composer, if possible. Several examples of typical musical graphics scores, showing a variety of uses, are included in Karkoschka (1972).

5. Electronic tape synchronization

A pictorial representation of live and prerecorded events. This kind of score can be "read" in much the same way as a musical graphics score. Verbal or notational cues are given for the coordination of the live and taped sounds. Pacing is often gauged in seconds. If so, the score will indicate the number of seconds for each timed segment. Sometimes improvisatory pitches or directions are given for the performer. The performer must fit them into the space indicated on the score. This is often a trial-and-error process. The space may look small on the score but may actually be quite long, requiring a slower pacing of the pitches or sounds the performer is required to make. This type of coordination often demands numerous rehearsals with the tape in order to smoothly synchronize the various events that may be occurring in both live and taped sound.

PROPORTIONAL NOTATION

Cope (1976, p. 7) points out, "Rhythmic notation has in many ways come full circle: from the nonmetered Gregorian Chant, through the mensural period (notation established, some say, by Franco of Cologne around 1250, which employed for the first time different noteheads for different durations) and the bar-line structure (around 1450 or earlier to the present day) to the proportional non-metered scores of many of today's composers."

Proportional notation is part of a compositional trend toward less notational precision and greater interpretative freedom. "It represents a fundamental break with all previous notational systems: the change from symbolic durational notation (quarter notes, eighth notes, etc.) to spatial (or proportional) notation in which durations are indicated through horizontal spacing of sounds and silences" (Stone 1980, p. 96). It generally does not contain bar lines or meter signatures but is organized around some internal controlling structure. That structure may include the timing of a pitch, phrase, or section into seconds, which are notated in the score, as in example 5.1.

Pitches are printed as whole notes using a traditional five-line staff. The numbers printed above the staff indicate the length of each pitch in seconds. Notice that rests (or silences) between tones are also given a length in seconds. The text is printed directly under the pitch on which it should be declaimed. This technique for depicting space and time has been used in vocal scores by many composers, such as Kenneth Gaburo (Two) and George Rochberg (Eleven Songs for Mezzo-Soprano).

What should it sound like?

The visual notation is proportional to a *sense* of time, not an exact or rigid number of seconds. In proportional notation of this type, there may or may not be a mathematical relationship between the length of consecutive pitches and silences. All tones specify exact pitch and should be sung in a traditional manner, including legato tonal attacks and use of vibrato. Specific dynamic levels are given for each pitch. If expression marks or vocal color indications are included, as in example 5.1, definite contrasts must be developed and projected with the voice.

Example 5.1   Proportional Notation

How do I do it?

1. Learn the exact intervals printed. This is not ad lib or indeterminate as to pitch.

2. Determine vocal registration (head or chest) for individual tones and rehearse them with attention to tone quality, legato attack, and normal use of vibrato. Do not delete the vibrato unless directed to do so in the score.

3. Modulate the voice according to stated dynamic levels, never pushing the voice beyond its natural limits of volume.

4. Use a stopwatch to determine the length of time for each tone. Do this only in the early rehearsals in order to get a feeling for the length. Once you have a good sense of the length of individual tones and silences (for example, eleven seconds), discard the stopwatch and rehearse, relying on your inner clock to determine an approximation of the seconds.

5. Add expressive qualities requested in the score. Mental imagery and vowel modification are two techniques that are useful for depicting vocal color and mood changes, as discussed in chapter four.

6. If singing alone, allow intuition to set the overall pace of the work within its general proportional sketch. However, if other voices or instruments are involved, then be aware that proportional time should be broadly interpreted without rigidity or metronomic spacing with accompanying parts.

A different kind of organization for proportional notation is shown in example 5.2. Here notes are placed on a five-line staff and connected with thick black lines of varying lengths. The length of the connecting line indicates the length of tones, as well as accelerando and ritardando. For example, if the lines between notes become increasingly longer, then a ritard is being indicated. Conversely, shorter lines mean a faster pace. This kind of proportional notation is seen with and without specification of the total length of a musical segment in seconds. In the example, a certain number of seconds is designated for an entire segment of the music and printed at the beginning of the line. At the end of the section, another time designation may be stated for what follows, and so on.

This boldly drawn notation is an excellent visual gauge for duration and rhythmic movement. As Stone asserts (1980, p. 137), "Spatial notation is the ideal graphic vehicle whenever rhythmic flexibility or durational vagueness is desired." Composers such as Penderecki, Ligeti, Rochberg, and Berio found it useful, providing a consistent and easily realized unmetered notation. It is fairly simple for

Example 5.2   Proportional Notation

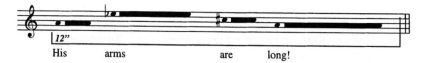

the performer to determine which tones should be held longer than others and paced accordingly within the time indication for the whole phrase or section.

As in other types of proportional or spatial notation, pacing in terms of seconds or black horizontal lines of varying lengths is only an approximation. No rigidity or artificiality must enter into the interpretation. Fluidity of line and a felt sense of time are the crucial elements involved in interpretation.

What should it sound like?

When rehearsing notation of this type, be aware that exact pitches are notated. As in example 5.2, there is no room for ad lib or approximation. The vocal technique needed for tonal attacks and for sustaining pitches is exactly that of traditional singing. The dark connecting lines merely indicate how long each tone is sustained in relation to the other tones in the phrase and to the segment's time allocation. It does not have any significance for dynamics, vocal color, or the use or deletion of vibrato. A typically encountered error in production of this notation is the assumption that all vibrato should be deleted, singing with continuous straight tones. Deletion of vibrato may be marked in the score. In that case, it should be deleted. The performer may elect to eliminate vibrato on individual pitches or words for expressive reasons. Otherwise, the singer's natural vibrato should be the norm for the production of all tones.

Unless there are obvious breaks, breath marks, staccatos, or grand pauses, each tone should move smoothly into the one following it. Always assume a legato attack and tonal connection unless otherwise marked.

How do I do it?

1. Scan the score, noticing whether the proportional notation contains both continuous horizontal lines of varying lengths and time zone indications in seconds. Highlight or circle any segments designated in seconds.

2. Analyze the use of the text. Is it a typical syllabic declamation? Does it contain melismatic vocalization on a single vowel? Is it built on nonsense sounds or IPA phonemes that weave through the pitched notation and horizontal lines? There could be variables in the text setting within the same work. If so, mark those contrasts with a check mark or colored pencil so that the eye and brain can quickly find and assimilate the changes during subsequent rehearsals. A set of color highlighters is a helpful tool when rehearsing music with this type of notation. They can be used to set off different kinds of notation within the same piece or to cue the eye to quick changes in articulation.

3. Signify with a check mark or other symbol (such as a short, straight, vertical line) the point of attack for each syllable or phoneme.

4. Learn all pitches on a neutral vowel until intervals are ingrained. Dissect any unusually difficult to hear intervals or passages and use them as part of your daily vocal warmup. Short exercises can be constructed from these intervals or recurring motives and patterns. Start the exercise in the middle range of the voice

and move up and down by half-steps as one would use any typical vocalise (i.e., five-tone scale or triad). This will accustom the ear to the pitches in question, eventually making them seem more natural and easier to find when returning to their original context. At this stage, disregard pitch length or time zone designations.

5. If there is a time designation in seconds, use a stopwatch to rehearse all the pitches within each time frame. First, sit quietly and, without looking at the score, start the stopwatch and let it run for the allotted number of seconds while you absorb the physical feeling of the length of the segment. Stop the watch. Do this several times until your inner clock seems to understand the approximate length required.

Now do the same exercise while watching the score, mentally placing the tones within the time zone. It will take several repetitions to visually fit all pitches within the space desired.

The final mental step is to give each pitch its written horizontal length, fitting it into the designated time frame. This mental preparation will save the voice from repeated attempts at pacing and will allow for physical and mental flow of tone when the voice is applied.

6. At this point, the mind and body should have an excellent kinesthetic feeling for the allotted time zone and the pacing of pitches. Discard the stopwatch. Begin to mouth silently (do not whisper) the text as it relates to the pitches. Repeat until each syllable or phoneme falls in place automatically.

7. Sing! Put it all together and do aloud what you have so meticulously rehearsed mentally. Check pitches and intervals for accuracy and correct placement of text. Add any expression markings and dynamic contrasts while approximating the designated time frame. Record your efforts at this stage, being mindful of time parameters and subtle vocal shadings that may be verbally notated.

A third common use of proportional notation is seen in example 5.3. These three examples of accelerando and ritardando are efficient, visually logical replications of the desired effect. Usually, proportional notation depicting speed and its relationships to individual tones is found using all black notes. They may be variously spaced to show pacing. The interpretation of the pacing in the three examples is similar, though the pitches are different. Each visually signifies a ritardando.

This pictorial notation for tempo change is interpreted in the following ways:

1. If the notes are spaced closer together, then the tempo is quick. More space is gradually added between notes to signify a slowing pace. The opposite indicates an accelerando.

2. If the beams are gradually spaced closer together, a ritardando is indicated, and vice versa.

3. If the tones are beamed and the number of beams gradually decreases from several to one or two, then ritardando is desired. The reverse signifies an accelerando.

Example 5.3a Proportional Notation

Example 5.3b Proportional Notation

Example 5.3c Proportional Notation

These symbols usually occur in works without metric organization and are based on the same principles found in the verbal cues (ritard and accelerando) over traditional metric structures. In either case, exactness is not possible or desired. Assess the tempo change according to the style of the composition, coordination with accompanying instruments, and a general sense of the purpose for the tempo change within the phrase or larger musical context. A sensory reflex and a matter of musical taste or nuance primarily govern interpretation of such symbols. They should never be matter-of-fact, guarded, or disconnected. Rather, they need to have a continuous feeling of tempo variance, giving the demarcations of speed a gradual and approximate realization achieved mostly through intuition and knowledge of the musical context.

There are two vocal considerations to take into account here. The first refers primarily to the physical and mental coordination of the breath. Breath pacing and support is always of prime importance when maximizing the effect of any notation. If the music requires a ritard, then the breath system must be coordinated with tone production in order to achieve a satisfactory conception of the ritard. It does not matter what notational device or verbal cue signifies a tempo change; the vocal technique used to achieve it remains the same.

Second, the singer must seek the physical and mental freedom to achieve the desired flexibility in tempo and nuance. Slowing down or speeding up, perhaps spontaneously and extemporaneously, is a characteristic of much of this type of musical writing. Being mentally and physically prepared for fluidity of pacing is very important. One's psychological response to indicative notation is crucial to its realization. A seasoned performer may be able to shift gears quickly, but for most singers, a practiced and learned response to the visual musical gestures produces polished results.

A fourth type of proportional notation that gives possibilities for choice and allows for improvisation is frame notation. According to Karkoschka (1972,

p. 55), the term *frame notation* was first used by Boguslaw Schäffer in the preface to *Topofonica*.

This is a significant innovation for the notation of a free and elastic realization of rhythm, pitch placement, pacing, and dynamics. In frame notation, all notes, dynamics, and activities contained within the box are to be improvised, sung randomly, in any order and nonmetrically. Any notes, dynamic markings, rhythms, or verbal instructions located outside the box remain constant and exact.

In most cases, if the noteheads are connected by a beam, either dotted or solid (example 5.4), the performer may start on any pitch within the pattern, but the original sequence of the pattern must be followed. Subsequent repetitions can start at a different point in the sequence, but the original pattern must continue to be followed. Some composers may not follow this plan exactly as stated. If not, the composer's usage should be explained in the score.

If the pitches are not connected, as in example 5.5, then the interpreter is thrust into the act of composition. For the elements of chance, changeability, and personal interpretation become involved in the performance outcome.

As shown in example 5.5, the box or frame surrounds a group of notes that are approximated (no note stems are printed). The length of the frame shows the approximate duration of the sequence within it. The frame is then connected to a black horizontal line that indicates the continued repetition of items within the box and the duration in proportional terms. There may also be a designation in seconds for the total time allotted for the improvisation of ideas within the frame.

This kind of notation has unlimited possibilities for improvisation of notes, rhythms, dynamics, articulation, and special effects. The performer's primary consideration is to determine what significance the frame has to the outcome of the performance. In addition to the items shown in examples 5.4 and 5.5, composers have used other means to indicate choices within the boxes, such as arrows showing the direction of pitches to be improvised; brackets that set off individual

Example 5.4   Frame Notation

pp – mf

Example 5.5   Frame Notation

30"

tones to be transposed or repeated; wavy lines, brackets, or letters showing a range of tones that can be improvised; and diagrams, colors, or numbers indicating choices for selection or repetition. Examples of frame notation can be found in numerous works written since 1950. Luciano Berio, Pierre Boulez, Karlheinz Stockhausen, and Rhian Samuel are but a few of the composers who experimented with this element of chance that allows the interpreter to be included in the creative act.

What should it sound like and how do I do it?

Within the general category of frame notation, a considerable variance of exactness and freedom is allowed the performer.

1. The box or frame determines what elements can be improvised. Read all interpretative directions given in the preface or within the score. Analyze the structure of each frame. Mark with a color highlighter any elements that are exact. Choose another color highlighter and mark all indeterminate elements so that they are easily differentiated for a quick response. Note that some aspects of the music may be completely controlled (pitch, articulation, dynamics) while other elements (tempo, note patterns, special effects) may be randomly and spontaneously interpreted.

2. A designation in seconds, a black horizontal line, or verbal instructions indicate the approximate duration of the combined repetition of items within the frame. As in previously discussed forms of proportional notation, the designation in seconds is a "felt" or approximated length. Again, use a stopwatch in the beginning rehearsals to acclimate your entire being to the specified length of phrases or sections. Once you feel comfortable with that time frame, discard the stopwatch.

The black horizontal line signifies the length of time in which the music patterns found within the frame should be repeated. The number of repetitions needed to fill the space signified by the black line will depend on the length of the original musical pattern found in the frame and the pacing of those pitches or events. If these repetitions are being accompanied by an electronic tape or live performers, beginnings and endings of frames must be coordinated with printed tape cues, verbal instructions for concurrence of instrumental and/or vocal lines, and section divisions.

Frame notation presents some intriguing performance problems. Coordination of events between individual performers in an ensemble may require extensive cuing from a conductor or one of the performers. All members of the ensemble must be attentive to the other players' or singers' parts. For this reason, the individual performer will need to thoroughly and creatively prepare his or her line, determining the general length, pacing, and number of repetitions of items within a frame before rehearsing with others. Adjustments may be necessary when full ensemble rehearsals begin, but a well-prepared plan, decided upon during early rehearsals, will give the singer much more confidence when faced with the complexity of the addition of other performers. They will likely have frames of notation quite different from the singer's. Having secure parameters in mind will allow the singer to be more flexible with other performers and less distracted by what they are playing.

3. The frame or box can be small, containing only a few pitches and musical ideas, or it can be quite large, encompassing substantial sections of the score. These large frames may contain smaller boxes within them. It is possible to have small, germinal ideas requiring repetition (small boxes) within larger musical sections (large boxes) that also require repetition. This kind of notation can get quite complex because there are several levels of decisions to be made. The decisions one makes will change the overall outcome of the piece. Some things to consider are:

   a. Approximately how long is the time zone?
   b. How many repetitions of the small boxes and large boxes need to be made in order to fill the time zone?
   c. Should some small boxes be repeated more than other boxes?
   d. Do any of the boxes (small or large) need to coincide with musical events of other performers?

Highlight any parts of the score that contain complications like those described above. Assign separate colors to small boxes located within larger boxes. Notice whether there is also a time zone designation in seconds for either the small or large boxes. This will be important as you decide on the number of repetitions required to fill the time zone. It will also affect the repetitions of the small boxes and how they relate to the full length of the large section.

4. There may be a combination of approximate and exact pitches and/or rhythms within the frames. Learn all exact elements first (pitch, rhythm, tone color, dynamics). It does not matter whether they are connected or separated. Having a solid ground for pitch reference is essential at the beginning. Always habituate exact pitches, securing them vocally (placement, registration) before adding any approximated pitches. This will allow for better aural orientation when the approximated tones are inserted later.

5. Allow for spontaneity. It is quite all right to change one's mind about the interpretation of elements that are not intended to be exact. Even though certain decisions might have been made during rehearsals concerning the number of repetitions for boxes or choices of improvisatory elements within them, they should not be set in stone. The beauty of frame notation is that it gives the performer some compositional creativity and fluidity to change on a whim. So use it to your advantage. If your current mood tells you to repeat an idea four times instead of a previously decided three, then go with your intuition. This might change the pacing in a dramatically different way and may coincide more agreeably with the other lines being played or sung around you. If the other musicians are working with the same flexibility of interpretation in mind, then

no two performances will ever be the same. As a matter of fact, the performance may change considerably in length and dramatic nuance due to a change in the alignment of voices or instruments as each invents its own patterns for details within individual frames.

Don't be afraid that you will be wrong! As long as you keep the exact elements and the improvisatory elements separate, never mixing up the two, you can simply follow your creative flow and allow it to direct the interpretation. There is no one way to produce this notation. The inherent freedom must be seized upon and used as a liberating force, drawing out otherwise masked, truncated, or hidden creativity in the singer.

PROPORTIONAL NOTATION AND THE VOCAL STUDIO

The inherent freedom in proportional notation is ideal for exercising the voice through the imagination. This nontraditional way of thinking about musical organization can easily be incorporated into a singer's daily rehearsal routine. Since the strictness of traditional music notation is not present, this license to be compositionally creative can be used to devise vocal, mental, and physical exercises that will liberate the psyche, the voice, and the muscles that control the body. This freeing of the imagination and inhibitions can then be transferred to other kinds of music. After all, versatility is an important factor for the training of singers in the twenty-first century. Most singers today do not select one musical style, composer, or era of music and perform that exclusively, as was the case for much of the history of vocal music. Instead, today's professional singer may sing a variety of repertoire from the operatic, folk, popular, art song, and ethnic literature.

The following exercises assume an erect (not rigid) posture throughout. Keep the feet slightly apart, the neck and spine aligned, and the chin level. The head should feel as if it is lightly hanging from a string attached to the ceiling. Maintain this "singer's posture" while quietly taking several deep breaths. Be sure to keep the chest still (neither rising nor falling) and allow the rib-cage (diaphragmatic-costal) area to expand on the intake of air.

Some of the exercises are built on the use of a stopwatch. However, a watch with a second hand could be used and the exercises adapted, if necessary, with the only difference being the ability to stop and start the timing sequences. If using a stopwatch, always hold it in one hand while the rest of the body remains relaxed in the singer's posture. Each exercise progressively attunes the mind, body, and breath cycle (inhalation, suspension, and exhalation) to a feeling or "felt sense" of approximate lengths of time.

EXERCISE 5A (TIMED BREATHING)

1. Start the stopwatch and let it run. Watch the hand as it moves, stopping the watch when it reaches five seconds. Relax and breathe normally during this process. Repeat the procedure, letting the watch run for ten seconds and then fifteen seconds, noticing the sensation of time as it passes.

2. Start the watch as you inhale through both nose and mouth. Observe the seconds ticking by. Inhale for the first five seconds, suspend the air for the next five seconds, and exhale for the last five seconds. Stop the watch at fifteen seconds and relax. Repeat several times until the process is automatic and flows smoothly.

3. Now that you have a physical and mental feeling for a fifteen-second time zone, repeat the exercise without looking at the stopwatch as it runs. When you get to the end of your exhalation, stop the watch and check how many seconds passed during the breathing exercise. See if the number is approximately fifteen seconds. After doing an exercise like this for any number of seconds you choose, the body and mind will more easily be able to simulate time frames without relying on a stopwatch.

EXERCISE 5B (TIMED SINGING)

This exercise has several benefits, including ear training (interval recognition and recall); development of mental concentration; and coordination of breath control with the length of phrases. In this case, each of these elements is related to time zones rather than meters or traditional musical phrasing. The physical, vocal, and mental coordination improvements will be similar to those encountered when doing traditional vocal exercises built on counts, meters, or measured phrase lengths. An added benefit will be in the realm of imagination, since the singer is encouraged to create many of the elements of the exercise. He or she begins to think of musical pacing in a different way and feels freer to experiment when the opportunity arises in a piece of music.

The purpose of the exercise is to coordinate several elements of vocalization. As you proceed through the steps of the exercise, follow principles of well-balanced singing. Attack all tones clearly and evenly, and sing with vibrato. Use the rests for breath preparation and concentration on body relaxation. Place each tone in the proper vocal registration. Be relentless in pitch accuracy, never scooping into tones or casually assuming an interval is correct. Finally, and perhaps most importantly, keep the mind fully attentive to every detail of the process. This is necessary for the development of immediate responses to visual stimuli and enables the singer to quickly become adept and facile when habituating new ideas.

1. Warm up the voice lightly throughout your normal singing range.

2. Choose five pitches at random that occur in the middle octave of your voice. Place the notes in a sequence that contains large and small intervals. No interval should occur twice. Write the pitches on staff paper in the chosen sequence so you can look at them as you sing.

3. Assign a specific number of seconds (between one and ten) to each tone. Write the number under the tone.

4. Separate each tone with a rest and designate a specific number of seconds (between one and five) for each rest.

5. Use a stopwatch as you sing on "ma" or "mo" through the phrase you have created, moving from tone to rest to tone, and so on. Abide by the time zones you have designated for each.

6. Check all pitches for accuracy, especially large skips or intervals that are difficult to hear.

7. Add specific dynamic markings to each note, using a range of P to F, and retrace the exercise, adding the dynamic contrasts. Continue to use the stopwatch until you have a keen sense of the approximate time value of each note and rest.

8. Discard the stopwatch and rehearse the phrase with a felt sense of the time zones indicated.

EXERCISE 5C (VARIATIONS ON TIMED VOCALIZATION)

The following exercise relies on the principles established in the previous exercise and uses them to stretch the singer's ability to mentally change directions, quickly become more flexible with aural recognition, and expand the felt sense of timing.

1. Use the sequence of pitches you previously learned (with the original time zone designations for tones and rests).

2. Next, sing the pitches on ma or mo from right to left (in other words, backward). New intervalic relationships are created and the sequence of time zones is now reversed, giving a different felt sense as you move through the phrase. Rehearse with the stopwatch if needed, but discard it as soon as possible.

3. When this new pattern is easily accomplished, create still another pattern by singing the tones in a random order (for example, 1, 5, 3, 4, 2). Always place one of the rests between the tones. Several random orders can be created from the five tones and four rests with their designated time zones. Simply decide on the order and see how quickly you can accomplish the new patterns.

PITCH

As contemporary composers were inventing new notations for rhythm and spacing, so too were they experimenting with shadings of pitch within the traditional tempered system. One approach involved the manipulation of the diatonic scale, which forms the basis of classical major and minor scales. Composers altered the scale, normally divided into twelve equal parts, to produce smaller increments than the normal half step; thus, the use of microtones.

MICROTONES

Microtones, though uncommon in Western musical heritage, are incremental variations in pitch frequently used in the music of India, China, and other cultures. As it relates to vocal music of the period, composers often drew upon cultures with different musical organizational systems or tuning systems than that of equal temperament in the Western tradition, to provide variety in vocal declamation and color nuance.

"Microtones result from normal intonation variations, tuning systems that employ a limited number of overtone series elements, the raising or lowering of standard equal-tempered pitches, or the use of equal-tempered systems employing more or less than twelve divisions of the octave" (Cope 1997, p. 122). A few composers, such as Benjamin Johnston, devised microtonal pitch variations based on just-intonation rather than equal temperament. The just system is based upon justly tuned major thirds and perfect fifths. Therefore, the system of accidentals produced means that the corresponding sharps and flats are not the same (Risatti 1975, p. 17).

As Cope points out (1997, p. 125), "Many microtonal tuning systems have been proposed . . . with divisions of the octave ranging from 14 to 144. However, many problems confront those using microtonal systems, including those of notation and performability on conventional instruments. The pervasive, if often subliminal, influence of equal temperament will cause many performers to attempt to round pitches to their nearest equal-tempered equivalents. The limits of the ear to appreciate fine microtonal differences should also be evaluated; since human responses to pitch vary widely, it is impossible to set an objective limit to the number of useful subdivisions of the octave."

Though some composers have chosen to immerse themselves in microtonal complexities, the majority have used microtones to create a new vocabulary of sound possibilities within a more traditional context. Of the many microtonal possibilities, quarter tones are found most frequently in the existing repertoire for the voice.

Composers use quarter tones for different purposes: to give special importance to a given pitch, work, or metrical accent; in certain contexts, as primarily ornamental sounds; as surprising aural elements in the midst of an otherwise traditional diatonic scale; or as a germinal element of a compositional structure built on microtones.

Individual composers have invented a multitude of notations to depict microtonal pitches. Risatti (1975, pp. 16–17) lists twenty-four systems for indicating accidentals by various composers. Always check the preface or page of directions in any score for information concerning these notations and others that may not conform to the standard usage.

Two notations have been used most often and have generally become standardized and promoted by writers on the subject. The most prevalent and, perhaps, preferred is the arrow system. "Among the many quarter-tone accidentals invented over the years there is none with identical alterations for both sharps and flats except the arrow system. Nor is any system quite as self-explanatory" (Stone 1980, p. 68).

Example 5.6a provides standard arrow notations for raising the pitch a quarter tone higher than printed on the staff. If the note were to be lowered by the same amount, the arrow would point downward. This system is seen most often in music for the voice. Some composers print the number "4" over or under the arrow. George Rochberg used this effect several times in his *Eleven Songs for Mezzo-*

Example 5.6   Microtones

quarter tone   one-third tone   quarter tone   quarter tone
  higher   higher   higher   lower

Soprano, as did Nicola LeFanu in *Il Cantico Dei Cantici II*. This bending of the tone does not become a fetish in the work. Rather, it gives a soulful quality to a few key words of the text. If a composer wishes to raise or lower the pitch in increments other than a quarter tone, a number will be printed and attached to the arrow, as in example 5.6b.

The plus sign system is used more often in instrumental music, but occasionally in vocal music as well. It can be seen in the music of Bussotti, Xenakis, and Penderecki, among others. If the plus sign is used for raising the pitch, there is generally no corresponding plus sign that appears under the note for lowering the pitch. Instead, the composer prints a normal flat sign or a hollow, backward flat sign under the note. As Stone (1980, p. 69) points out, the normal flat sign can easily be mistaken for sloppily written regular ones and cause confusion in the performer. The plus sign and hollow, backward flat sign are shown in example 5.6c.

What should it sound like and how do I do it?

The idea of singing absolutely "in tune" has no basis in reality, no matter the system under which the composition was written. Several factors affect this. In tonality, some tones naturally lead toward others. Singers tend to vary the intonation and lean toward the octave, making leading tones, such as the seventh, slightly sharper than others in the scale. Acoustics play a major part in the achievement and perception of intonation. Even the most acoustically perfect halls create performance differences due to reverberation and resonance variations. The vibrato of a singer or the combination of several singers and their vibratos cause great variations in pitch and pitch perception. And as Cope remarks (1997, p. 125), "Because performers of instruments capable of varying intonation typically combine just and equal-tempered systems intuitively, microtones in actual practice are the norm rather than the exception."

Suggestions for practice

1. The original tone, as printed, should be raised or lowered slightly according to the symbol printed above or below it.

2. The pitch should sound slightly sharp or flat to the original tone without moving a complete half step away from it.

3. The microtone indication does not affect tone quality. Continue to sing the tone in a normal voice quality unless other indications, such as white tone, nonvibrato, or stark are also present.

4. When rehearsing music with microtones, learn the score first with the original pitches only. After the pitches and intervals are secure, begin to alter each one with its designated microtonal effect. Do not guess or try to sense where the pitches are. Frequently check them with a pitch pipe to make certain that you have not altered them too drastically, thereby moving too far away from the original pitch. Be aware that rehearsing with an out-of-tune piano will be pointless and frustrating when working on microtone increments. Learning to sing in microtones is an excellent ear-training exercise.

The concept can be practiced in a very simple way. Choose three notes in the middle octave of the voice. They could be in the form of a simple triad in any key. Sing each of them squarely on pitch, holding each tone for four counts. Do this several times until the pitches are secure. Next, as you sustain each pitch for four counts, move the pitch up or down a quarter tone. Check with a pitch pipe to make sure you have not moved a complete half step away from the original note. Do this several times on each pitch until you have a good sense of distance in the quarter tone adjustment of pitch.

This exercise can be applied to pitches in any part of the vocal range or to specific pitches in a well-known song. By adding this kind of ear training to a practice session, the singer becomes more secure with all intervals and gains a better kinesthetic feeling for pitch distance.

5. If accompanying instruments are also playing microtones, make a tape of their accompaniment for rehearsal purposes so that you can train your musical ear to the new configuration of intervals created by the combination of the voice and instruments moving in microtonal increments.

chapter 6

Vocal Hybrids:
Sprechstimme and Recitation

Several hybrid and alternative forms of vocal declamation were developed and exploited during the twentieth century and continue to be used by contemporary composers. None of them could be called normal singing in the traditional sense. These mixtures of speech and song rely on aspects of both functions of the voice, exhibiting characteristics of each. Composers who incorporated some type of speech-song in their music were doing so in an attempt to heighten dramatic, conversational, or coloristic elements of both text and music. Though several terms and notational devices have been used to describe these composite vocal styles, the two most important and frequently seen innovations are *sprechstimme* and recitation.

SPRECHSTIMME (FIXED PITCH NOTATION)

Composers began experimenting with new treatments of the voice as early as 1897 with Englebert Humperdinck's use of *sprechstimme*, speaking in rhythm on a monotone, in his opera *Königskinder*. Humperdinck indicated approximate pitches by notating the vocal lines with x's instead of note heads. The singers were doubled throughout by instruments playing exact pitches. The composer abandoned *sprechstimme* when he revised the opera in 1910. All approximated tones were changed to exact pitches.

This type of vocal experimentation continued throughout the twentieth century and has been referred to variously as *sprechstimme* (speaking voice) or *sprechgesang* (speech-song) and recitation. The term *sprechstimme* has become standardized when describing contoured speech-song. For the purpose of clarity, *sprechstimme* will be used to refer to all examples concerning fixed pitch notation. *Recitation* will be used for other types of spoken or half-sung notation. The notation and desired realization of these vocal hybrids between speaking and singing have been handled in diverse ways.

Sprechstimme owes its development to one composer in particular, Arnold Schoenberg. He was influenced by the popularity of the German melodrama that typically was of two types: those with a text spoken to musical accompaniment and those with musical interludes between the spoken sections. The melodrama was quite successful as a vehicle for the interpretation of magical, supernatural, atmospheric, or mysterious texts, since the voice was not restricted to particular tones or rhythms and had total freedom of expression and nuance. It offered a more spontaneous and descriptive expression for emotions than did the era's stylized conventions of opera and solo song.

Schoenberg attempted to combine the emotional expressiveness present in the text of the melodrama with the musical expressiveness present in his instrumental writing in works such as *Erwartung* (1909) and *Die glückliche Hand* (1910–1913). But he established the closest relationship between words and music with the use of *sprechstimme* in *Pierrot Lunaire, Op. 21* (1912), the final composition of his atonal period, 1908–1912. This period of experimentation dealt with the suspension of traditional tonality and preceded Schoenberg's development of twelve-tone or serial composition.

Schoenberg notated exact pitches and rhythms in *Pierrot Lunaire, Op. 21*. Accidentals are indicated throughout and *x*'s appear on note stems rather than note heads. A *sprechstimme* style is used for most pitches, though a few are to be sung normally. The sung tones are clearly differentiated by the absence of *x*'s on note stems and the addition of the word *gesungen* (sung) written over them.

Example 6.1a shows a notation similar to Schoenberg's. Since specific rhythms are indicated, the reciter should adhere strictly to the rhythms marked in the score. In this type of notation, improvisation should not be part of the interpretation. The composer has chosen to maintain precise control of rhythmic values, coordination with other voices or instruments involved, and the overall progression and pacing of the work.

The *sprechstimme* (fixed pitch) style developed by Schoenberg has been embraced and used widely by many twentieth-century composers. Some have continued to notate approximate pitch with a small *x* through the stem as Schoenberg did, while others have used the *x* as the notehead, flagged or beamed, to show time duration, as in example 6.1b.

Example 6.1a, 6.1b   *Sprechstimme*

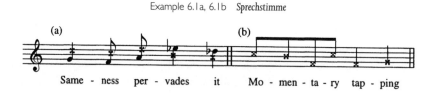

Unfortunately, Schoenberg did not give explicit instructions in the score for the production of *sprechstimme*, only the desired effect, stressing an interpretation between song and speech. He makes the following statement concerning *sprech-stimme* in the preface to the work, stressing an interpretation between song and speech (Mabry 1977, p. 179):

> The melody indicated for the speaking voice by notes (apart from a few specially indicated exceptions) is not to be sung. The reciter has the task of transforming this melody, always with a due regard to the prescribed intervals, into a speaking melody. That is accomplished in the following way:
>
> 1. The rhythm must be kept absolutely strict, that is to say, with no more freedom than he would allow himself if he were just singing the melody.
> 2. To emphasize fully the contrast between the sung note and the spoken note, whereas the sung note preserves the pitch, the spoken note gives it at first, but abandons it either by rising or falling immediately after. The reciter must take the greatest care not to fall into a sing-song form of speaking voice; such is absolutely not intended. On the contrary, the difference between ordinary speech and a manner of speech that may be embodied in musical form, is to be clearly maintained. But, again, it must not be reminiscent of song.

One cannot assume that Schoenberg or any of the composers who employed this technique after him were seeking an extension of the singing style by using *sprechstimme*. Rather, it was more likely used as a solution to dramatic declamation and color differentiation, creating a stylized and exaggerated application of the voice through the production of sounds unlike that in normal singing. As seen above, Schoenberg insists that the reciter adhere to precisely notated intervals throughout while transforming the melody into a "speaking melody." The reciter's dilemma is to determine what constitutes a speaking melody. As a result, reciters have approached the realization of Schoenberg's *sprechstimme* in different ways with quite varying results. Some have disregarded Schoenberg's directions altogether and have chosen to sing all the pitches in a normal singing voice. Others made no attempt to simulate the melodic contour written in the score, declaiming the whole work within a narrow speaking voice range. Schoenberg's own words illustrate that neither is what the composer had in mind.

What should it sound like?

Several issues involved in the production of *sprechstimme* must be considered. They concern specific characteristics of the *sprechstimme* vocal style: use of glissando connectors, elimination of vibrato, natural inflection of the text, and the effect of vocal registration on the notated melodic outline.

The use of glissando connectors

In order to follow Schoenberg's definition of the difference between a sung tone and a *sprechstimme* tone, the following concepts must be kept in mind: (1) Pitch remains constant in the sung tone for its full rhythmical duration. (2) In a *sprechstimme* tone the pitch is sounded and then allowed to change by letting the voice rise or fall before the tone ends.

As Emmons and Sonntag (1979, p. 228) reported, "Jan DeGaetani, specialist in modern music and brilliant at many other styles, describes her method for practicing *sprechstimme* thus: . . . learn to attack each note on pitch and immediately leave the pitch, keeping it in flux as you approach the following note, where you do the same thing. The end result is a legato line with approximate pitches." Both Schoenberg and DeGaetani stressed that the voice rises or falls after each pitch. The most logical way to achieve this is with connecting glissandos that will help to achieve the legato line DeGaetani describes.

When the melodic line is carefully notated, the glissando at the end of a *sprechstimme* tone should move up or down according to the direction of the next tone. If the glissando were allowed to slide downward after every tone, as some reciters have interpreted, then an entirely new melodic line would be created and the contour of the vocal inflection outlined by the composer would be totally destroyed.

The use and direction of the short glissando decidedly changes the vocal declamation to a style somewhere between normal speech and normal song. It is also a vocal inflection that will be familiar, when one considers its relationship to other uses of the voice. As Emmons and Sonntag point out (1979, p. 225),

> It is important for the neophyte singer of *sprechstimme* to realize that she has encountered it before in other forms: the slight exaggerations of great recitative singers who achieve a result more in the direction of speech than singing; the "dirty" intonation of jazz singing; the sound nonsinging conductors and instrumentalists create when they try to indicate rapid musical passages with their voices; and the *sprechstimme* produced by young children, fluent as imitators of speech intonations but not yet proficient at real musical scales or intervals. Thus, for a singer who is master of recitative singing, *sprechstimme* is simply a more methodical and less instinctive matter of learning to sing the line, break it into speech, and finally to sing/speak by hitting the pitch and leaving it. Nonsingers like Rex Harrison do the opposite. If he can manage, so can you.

This technique gives the reciter considerable freedom of interpretation between tones, which is not afforded the singer of traditional song literature. The direction of the glissando following the final tone before a rest should move up or down according to the dramatic stress of the word being spoken. For instance, if the mood is one of joy or exhilaration, the glissando would ascend. If the phrase ends in a melancholy mood, the glissando would descend. This seems necessary in order to adhere to the natural word inflection and dramatic intent that would be portrayed if the text were being spoken in a theatrical monologue. The glissando at the end of a short tone should be lighter, more delicate, and less noticeable than one that spans a long tone. At the end of a long tone, the glissando could continue through the full note value.

The approximate intervals are achieved by accurately placing each word or syllable of the text on its designated pitch before gliding in the direction of successive pitches. This prevents a continuous crooning or sliding through an entire vocal line without ever establishing a distinct pitch definition. Such an affectation would become monotonous, giving a sing-song and perhaps unwanted humorous effect. Therefore, the glissando merely serves to connect the indicated pitches with an exaggerated legato. A vocal legato should be maintained unless rests, staccati, or other indications to do otherwise are given. Avoid harsh glottal attacks (a hard, explosive initiation of tone caused by the buildup of too much air pressure below the vocal cords that suddenly blows them apart). This attack, if used consistently, will tire the voice, cause increased tension in the overall vocal production, and disrupt the desired legato connection between tones. Though some languages, such as English and German, naturally contain glottal attacks when spoken, it is possible to sing them with a beautiful legato connection. The same can be said for the production of *sprechstimme*.

Elimination of vibrato

The second element crucial to the production of *sprechstimme* is the elimination of vibrato. When vibrato is eliminated, the voice quality will more closely approximate that of the speaking voice. In works that contain both sung tones and *sprechstimme* tones, the reciter should apply normal vibrato to the sung tones, keep the pitch sustained full value after the initial attack, and use no glissando for connection of pitches. This flexible technique will bring about maximum contrast between sung tones and the *sprechstimme*.

Text inflection and vowels

Strict adherence to natural text inflection is of paramount importance to the *sprechstimme* style. In traditional singing, elongation and purity of vowel formation is important when sustaining pitches or singing a typical legato vocal line. But in everyday speech, no conscious effort is made to elongate vowels as they are spoken nor to prevent their decay into succeeding vowels. In *sprechstimme*, vowels may be allowed to morph (to gradually change color, fade, become smaller or larger) through the length of the connecting glissando, giving a more speechlike effect. In other words, normal speech inflection dictates the length of the vowel as well as its dissipation, migration, and decay between tones. One must be careful not to anticipate consonants, thereby cutting the vowel short at the end of a glide.

The mouth space used for the production of this vocal style is generally slightly smaller than the full voice singing style. This gives the vowels a quality and space similar to speech. However, the reciter must be careful to open the mouth enough to allow for vocal flexibility throughout his or her entire vocal range. Extremely high tones or those marked mf–fff need more mouth space for resonation and projection than lower, softer tones. The reciter may also need to dispense with the use of a raised soft palate, especially in the middle and lower registers. This is opposite from the approach most singers use when vocalizing in a traditional manner, where the palate is usually kept raised in all vocal registers. However, by using more of a "spoken" space, a significant and distinct difference between normal singing and *sprechstimme* is established.

Vocal registers and sprechstimme

In order to approximate intervals and carefully follow a prescribed melodic line while reciting in *sprechstimme* style, the female reciter can make full use of the chest, middle, and upper (or head) registers of the voice exactly as one would vocalize a traditional melodic line. Though much of the repertoire in this genre calls for a female voice as reciter, men occasionally perform works of this kind. A male voice would use mostly chest and head registers unless extremely high tones were written that could only be accomplished by using the falsetto. A flexible and balanced approach to the use of all vocal registers seems more appropriate for fixed pitch *sprechstimme* notation. Confining the voice to chest tones only, keeping all pitches within the bottom octave of the voice, completely negates a printed melody that contains tones in the upper voice. Also, if one limits the voice to head tones, never using any pitches in the lower voice, the more percussive, contrasting speech sounds possible in the chest voice are eliminated. Both of these limited approaches fail to achieve the multitude of vocal colorations and contrasts available through the use of the reciter's entire vocal range.

By using the three generally recognized singing registers for both men and women, the reciter is able to negotiate a wide vocal range and create elaborate vocal shadings. A vocally damaging scenario would be to use only the chest voice while attempting to approximate the melody as written, taking the chest voice up to pitches that are out of the normal chest voice range. For vocal security, longevity, and overall vocal health, the chest voice should not be taken higher than G4 (fourth G from bottom of keyboard) for females or above the upper end or cut-off point of the male speaking voice range (an individual characteristic that is widely variable for bass, baritone, and tenor). Unless a gradual transition is made through the middle voice, F5 to C5 (for women), and then up into the head voice for high pitches, the voice will begin to shout, become muscularly stressed and tired, and eventually "break" abruptly into the head voice. Negotiating the register transition between chest and head voice is crucial to a fluid vocal production. It requires attention to factors that affect it, such as dynamic levels, placement of the tone, relaxation of the tongue and surrounding musculature, and the formation and resonance of specific vowels being sung. All of these factors must be dealt with in a commonsense, vocally healthy fashion, as one would when technically preparing music of any stylistic period. Proper vocal technique transcends eras and styles.

The use of extreme ranges in both voices and instruments and the combination of various vocal and instrumental timbres contribute to the constantly changing colors and unique qualities heard in this vocal style. However, composers must be aware of the natural capabilities of a particular voice type, especially its range and register transitions, in order to achieve a realistic interpretation of the score. If the score demands something unnatural to the voice, such as asking a soprano to produce high notes above D5 with the chest voice, then physical damage could occur. In this case, the reciter must rely on good vocal sense and decline to do as directed, either substituting a head tone for those pitches or leaving the work out of her repertoire. The composer's understanding of the voice, with all of its attributes, complexities, and faults, is crucial to the development of notation that will be understood and possible for the performer to interpret satisfactorily and with confidence.

Though all notational systems have weaknesses and ambiguities, the composer has a great responsibility to construct the notation as accurately as possible in order to signify what kind of vocal declamation he or she desires. If fixed pitch notation is used and indicates a wide vocal range, logic will tell the singer to try to produce the melodic outline printed on the page. So if the composer prefers that all *sprechstimme* be limited to a relatively short speaking range, then the notation should be confined to that range. To do otherwise gives the wrong impression and may cause the singer to engage the voice unnaturally, using the chest voice too high, especially if additional descriptive directions, such as *declaim* or *speak on pitch*, are printed in the score. If true recitation is desired, rather than a Schoenberg-like *sprechstimme*, then a more indeterminate notation may be the solution. To quote Gardner Read (1979, p. 453), "The first responsibility, then, is the composer's, not the performer's . . . to master the proper written language of his chosen profession is the minimum obligation of the aspiring musician to his art."

How do I do it?

Singers who wish to expand their vocal skills into experimental areas need to have a plan for developing those skills. It is true that some vocalists seem to have a natural affinity for experimentation and are quickly able to translate novel vocalizations into performance. As with other skills, people learn them in different ways and are not created equal in their ability to do so. Each singer has his or her individual vocal strengths, weaknesses, and interests. The same is true of other aspects of musical performance. Some performers are facile sight-readers, while others struggle. Some have difficulty interpreting rhythmic structures, even at an elementary level, while others immediately feel the rhythmic message. Some have a quick recall of language phonemes and can sing easily in French, Italian, German, or Spanish, while others labor over what seems to be the simplest combination of vowels and consonants. In the final outcome, those with strong intuitive abilities will probably master the task faster, but those who require a more methodical approach will often become the keener interpreters, due to a stronger commitment to the achievement of the goal. In either case, preconceived notions must be shed for successful vocal experimentation, and a definite rehearsal/study plan is needed for the development of the vocal and musical reflexes inherent in the new technique. The following section presents several ideas for expanding interpretative skills and for developing a specific practice routine in order to master the production of *sprechstimme*.

Developing a study/practice plan

1. Carefully analyze how the voice is used throughout the score. Determine if there is a continuous use of *sprechstimme* or if it is alternated with sections or individual tones to be sung, spoken, or produced in other ways. If there are only a few *sprechstimme* tones, mark them clearly, perhaps highlighting them with a light yellow marker so that the eye and mind become used to where they belong in the vocal line.

2. Read the text aloud in its poetic form. Then practice speaking it, using the exact rhythms notated. Speak the entire text, even though some of the tones may be eventually sung in a traditional manner. For an extended work, this process can be done in short, manageable sections. When reading aloud, always speak in a normal speaking register and a medium volume. Do not whisper or allow the pitch of the voice to become low and raspy. The voice will tire under those conditions. Keep the placement of the voice forward, ringing in the front of the face. Concentrate on clarity of tone and freedom of the articulators (lips and tongue) as the text is being delivered.

3. Since fixed-pitch *sprechstimme* notates specific pitches, learn the indicated melody line as you would with traditional notation. Do not guess or assume that pitches are near those notated. Use the piano keyboard as a pitch reference and continually check intervals for accuracy. Learn to play some of the accompanying figures, if possible, and occasionally play a chord, ostinato pattern, or whatever is occurring while you are delivering the *sprechstimme* line. This practice routine will orient the ear to musical material accompanying the voice and will help lessen the impact of distraction and psychological overload or panic when re-hearsals begin with the other instruments. During the early practice sessions, disregard the tempo marked. Practice at a slow enough tempo to allow the voice and ear to become accustomed to what may be a very angular melodic line.

4. From the beginning, practice the melodic line with a beautiful legato con-nection between pitches, allowing the voice's normal vibrato to be present at all times, keeping dynamics within a medium volume throughout until all intervals and rhythms are learned. Pay close attention to vocal register adjustments, deter-mining during this stage of rehearsal exactly where and when to shift from chest voice to head voice. Mark these transitions on the score and rehearse them con-sistently, using the same technique so that the connection will become smooth and automatic. It may be helpful to use shorthand, such as a c for chest voice and an h for head voice, printing them above notes that lie in the lower passaggio.

Continue to keep the tempo slow and the dynamic levels moderate throughout this process.

5. Once the voice and ear are secure with the intervals, the next step is to allow the voice to attack each note on pitch and immediately leave the pitch by incorporating the glissando (or short glide) in order to reach the next pitch. Always allow the glissando to glide in the direction of the following pitch, unless an unusual dramatic effect is needed (for example, an element of surprise or a sigh). Keep the glissando elegant, even, lyrical, and floating on the air stream. Allow it to merely skim the notes in between pitches, never halting or squarely landing on any pitch other than those notated. Delicacy of attack is essential during this stage of technical development. Continue to practice at a slow tempo and in a light- to-moderate dynamic level until the glissando connection between tones is automatic. During this stage of rehearsal, delete the normal vibrato as would traditionally occur in a glissando connection.

6. Once pitch, rhythm, voice placement, and glissando connections have become automatic, other subtleties of declamation and score realization can be tackled. Divide the work into short sections and incorporate the elements of dynamics, vocal color nuance, and dramatic interpretation. Look at the dynamic scheme of the work. Decide where the softest and loudest points are and mark them clearly. Determine the volume used most frequently in the work. Normally it will be a medium volume. Find that medium volume, natural to your voice, and rehearse those sections of the work first, becoming comfortable with the *sprechstimme* technique before applying dynamic adjustments. Some pieces from this period call for an extreme dynamic range. If that is the case, be careful to find a relaxed, focused placement for those tones, never allowing the voice to get too soft or breathy to be heard, nor forcing the voice to sing louder than its natural resonance capabilities. Markings such as *pppp* or *ffff*, occasionally found in contemporary music, should be assumed to be the softest and loudest tones in the voice's natural dynamic range, not inaudible or screamed. To do the latter puts undue physical and psychological stress on the performer. If the composer wishes the voice to be heard easily above accompanying instruments, then those instruments must be adjusted so that they do not overpower the voice, rendering it inaudible or causing the singer to push the voice beyond its limits in order to compete with the collective instrumental sound. In some cases, the voice is not meant to be heard in the forefront of the ensemble, only as a contributor to the general coloristic effect. In that situation, the singer must adjust all dynamic levels so that the voice simply coasts within a framework of instrumental sound. This is a good time to relax and let the voice rest for an upcoming dramatic spot requiring more vocal stamina and projection.

Rehearse with the proper dynamic scheme until it is automatic. Then begin to add vocal color contrasts where indicated. Some composers mark the score with descriptive adjectives indicating a desired color change. This could occur on one note or over an entire section. Even if there are no color markings in the score, the reciter should feel compelled to approach the text as an actor, rather than as one who merely vocalizes tones. Concentrate on the dramatic import, with all of its subtleties, in order to express the innate meaning of the text and its setting. Only then will the audience fully appreciate the text's dramatic significance. This concept of meaningful text delivery applies to the performance of works from several eras and styles, as well as *sprechstimme*.

7. Relate vocal color changes to the text. Since the voice is now combining elements of speech with those of singing, most of the color contrasts will come directly from the dramatic intent of the text and how it would be inflected if it were spoken, not sung. Time was spent at the beginning of this rehearsal process reading the text aloud for familiarity, fluidity, and voice placement. Now go back and read it aloud solely for dramatic intent, taking time to locate important action words; words or phrases with heightened emotions; moments of unbridled joy, sadness, or depression; and words that depend on their percussive or suave sound for a unique vocal effect. Mark these areas in the text, making notes and assigning coloristic adjectives to each. Then rehearse them one at a time until a broad spectrum of colors is reached by using vowel modification—elements of regional accents where appropriate—or by allowing the voice to mimic a sound that is being described. Mental imagery and imitation are as important as vocal technique when portraying a large palette of vocal color. Refer to chapter 4 for ideas about the general development of tone color variation.

Singers are constantly being admonished to "spit out the words" so that the text can be understood. That is crucial with the interpretation of *sprechstimme*. Consonants must be clear and crisp, and delivered precisely and quickly with the tongue and lips. Don't allow the jaw to become involved in the production of consonants. If the jaw opens widely on every syllable, producing a flopping or chewing effect, words will be distorted, voice placement will suffer, and vocal register breaks will be more noticeable. Keep the jaw stable and relaxed, not stiff or held, as in normal singing.

8. The final element in the rehearsal process is to allow the vowels in each word to elongate or decay, as in normal speech, while connecting the tones with a glissando. In normal singing each vowel is held until the last possible second before inserting the consonant following it, and mouth space does not change while vocalizing the vowel. This is an important difference between normal singing and *sprechstimme*. In this final stage of preparation, allow the single vowels and diphthongs to gradually change shape during the length of each tone, mimicking normal speech. If this still seems unnatural, speak the phrase, noticing how the vowels and mouth space are in constant flux. Then intone the phrase on a monotone pitch until the effect is achieved. Finally, reapply it to the pitched notation marked in the score.

Once this practice routine has been accomplished for one piece of music, it will eventually become automatic as the singer uses it for other repertoire. At that point some of the intermediate steps can be eliminated and perhaps the routine may not be necessary, because the mind, muscle structure, and vocal apparatus will have become familiar with the process, the sound desired, and the technique required to produce it.

RECITATION

The term *recitation* has been used to signify an assortment of hybrid vocalizations since composers began to experiment with notation calling for vocal declamation other than normal singing. Individual composers devised their own notational systems for this vocal treatment, and few have given explicit directions in their scores as to its performance. Interpreters have had to rely mostly on native instinct and creative experimentation in the realization of these works. Some have fared well and produced thoughtful responses to the unusual visual and aural demands made by this kind of text setting, but many have felt the need for more specific directions.

Since the voice is capable of making numerous sounds that could be called *recitation*, composers have continued to search for more accurate ways to notate subtle, sometimes elusive, qualities of the voice. Even if the composer's notation and explanations are precise, no two performers will achieve the same sound or exact articulation due to the vast differences in the performers themselves: their interpretation of the composer's directions, and their psyche, voice range, vocal timbre, natural resonance capabilities, acting ability, and willingness to improvise and experiment with the voice.

Composers have tried to allow for divergent realizations of recitation by moving away from the precise notation of pre-twentieth-century eras to several kinds of indeterminate notation. Some of this new notation is nonspecific as to pitch and rhythm and merely *indicates* shapes, colors, pitch relationships, rhythmic values, or the musical organization itself. This kind of notation has been called "indicative notation" or "musical graphics." As discussed in chapter 5, the lines between precise notation, indicative notation, and musical graphics are occasionally blurred, the latter two being degrees of freedom allowed the performer.

The most commonly seen vocal articulations included in the recitation category are unpitched, rhythmically free speaking (with or without musical accompaniment); unpitched speaking on designated rhythms (with or without musical accompaniment); and pitched or intoned speaking using either the speaking voice only or the entire speaking and singing vocal range.

UNPITCHED, RHYTHMICALLY FREE SPEAKING

Generally, two types of usage are found for unpitched, rhythmically free speaking. In the first type, individual lines or large sections of text are used either to interject a momentary change of direction in the musical organization or to provide dramatic contrast and commentary between divisions of an extended work.

The text is generally printed in its poetic form, without any reference to pitch, pacing, or rhythmic structure. The composer may give a verbal indication, such as *speak, narrate,* or *recite.* Sometimes there is no musical accompaniment during this form of recitation, except perhaps an interjection of sound at certain points to emphasize a sudden dramatic intensity or calmness. For instance, a gong, finger cymbals, wind chimes, or other percussive effects might be sounded, providing a short space of lingering atmosphere underneath the spoken words.

The interpretation of this type of recitation should be totally controlled by the dramatic intent of the text. Use the voice within its normal speaking range in an oratorical (stage-theater) manner, well-projected and with dramatic nuance. Pacing of the text must be taken from the actor's viewpoint, stressing appropriate lines or words and spacing sentences according to dramatic flow. Project the voice clearly, with precise diction, and modulate it to a medium volume except for more dramatically intense words or phrases. Never let the voice become raspy or speak in a whisper unless a specific dramatic contrast is called for or there is direction in the score to do so.

An excellent example of an effective use of unpitched rhythmically free speaking occurs in Elizabeth Vercoe's dramatic monodrama *Herstory III: Jehanne de Lorraine* (appendix B). The work is divided into twelve contrasting sections that use the voice in both traditional and novel ways. Vercoe uses speaking as a connecting device in three critical areas of the work. None of the spoken sections is accompanied by the piano or percussion instruments otherwise used in the work. Each presents a facet of Joan of Arc's transformation from innocent young girl to stirring warrior leading troops to free her country of an occupying army. The speeches are sympathetic, sometimes stark, and provide emotionally charged contrasts to the sung portions of the work.

Another type of unpitched, rhythmically free recitation popular with twentieth-century composers differs from the first in its placement of the spoken text and the use of accompanying instruments. In this case, the text is generally used as an integral part of the musical organization rather than as a connector of sections. It may suddenly be inserted into the middle of an otherwise traditional use of the voice. The spoken section provides a distinct contrast to normal singing, *sprechstimme*, or other vocal devices that might occur.

What should it sound like?

Characteristics of this type of recitation are:

- Verbal cues are given for the type of declamation desired, such as *spoken, recited, yelled, speak (ad libitum)*, or *declaim*.
- No pitches or rhythms are provided for the pacing of the text.
- The text is generally written below the normal vocal staff and above the staves containing accompanying lines. However, it is sometimes written on the page in place of the normal vocal staff.
- The accompanying lines may or may not continue in definite rhythmic patterns. The compositional style will determine whether the music contains consistent metric movement, meters interspersed with indeterminacy, or whether it is altogether aleatoric. In either case, the recitation will need to be paced to fit into the pattern accompanying it, whether metric or aleatoric.

It will be a felt or intuited declamation, not one precisely notated and produced.

How do I do it?

When preparing this style of recitation, pay close attention to all composer-generated directions for interpretation. Some composers are quite prolific and helpful in their verbal notations for the performer. For instance, in the song "spoke joe to jack" from *cowboy songs* by Karen P. Thomas (appendix B), the composer is quite clear about words to be stressed, particular moods that should be developed, and specific vocal color nuances desired. In the course of thirteen fast-moving measures marked "spoken", Thomas writes the following interpretative directions over specific words: "questioning," "biting," "inquiring," and "whispered." The voice declaims melodramatically over a sharply punctuated, angular accompaniment, strategically placed to add dramatic impact to the text. Dynamic levels range from FF to PP in the accompaniment, so the voice must follow suit in order to match the mood created by the piano and be heard as an equal with it. When a composer carefully marks the score with dynamic, expressive, theatrical, and interpretative directions, the reciter's responsibility is to find and rehearse those contrasts within his or her own range of possibilities. These markings are particularly helpful to novice actors who may not have discovered the depth of their ability to imagine and create contrast in the projection of drama.

Recitation that is spoken in competition with accompanying instruments must be done judiciously. If one normally has a weak, light, or unprojected speaking voice with few dramatic resonance colors (such as a light coloratura soprano or a light lyric tenor or countertenor with a very high, light speaking voice), this type of declamation may not be suitable. It could even be injurious if the ill-cast reciter tries to deepen or force the voice unnaturally in order to be heard. A few words recited in this fashion might not be a problem, but more than a few could be cause for choosing another work for performance. Melodrama of this kind needs a speaking voice with considerable resonance, a fairly wide range of easily produced dramatic colors, and the flexibility to move quickly from one to the other in a theatrical manner. The rules for voice placement and projection stated earlier for *unaccompanied recitation* apply here, as well. The major difference in the interpretation involves pacing and coordination of the dynamic levels in the speaking voice with those of accompanying instruments.

A study/practice plan
EXERCISE 6A (DEVELOPING A SENSITIVITY TO MOOD)

Find a short poem of four to eight lines or part of a longer poem that is characteristic of a contemplative, sad, melancholy, or depressed mood. Read the text silently, paying attention to how the words make you feel. Think of a piece of instrumental music with which you are familiar (it could be a piece from any musical era or any musical style, such as classical, jazz, new age, or folk music). Once the selection is made, play the music at a moderately soft level while reading the text silently. Make sure the moods fit together. If so, repeat the process, hearing your own inner voice. Read the text and picture the volume, color, and pacing you feel would be appropriate for the music. This could be done several times before moving to the final stage of practice. Self-visualization of physical appearance and sound qualities has been used successfully by vocal pedagogues and singers for the interpretation of both singing and acting. Balk (1978, p. 63) believes that "emotions must be aroused indirectly . . . if one wishes to draw upon a personal event, one must not think about the event itself . . . if one can visualize it, hear it, smell it, and taste it, the emotions connected with the event will return of their own accord . . . one can only lure them with sensory stimuli." This mind-body theory applies equally well to the development of appropriate moods for this exercise.

Having gained a clear picture of the type of recitation you desire to produce over a chosen musical background, begin to read the text aloud while the music is playing. Check the placement of the voice for clarity. Moderate the volume of the voice as you progress, adjusting it if the text or music contains subtle differences. During successive repetitions, continue to check decisions you made concerning pacing, volume, etc., and adjust them as your natural creativity becomes freed and spontaneous ideas for interpretation appear. Ideally, each reading will be slightly different as you become less inhibited and rely increasingly on intuition for vocal declamation.

This kind of thought (mind) rehearsal, ending with the overt production of sound, is helpful in the expansion of imagination, mental imaging, and the ability to connect the voice and its subtle properties with outside musical sources. Because much of the exercise is silent, a great deal can be accomplished without tiring the voice.

EXERCISE 6B (EXPANDING MOOD SENSITIVITY)

Follow the guidelines for exercise 6a and choose one additional short text of four to eight lines for each of the following general dramatic moods: excitedly happy; serene (at peace); agitated (perhaps defiant or angry); hysterical (frenzied or mad, out of one's mind); and bitter (full of regret). Again, choose an instrumental or electronically produced piece as a musical companion for each. Work each text as you did with the original example, varying the order in which they are rehearsed. Once you have chosen the musical selections and they seem perfectly satisfying for each mood, record them on a cassette tape in any order you wish. Having this repertoire of recorded examples of emotional and dramatic contrasts will be valuable as a rehearsal tool and can be readily called upon when you need a quick reminder of a particular psychological disposition.

It would also be enlightening to record yourself as you read each text with its accompanying music. We often think we are achieving great contrasts in color, mood, and so on until we hear ourselves on tape. It can be a revealing experience and elicit more subtleties of declamation than we originally felt were necessary. Listening to one's voice on tape can also be helpful in determining natural and appropriate pitch levels for speaking. Becoming aware of speaking faults, such as nasality or the use of glottal attacks and fry tones (vocal sputter), is vital to vocal health and longevity. Finally, clarity of enunciation—the ultimate communication device—can be verified through this method.

EXERCISE 6C (DEVELOPING FLEXIBILITY OF MOOD)

Now that you have chosen and thoroughly ingrained short texts for a variety of dramatic moods, select one line from each text for this practice phase. Obviously, the individual lines will no longer be connected by meaning, mood, pacing, or poetic style and rhythm. The more contrasting the lines, the better.

Place the lines of texts in any order you wish. Read them silently in succession, remembering the dramatic characteristics of their original context. Picture the tempo, pacing, vocal resonance, dynamic levels, vocal colors, and shadings orig-inally used for each. Try to recall the musical selection originally chosen to fit each mood. Hear it in your mind. Getting a sense of its mood will help to trigger an emotional response.

In the beginning, take your time between lines if it is difficult to make the sudden change from one mood to the next. But with each repetition make a mental shift in psychological tone or feeling as you silently read the lines, trying to switch more quickly between disparate moods. You may feel a shift in physical energy. Your pulse may quicken and your body language change as you remem-ber how you felt while speaking each line with the original music. There is no need to actually play the music at this point. Pay attention to how the body reacts to excitement, sadness, or anger. Changes will occur in breath flow, muscle ten-sion, body position, and facial expression. Each of these reactions is an integral part of the development of sensory triggers that enable the coordination of mind and muscles. It is important to divert the mind from reactions that do not apply to the dramatic response you are trying to achieve and to increase awareness of those that are essential in producing the desired response.

When this flexibility of mood seems comfortable, change the order of the lines and rotate them into several different sequences until it is effortless to depict the mood of each, no matter the order in which they appear.

Once this process can easily be accomplished in silence, begin to speak the lines aloud, returning to their original sequence. Having satisfactorily mastered it, rotate the lines, as before, until they can be quickly and easily dramatically differentiated in any order.

Record the spoken portion of this exercise. Listening to one's voice as it ex-presses sudden shifts in dramatic declamation will further imprint vivid imagery in the mind, allowing for quick recall.

UNPITCHED SPEAKING (WITH DESIGNATED RHYTHMS)

The second type of recitation frequently used by twentieth-century composers is unpitched speaking within a notated rhythmic pattern. No longer is there total freedom of pacing as in unpitched, rhythmically free recitation. Some composer-generated system is now in control of the flow of the declamation.

The rhythms may be notated on a five-, three-, or one-line staff. Sometimes the rhythms are notated as if in limbo, with no staff lines at all. The notation can be of different types and still signify unpitched speaking: note stems without note heads; note stems with x's as heads; note stems with hollow heads; or note stems with square heads (see example 6.2). If spoken phrases using x's as note heads appear amid traditionally sung pitches, the word *spoken* should be written above them to avoid confusion with *sprechstimme* notation (Stone 1980).

What should it sound like?

The note stems and heads do not move up and down on the page or on staff lines indicating specific pitches. Rather, they are in a straight, even line moving left to right. This indicates that the voice should be kept approximately within a major third of the normal speaking tone. The note stems, beamed and flagged, signify definite rhythmic values, whether the note heads are missing or appear in a nontraditional shape.

A fine example of this form of recitation is found in Charles Ives's well-known and much performed song, "Charlie Rutlage," published in his *114 Songs*. The lengthy spoken section occurs in the middle of this cowboy song and must be

Example 6.2a   Unpitched Speaking: Designated Rhythms

Mo - men - ta - ry tap - ping, tap - ping!

Example 6.2b   Unpitched Speaking

Mo - men - ta - ry tap - ping, tap - ping!

Example 6.2c, 6.2d   Unpitched Speaking

Mo - men - ta - ry   Mo - men - ta - ry

declaimed over a forceful, dense, and raucous piano accompaniment. The reciter is given specific rhythms throughout, notating them with stems and flags but no noteheads. There is also a direction to *follow the piano*. The singer could use a southwestern Texas accent to bring out the flavor of an off-handed cowboy spirit so beautifully captured in this humorous piece. Also, notice the seven tempo and dynamic markings within that section (*hold back, fast, a little slower, fast again, faster and faster, louder and louder, and slower*). They guide the voice beautifully as to dramatic intent, pacing, and vocal intensity and aid in the coordination of the spoken text with the piano, since each coincides with a similar marking for the piano.

Occasionally, performers encounter confusing notations for unpitched speaking. Gardner Read (1979, p. 298) points out that composers must "assist the performers by aiming for impeccable clarity" and by understanding the voice and how it works. Unfortunately, this is not always the case. A particularly problematic notation for unpitched speaking is the use of *sprechstimme* notation (which contains fixed pitches) combined with written directions to speak in a normal voice. These two directions are at odds if the fixed pitches move considerably outside the normal speaking range. In a case such as this, contact the composer if possible. If not, then adhere to the written directions to use the normal speaking range instead of the melodic outline of the notation. This is a composer/notation problem, and without input from the composer, it is impossible to know exactly what was intended. In no case should the speaking voice be taken up to high pitches, in effect shouting above the normal speaking voice cut-off range. In particular, this pertains to female singers who speak primarily in the chest voice. Carrying the chest voice too high can put stress on all facets of vocal production, tiring the voice and perhaps leading to vocal abuse.

How do I do it?

Developing a practice routine for this type of recitation is quite simple and may already be part of a singer's rehearsal pattern. A familiar pedagogical suggestion for learning music of any era or style is to practice speaking the text in the rhythms designated in the music. It is traditionally one of the first steps used when dissecting a new piece.

Look carefully at the application of unpitched speaking in the work. Determine if the rhythmic movement is organized within meters, freely inserted over accompanying lines, or altogether indeterminate. Whatever the case, the most important aspect of the rehearsal strategy is to become familiar with the look and organization of the score.

Compare the visual effect of the notes and their stems, heads (or lack of), and flags or beams to the accompanying material. Specific notational devices likely to be found in such situations are discussed in chapter 5 and may help with the deciphering process.

Read all printed directions for realization, either in the preface or over individual pitches or phrases within the score itself. Once you have made decisions concerning the rhythmic flexibility, pacing, and coordination with accompaniment, establish a practice plan and rehearse each phrase with a specific intent.

Practice plan

1. Divide the work into short sections. Never attempt to *read through* an entire work with this kind of notation. Small bits of new material will be easier to absorb and leave the mind freer, fresher, and in a more positive attitude for later, more comprehensive rehearsal sessions.

2. Indicate the note values, beats, or rhythmical pulse over any complicated, irregular, or visually confusing rhythmic structures. This applies to any work containing meters, measures, or merely a line of pitches built on note value relationships (eighth notes, quarter notes, triplets, duplets, etc.). Use numbers to mark beats within measures or choose another sign, such as a check mark, to signify strong rhythmical pulses in unmetered music.

3. Notice the beaming of notes, slur lines, dynamics, accents, or verbal indications and mark them clearly for textual stress or emphasis. Placement of text is crucial to the realization of these notations. For instance, if a word is rehearsed and learned on an incorrect portion of a beat (not the one indicated in the score) or a tie sign is ignored, it would change the intended rhythmic pattern of the phrase as a whole. Ingrained bad habits are hard to break. Careful attention to details in the early stages of preparation will save painful relearning later on.

4. If the text is written in a foreign language or contains foreign words, translate the text before proceeding with a vocal rehearsal. Write the translation above the printed text so that word and phrase meanings will be established psychologically from the start of the practice session.

5. Silently read the text without reference to the notated rhythms, developing a sensitivity to its mood. Pay attention to bodily reactions to mood as mentioned in exercise 6c.

6. Read the text in rhythm, mouthing the words silently. Do not whisper. Whispering for long periods causes the voice to tire. Clap the rhythms or conduct (if there are metric patterns) as you silently vocalize. Continue this phase of the rehearsal until the rhythms of the spoken text are secure.

7. Continue to rehearse silently, combining the learned rhythmic designations with dramatic expression. Putting the two elements together at this stage will save time later when you are speaking aloud. Also, the speaking voice will be spared numerous repetitions, allowing for a longer rehearsal period.

At this stage, preparation of mental imagery will result in a quicker response from the speaking voice when it does become involved. Physical and mental reactions to changes in mood will already be automatic. Use all of the senses when doing imagery work. Try to work in detail and bring forth every vivid aspect of the text until the mind can recall them at will. Your ability to image will improve with practice. It is a skill like any other in singing and requires consistent practice until it feels normal and is easily accessed.

8. Now you are ready to engage the speaking voice. Rehearse in a medium volume, using a clear, well-projected tone. Concentrate on precise, clean articulation of consonants, correct pronunciation (foreign or domestic words), and declamation of text on designated rhythms. Notice that all syllables are rhythmically placed exactly as printed. When the rhythms are complex, declamation becomes much more difficult. If the tongue and lips have problems articulating fast-moving or complex rhythms, slow down the tempo until they easily respond to the rhythmic patterns. Pull out any particularly complicated, intricate rhythmic combinations and practice them separately as an individual exercise. Keep these excerpts short so that you can do them casually as you are doing other chores during the day, unrelated to a true rehearsal session. The pattern could be as short as one or two words that can be repeated over and over, much as one would practice a diction exercise like "red leather, yellow leather," or "tikituta," to work the tongue and lips in a particular pattern.

9. As the rhythmic structure and precise diction are becoming fixed and automatic, draw your attention more closely to the use of the voice itself. Keep the voice within its normal speaking range, use appropriate color shadings indicated in the text, and modulate the volume so that textual stresses and dynamic contrasts become incorporated.

10. Add any unusual, exaggerated, or melodramatic declamations required. For example, some texts include dialogue that is spoken in a colloquial or regional accent, while the majority of the text is in a neutral, narrative style.

General recommendations

Record your rehearsal sessions for evaluation. Listen for efficient and ringing voice placement, precise articulation of text, appropriate dramatic expression, and rhythmic accuracy. Watch yourself in the mirror during this process in order to incorporate convincing facial expressions. Keep all unwanted physical tension out of the vocal production of this melodramatic style. Always pay attention to correct body alignment, especially the neck and head. Use only those muscles most directly involved in the production of a sound, articulation, or physical movement. Try to release excess tension in muscles that should be at rest during vocal activity. Any unnecessary muscular activity or tension tends to grow and become difficult to release if habituated. Efficiency and proper balance and coordination of the muscles and articulators will result in a clearer, more relaxed vocal production.

If you find that a rehearsal session is mentally or vocally tiring, stop immediately. Vary your routine. Take a few moments to release pent-up tension by meditating, doing light physical exercise (walking down the hall or up and down a flight of stairs), or practicing a relaxation-response exercise (tensing the body from head to toe for five seconds and suddenly letting go, followed by exhaling and taking in a slow, deep breath, feeling the physical release of tension). Simple stretching, rolling the shoulders forward and back, or bending forward at the waist for a minute, with your arms dangling toward the floor, will help to rid the body of rigidity and stress. It also helps to vary the content of any practice session involving new vocal or musical ideas. Intersperse familiar songs or vocalises, giving the mind a moment to shift its focus and lessen the intensity of the rehearsal.

PITCHED RECITATION/INTONED SPEAKING

The term *intoned* has been used for centuries in reference to the vocalization of Gregorian and other kinds of religious chant, especially the vocalization of the first few notes of a line of chant sounded by a priest or celebrant. It has become synonymous with a half-sung, half-spoken monotone vocal production that does not contain vibrato or vocally expressive emotion. This type of vocalization is familiar to those who have been exposed to religious ceremonies containing the intoned recitation of sacred texts or to those who have studied them for research purposes.

Since the origin of pitched, intoned speaking goes back hundreds of years, it cannot be said that twentieth-century composers created it. However, they have invented numerous creative approaches to its use in modern music. Some composers have treated intoned speaking similarly to its historical use, while others have experimented in terms of pitch variation, expressive qualities, and rhythmic contrasts.

As used in modern music, pitched or intoned speaking is a vocally liberating technique that affords the reciter-singer great freedom to express creativity, imagination, and extraordinary emotional contrasts. One of the psychologically freeing elements involves the very lack of a preconceived, precise, or traditional vocal production required for its interpretation. Knowing that one has great freedom to experiment with the sound, voice color, dynamics, pitch, and pacing can be an exciting prospect for the inventive, inquisitive performer.

What should it sound like?

Intoned speaking can be limited to a relatively small pitch area confined only to the speaking voice range, or it can include the entire speaking and singing range. The notation generally indicates which modulation of the voice is desired. Several notational styles have been used to depict pitched or intoned speaking. The most commonly encountered are shown in the following examples.

Example 6.3 (pitched recitation) shows a one-line staff with pitches placed both above and below it. Individual syllables of text are printed directly below

Example 6.3   Pitched Recitation

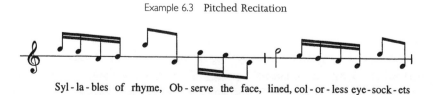

Syl - la - bles of rhyme, Ob - serve the face, lined, col - or - less eye - sock - ets

the pitch on which they must be declaimed. The staff line signifies the middle of the voice. The location of the pitches outlines the melodic contour and its relationship to the middle of the reciter's voice. For the reciter, the middle of the voice should include the top (or cut-off area) of the speaking voice and the bottom of the head voice, an area of about a major third. For female voices, that could be anywhere in the range from middle C on the piano keyboard to the A above, unless the voice is very high in pitch. The same principle would apply for male voices an octave lower. It will be slightly different for each voice type and for each singer within that type.

It is left to the singer to determine the approximate pitch of the notes written above and below the staff line. Pitches should be approximated according to their distance from the staff line. There are no absolutes involved in the printed pitches because the line indicating the middle of the voice is itself indeterminate.

Notation of this type can either be rhythmically free (no indication of specific rhythms) or built entirely on designated rhythm patterns. The compositional style or structure will determine which method is used. George Crumb used approximate pitch, intoned speaking with a notation similar to example 6.3, in several works, including *Ancient Voices of Children, Night of the Four Moons,* and *Madrigals, Books I and II* (appendix B). In the *Madrigals* he used the notation primarily for whispered or spoken sounds to be projected in different pitch ranges. He was able to create a successful marriage of song and speech, giving the interpreter great freedom to express subtle colors inherent in the composite musical and textual atmosphere of each piece.

How do I do it?

1. Divide the score into short sections for rehearsal.

2. Locate and mark all instances of intoned speaking.

3. Determine whether the intoned sections are free and indeterminate or have a specific rhythmic structure. Write in beats or rhythmic pulses over complicated sections. Clap rhythms and speak the text silently until it is rhythmically secure. Take care to give each syllable of text its full and correct rhythmic value. Properly position each syllable in its exact location, rhythmically and melodically, within the melodic contour (notice ties and beaming of pitches, which determines syllabic grouping and rhythmic intent).

4. Analyze the contour of the melodic line, noticing where and how far pitches move above and below the staff line.

5. Use a normal speaking voice range and practice reading the text aloud, keeping the voice within the top third of that range. Get used to the sound with its natural focus and modulation. On a piano, find the approximate pitches for the top of your speaking range. Add a major third above the speaking range and consider the whole area as the middle of your voice for this type of recitation. Begin to experiment with the reading of the text, allowing the pitch modulation of the voice to follow the contour of the melodic line. Check to make sure that

pitches printed on the staff line are being produced in the comfortable middle range of the voice. Make full use of the head voice for all tones above the staff line. Do not extend the chest voice higher than its normal singing range while reciting in this style.

6. Listen for vocal inflection, letting the voice follow the standard syllabic stress (dictionary usage) for each syllable. All syllables are not equally weighted when we speak, and thus they should not be intoned with equal weight. The combination of the naturally spoken inflection of the words, the use of singing style vocal placement, and the deletion of vibrato gives this recitation its unique quality. Since there is no vibrato in spoken tones, delete it completely unless the composer directs otherwise.

7. There is no inherent glissando in this form of recitation (as described earlier for *sprechstimme*). However, a lift or drop of pitch can occasionally be inserted lightly when moving from a high pitch to a lower one and vice versa, much as one does when answering someone's question with "yes." Practice saying "yes" as if confirming the answer to a question. Do this on several indeterminate pitches and notice how the voice lightly drifts down from its original pitch after it is sounded. Then pretend someone has called your name and you answer "yes." Allow the voice to lift up in pitch after striking the initial tone. It gives the effect of an inquiring "yes." That natural inflection of sound up or down is useful in intoned speaking, but it should not be used to connect every pitch in the melodic line nor be considered a real glissando, since it does not strike all notes in between the pitches of the melodic contour. Instead, it should be thought of as an inflection or color device, putting emotional character into the transmission of the text and making the language come to life.

8. Connect all tones with a smooth legato attack unless otherwise indicated. Eliminate glottal attacks and fry tones from the vocal production. Keep the breath flowing steadily as in normal singing, without stops and starts of the breath stream, and without gripping the throat muscles for the cut-off of tones.

9. Use a speaking (midmouth, no raised palate) placement of the voice when intoning within the normal speaking range. As the voice moves to higher pitches, use more mouth space and allow the voice to make use of the soft palate and sinus cavities for additional resonance, keeping the vowels placed high in the head for maximum ring in the tone. This combination of elements taken from speech and singing will promote freedom in the voice, especially in the upper range. To keep a speaking voice mouth shape throughout would confine the tone and create shrillness, nasality, and vocal constriction.

10. Vocal flexibility is very important for the production of intoned speaking, so concentrate on the relaxation of all physical elements of production. Walk around the room as you rehearse. Watch yourself in the mirror for any telltale signs of tension in the shoulders, neck, jaw, or face. Keep the lips and tongue loose and fluid, as in normal speech and singing. Never hold the lips in a fixed

Example 6.4   Intoned Speaking

Times were slow then dragging down jumpers,   No one gets it now.

position, trying to create a special vocal effect. This could become a habit and creep into every aspect of performance.

11. Record your rehearsals to see how the development of the intoned style is progressing. Listen for inappropriate syllabic stress, incorrect rhythms, contour of melodic line, vocal color shadings, and dynamic contrasts that still need some attention. Mark any problems you find, dissect them from the score, rehearse them separately until mastered, and then record the section again as a final check for accuracy.

12. Put all elements together and concentrate on intoning with only the drama in mind. Watch yourself in the mirror for the development of facial expressions appropriate to the text. If stage directions are involved in the piece, add them at this point.

Example 6.4 indicates a pitch range in which the text is to be intoned. In notation of this type, all words and syllables of the text are printed under the pitch on which they are to be recited. In this instance, two tones have several words of text under each tone, while other tones have only one word printed. The intoned melody moves from an original pitch to three higher pitches, then back to the starting pitch. Variations in this kind of pitch placement are limitless and are totally at the composer's discretion.

What should it sound like?

No individual rhythms are written for each word or syllable of the text. The pacing is a *felt* or *interpreted* flow according to the rhythmic structure of the accompanying lines, metric organization, metronome markings, and style of the composition. Each piece will be individualistic in its use of this type of recitation and must be analyzed with that in mind. The declamation of text should continue to adhere to the pitches indicated, staying within the printed pitch range.

This type of notation relies heavily on the speaking voice, keeping most of the pitches within the normal speaking range. Composers have used a variety of verbal instructions to describe the desired outcome for this sing-song, half-spoken, almost jaunty kind of intonation, with directions such as *spoken on pitch*, *intone*, *declaim*, *sing*, *casually sung*, and *talk on pitch*. The notation can be used to depict various dramatic intents, some solemn, some humorous. The voice is simply the conduit through which the dramatic intent of the text is expounded. It is a perfect example of a composer's desire to suppress the normally extravagant singing voice tone quality in favor of something more casual. This half-spoken sound calls for a specific definition of the desired personality to be conveyed, a keen understanding of the textual meaning, a finely rehearsed use of imagination, acting ability, and the forward bite of the spoken sound.

Darrell Handel used this kind of notation in "Cardinal," the second song in his song cycle, *Three Birdsongs* (appendix B). Handel chose to combine normal singing with interspersed short sections of pitched, intoned speaking. The dramatic contrast of the two vocal styles is quite effective in describing the violent death of a beautiful bird. Handel limits the intoned sections to a narrow, medium-low vocal range, while the sung portions of the piece span an octave and a fifth. Also, he saves the intoning for portions of the text that dutifully describe the invasion and vacating of the cardinal's body by a line of ants. The solemnity of the intoned, emotionless vocal treatment is most effective in painting a stark and tragic picture of one of life's everyday events.

How do I do it?

1. Keep all text declamation within the tonal range indicated, making certain to place individual words or syllables on the proper pitches. Recitation of this kind can be flexible in its use of vocal color, but it cannot deviate from the specific pitches printed. Improvising pitches should be saved for notation that encourages it.

2. No glissando connection should be used. Strike the pitches as they are written, pacing them according to the flow of the music and the compositional organization.

3. Use the speaking voice (no lifted palate, forward placement in the teeth and mask, no vibrato, and no fry tones and glottal attacks).

4. Fully support the voice with breath as in normal singing (diaphragmatic-costal breathing).

5. Thoroughly analyze the text in order to find a fitting approach to the interpretation. Read the text aloud to get a sense of the natural flow of the words, the overall mood, and any special characterizations or emotional "surprises" hidden within its lines.

6. Select at least two vocal colors and emotional intents that fit the mood you are trying to achieve. Practice reading the text with these shadings in mind.

7. Apply the vocal color you have chosen for the text and intone it on the printed pitches, a section at a time, until the words and pitches flow naturally.

8. Add any characterizations, regional accents, and word exaggerations that are important to the meaning and projection of the text.

9. Don't be afraid to experiment. Let the voice make a wide range of natural vocal sounds. Listen to the speech qualities of voices that are slightly different from your own. Analyze characteristics of those voices that you can easily mimic without causing vocal stress. These characteristics include projection or resonance qualities, articulation of consonants, formation of vowels, vocal color, pacing of words, vocal inflection, and speaking pitch range. Remember that the speaking

Example 6.5a   Indicative Notation

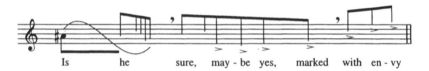

Is   he   sure,   may - be   yes,   marked   with   en - vy

Example 6.5b   Indicative Notation

O(oh)

voice is the window to a person's personality and reveals much about his or her inner emotional feelings and self-image. Recalling these elements in other voices can be useful when preparing to intone words that speak of situations, emotions, or moods that are foreign to the interpreter. Use the voice in a comfortable range of volume and keep the body relaxed while experimenting with sound.

10. Record your efforts at experimentation. Listen to the various attempts and choose those that seem right for the piece and give the desired character to the text and music.

Example 6.5 shows two additional kinds of indicative notation used by contemporary composers for intoned passages. In each case, the normal five-line staff is printed. A general melodic outline is indicated by means of either a wavy line or note stems without heads signifying pitch flow. Notation of this kind may include specific pitches among the indeterminate ones, as in example 6.5a, or may have no exact pitches printed, as in example No. 6.5b. In either case, the primary goal for the vocalist is to simulate the flow of the melodic line, keeping all vocal tones within the pitch range indicated on the staff. If the wavy line or note stems move up, the voice should mirror them and vice versa.

What should it sound like and how do I do it?

Works using notation such as in example 6.5 are generally improvisatory, allowing the interpreter freedom to experiment with rhythms, spacing, and approximated pitch. Use the following guidelines to decipher this notation. In example 6.5a, a wavy line begins after an exact pitch. The line connects several indeterminate pitches and then stops. What follows is a series of independent, approximate pitches. Here, a wavy line merely draws a picture of tone, signifying relative pitch and flow of sound in a continuous movement. If the line is continuous, do not take breaths, create ad lib rhythmic movement, or add stops and starts until the line breaks. Though the line indicates a continuous flow of tone, it may not indicate a specific tempo or spacing for the tones. If text is printed under the wavy line, the reciter has some freedom in the placement of the text. The wavy line could signify word stresses or heightened dramatic import within the phrase by moving up or down in pitch.

Read the text aloud. Check to see if the placement of the text dramatically fits the contour of the line as it is written. If the melodic contour of the line does not seem to coincide with the textual expression and drama, concentrate primarily on the expression of the text. Give detail to natural word inflection and emotional/dramatic contrast, allowing the words to fall at whatever pitch level occurs as you recite while following the contour of the printed line.

This kind of notation has been used frequently with phonetic vocalization, rather than in a traditional syllabic text setting. Notice in example 6.5b how the "o" vowel is carried through the entire phrase of indeterminate pitches and glissandos. The voice does not reattack each tone within the glissando/wavy line. It glides in a swooping fashion, following the curve of the line and "glissing over" notes (like a sigh with an up-and-down sweep through several approximated eighth-note tones).

The singer should assume a normal legato connection between all tones within a wavy line and all rhythmically designated tones with note stems only. Separations, lifts in phrasing, breaths, and staccato attacks will be notated, if desired by the composer.

Music such as this is not meant to be metronomic. Though rhythmic values may be indicated in the notation, one should not be rigid in the interpretation of the flow of pitches. Rather, it is an imagery-guided flow. Indeed, some notes are faster than others, but they are not bound by a metronomic or consistent pulse. Instead, the vocal notation is coordinated and spaced in conjunction with any instruments or electronic tape accompanying it and in accordance with expressive qualities of the text that need to be emphasized or veiled in some way. If the voice is intoning without accompaniment, much greater liberty may be taken with pacing the pitches. Always consider any verbal tempo or expression markings in the score that will affect the flow. Some pieces give the performer license to become a composer and create fantastical, improvisatory elements in the realization of the work. But many pieces do not go that far and have a few built-in controls for pitch, tempo, declamation, and expression. The correct balance arises from meticulous analysis of each score. Never assume that because a composer allowed the performer great freedom to improvise in one work, all of that composer's works are constructed in the same manner.

A STUDIO APPROACH TO *SPRECHSTIMME* AND RECITATION

Singers can easily incorporate elements of *sprechstimme* and recitation into their daily warm-up routine, preparing the psyche and voice for the challenge when it arrives in a piece of music. The following practice hints are not necessarily new, innovative, or time-consuming, but they may be couched in a new context, making them seem unfamiliar. They are taken from time-honored principles of effective vocal training. Some, regularly part of a typical vocal warm up, are used for such technical issues as coordination of vocal registers, achieving a smooth tonal attack, or maximizing resonance. These exercises are meant to free the voice, develop mental imagery, and create spontaneity in the singer's approach to vocalization.

EXERCISE 6D (HUM-SIGH, GLISSANDO)

Begin by lightly humming an "m" on a pitch in the middle voice. Slowly glide down to the octave below, being certain to keep the movement legato. As the pitch descends, gradually open the mouth to an "ah" vowel before reaching the octave below. When the lower tone has been sounded, immediately begin to glide upward to the original tone, gradually closing the mouth to an "m" before reaching the top note. The exercise then can move up and down the scale by half steps, using the entire normal singing range of the voice. It can also be tailored to a specific interval, such as a minor seventh, which may be difficult to hear in a musical context. Vary the vowels, using "ah," "ay," "ee," "oh," and "oo." When the glissando connection has become uninhibited, try letting the voice choose random starting pitches, covering more than an octave expanse, and without attempting to strike specific pitches. This will develop spontaneity and rid the mind and muscles of the need to always have rigid pitch definition, which is unnecessary for the realization of approximated pitch notation. This exercise is also excellent for promoting a legato connection between tones and for blending vocal registers.

EXERCISE 6E (FINDING THE SPEAKING RANGE)

Choose a short line of poetry or prose, one not connected to a familiar existing song or melodic line. Read the text on a monotone without glottal attacks or fry tones in the production. (Fry tones occur when there is insufficient air flow to produce the sound or when the pitch of the voice is too low and unfocused to take advantage of resonance possibilities in the vocal tract.) Speak the words aloud, finding a comfortable, medium-range, well-focused sound. Use a piano to locate the approximate pitch of that easy, resonant speaking voice. Once that pitch is determined, read other texts at that approximate pitch level until the voice and ear are habituated to keep the voice within a major third on either side of that suitable pitch level. Practice in a medium volume throughout.

EXERCISE 6F (SPEAKING WITH MELODIC CONTOUR)

Use one of the texts chosen for exercise 6e and begin to design a melody for it ad libitum. Do not search for a "correct" melody. Simply allow the voice to rise and fall in pitch according to the dramatic image you have of the meaning inherent in the text. Let the voice move up into the head register at or about the normal transition level used in singing. With each successive repetition of the phrase, allow the voice to create an entirely different melodic contour. It may be helpful to draw the contour on paper or to outline it pictorially by moving the arms as the text is spoken, mimicking the upward and downward pitch levels of the voice. Close your eyes as you draw this vocal melodic outline in midair. Visualize the contour in your mind's eye as you go through each phrase vocally and physically. A visual connection to the sound will be enhanced by the use of physical memory, creating a mental frame of reference for re-creating this effect in a musical context. Continue to vocalize in a medium volume.

EXERCISE 6G (SPEAKING CONTOUR WITH GLISSANDO)

Continue with the same text or choose a new one. After developing a satisfactory contour for a given phrase, having drawn or outlined it physically, begin to exaggerate any dramatic elements present in the text. Recite with a heightened resonance or dynamic level for particularly active or intense words. Conversely, allow the voice to become more subdued for introspective or sad words and ideas. After the dramatic choices have been made, add a glissando connection between all words, always maintaining the glissando in the direction of the melodic contour. Continue to monitor the production, being careful to use no glottals or fry tones and to make full use of chest, middle, and head registers of the voice. Falsetto may be included for men.

EXERCISE 6H (SPEAKING WITH MELODRAMA)

Choose a text with a broad range of emotional content. Read it in an exaggerated manner, as if reciting in a large auditorium. Allow the voice great freedom to imitate the voices of famous actors or singers who speak in a similar vocal range to that of your own. Do not try to imitate someone's voice by gripping or holding the articulators or musculature. Simply use the imagination, vowel modification, lip shape, and breath to accomplish the imitative sounds. Air flow must be increased for higher or louder pitches and decreased for lighter or lower ones.

Walk around. Gesticulate with the hands and arms, letting the face reflect emotions being expressed during this exercise. Never stand rigidly, purse the lips, or use the voice in a rough or unhealthy manner while exaggerating emotional content. Be constantly aware of proper body alignment, especially the connection between the head and the spine. The head should simply balance evenly on the top of the spine. It should not jut forward as the drama in the vocal sound is increased. Pretend that the head is attached to a string hanging from the ceiling, but not held tightly or pulled upward. Keep the shoulders and chest loose, hanging as if from a coat rack over a poised but flexible body. The legs and arms should be free to move without tension or stiffness.

chapter 7

Nontextual
Sonic Vocabularies

"What happened to the text?" "There is no text!" "This looks like a lot of gibberish."

These reactions and others like them have been uttered by singers when confronted with contemporary music built around the use of nontextual sonic vocabularies (texts based only on individual vowels, consonants, or non-language combinations of the two). As twentieth-century composers began to think of the voice as "just another instrument," capable of creating a multitude of extraordinary and contrasting colors, textures, and articulations, they reorganized the realm of text settings into novel configurations.

Traditionally, we think of a text setting in the poetic or prose sense—using an understandable sentence structure, portions of a poetic line, or individual words taken from an established vocabulary. Communication through language has been a key element of vocal music throughout history. The text of a song or aria, when clearly and expressively projected, can move the listener in ways the music alone could not accomplish. However, the vocalise, using only a vowel such as "ah" or "oh," can also be extremely effective in projecting beauty of tone, nuance of color, and emotional/dramatic contrasts. Composers such as Rachmaninoff (*Vocalise*), Chenoweth (*Vocalise*), and Villa-Lobos (*Bachianas Brasileiras, No. 5*) chose to write vocalises for the voice and did it with memorable and lasting results. All of these works have become part of the standard repertoire for soprano. Hearing these effective uses of pure vowel vocalization within a traditional context, one would have to say that there is communication even when no text is present. If that is the case, then it can be assumed that vocalization does not require a text (in the traditional sense) in order to be expressive, communicative, and to have artistic integrity.

It is possible for the voice to stir emotions, when required, or to be an equal contributor to an overall sonic experience that is basically nonverbal. The idea of treating the voice as "just another instrument" can be both positive and negative. If the voice is asked to do things unnatural to its basic principles of production, then only negative results will occur. But if the voice is used within its normal singing range and given freely produced articulations and sympathetic utterances, then the presence or absence of a traditional text is irrelevant.

As composers searched for new possibilities for vocal delivery, they began to rely on what is most familiar to singers: the colorful palette of sounds created by the combination of vowels and consonants. The term *nontextual sonic vocabularies* may sound daunting. But singers deal with this entity every day and are quite unaware that they are involved in a topic with such an intimidating title. Singers spend all of their performing lives warming up, vocalizing, and learning new music by using familiar vowel-consonant unions, such as "me," "ma," "mo," and "moo."

Traditional vocalises are built on a system of conjoined vowels and consonants, shifting effortlessly through variations according to a desired vocal outcome. Particular consonants are inserted for articulation efficiency of the lips and tongue. A singer might go through a series of exercises, within a ten-minute rehearsal period, designed to refine the precision of specific consonants and vowel combinations ("da," "pa," "la," "fa," "wa," or "sha," for example). The most sluggish articulation can be enlivened, freed, and made precise by practicing diction exercises that emphasize clean, quick use of the tongue and lips. Diction exercises of this sort inevitably include an extensive number of unique vowel-consonant combinations.

It has become the norm for vocal pedagogues and singers to devise combinations of speech sounds for their own vocal warm-up purposes and to solve individual articulation problems. Practice diction patterns often contain nonsense phrases or a series of nonsense syllables, such as "red leather, yellow leather," "unique New York," "tikituta," or "labadabawaba." They are practiced at various speeds until they easily roll off the tongue and lips. There are dozens of similar examples. None are meant to have textual significance. Instead they are intended to exercise the tongue or lips in a particular configuration, develop efficiency of vowel resonance, or quicken the singer's physical and mental responses while vocalizing.

In the past, vocalises were relegated to the vocal studio warm-up and not thought of as performance material. However, some inventive twentieth-century composers, mostly since 1950, seized upon this type of pedagogical exercise and brought it out of the rehearsal studio into the realm of musical performance.

When singers are confronted with nontextual sonic vocabularies, they may not be immediately aware that the principles involved in the vocal declamation are related to things they already do in their daily practice routines. Part of the confusion may lie in the fact that singers learn much of their warm-up routine by rote and do not read it from a printed score. They simply ingrain it by repetition over a period of years and relate it to nothing in print.

The realization that there is a similarity in the vocal, physical, and psychological approach to the performance of music of this kind and the singer's daily vocal warm-ups is often enlightening. What a relief to find that the voice can sing in its normal manner, though the music has a new look! It can free one of inhibitions, allow the voice and mind to make unconstrained associations with familiar patterns, and release the imagination for more specific and picturesque interpretations than with traditional text settings.

In addition to consonant-vowel combinations, nonsense syllables, and quirky phrases used for vocal warm-ups, serious singers often use exercises built only on vowels and their smooth connection to improve vocal placement, legato, and equalization of tone quality. Frequently, the five cardinal vowels ("ah," "ay," "ee," "oh," and "oo") are sung on a sustained tone without consonants or applied to a familiar pattern, such as a triad or 1-3-5-8 ("doh," "mi," "sol," "doh") pattern in each key, moving up and down the scale by half steps. This attention to vowel connection is effective for producing a lovely legato and evenness between the vocal registers.

The International Phonetic Alphabet (IPA), a worldwide standardization of phonetic symbols, is extremely useful for transliterating speech sounds from one language into corresponding sounds of another language. Singers are familiar with this system, which is a staple of modern vocal pedagogy and the instruction of foreign-language diction. Most foreign-language diction classes for singers require that students learn the system and use it to specify sound characteristics for vowels and consonants within the language being studied. However, as Ware (1998, p. 156) says, "students should be forewarned that IPA symbols are intended only as basic representations of the approximate sound characteristics for any given vowel or consonant. In reality, there are subtle differences according to specific language characteristics, such as regional dialects and accents." Voice teachers often ask students to write IPA symbols above all words in a foreign language song prior to attempts at overt pronunciation. This process saves much time in habituating sound qualities of syllables that may have unfamiliar spellings.

Modern composers also discovered the usefulness of this system. They realized that since singers around the world are familiar with IPA symbols and their meanings, it would be an extremely valuable tool for depicting vocal sound that was not built on a traditional poetic text. It provided a method of divorcing the voice from a text-dictated mood, story, character, or syllabic stress. In essence, it gave the composer a means of using the voice in a more chameleonlike fashion, tied to no tradition and owing no allegiance to preconceived sounds or textual projection.

Numerous examples of experimental textual applications can be found in twentieth-century compositions. Risatti (1975) shows more than twenty examples of nontextual sonic manipulation by Peter Maxwell Davies, Luigi Nono, Luciano Berio, Mauricio Kagel, and other composers. The experimentation takes many forms but primarily deals with the aforementioned consonant-vowel or vowel-vowel relationships, as well as the use of IPA symbols.

USE OF IPA PHONEMES

The IPA symbols provide a practical method for composers to organize vocal sound. Though the IPA is not absolute in its translation of exact vowels or consonants in any language, it does represent fairly specific sound characteristics that are recognizable to the listener. The complete IPA vowel and consonant system is published in numerous vocal pedagogy, language diction, and music notation sources. Some excellent ones are *Basics of Vocal Pedagogy* by Clifton Ware, *The Structure of Singing* by Richard Miller, *Diction* by John Moriarty, and *New Music Notation* by David Cope.

Examples 7.1, 7.2, and 7.3 show three ways in which text can be manipulated through use of the IPA. In each case, the purpose is to create a sonic vocabulary for the voice. No complete words are present. Individual vowels are printed, sometimes surrounded by brackets, and continuation and length of the vowel are indicated by wavy or straight lines, called extenders.

Example 7.1 demonstrates a continuous flow of vowels and consonants depicted by IPA symbols. There are generally no complete words or understandable syllables from any spoken language present in texts of this kind. An example of this usage can be found in Milton Babbitt's song, "Sound and Words" (appendix B). The vowels and consonants are used to promote vocal color and articulation, and to give texture rather than textual meaning to the composition.

Some composers, such as Thomas Albert in *A Maze with Grace* (appendix B), selected a text and then dissected it into specific phonemes. The phonemes taken from the text of the hymn "Amazing Grace" appear randomly throughout the

Example 7.1   IPA Manipulation: Vowel Sequence

Example 7.2   IPA Manipulation: Vowel Continuation

Example 7.3   IPA Manipulation: Vowel Morphing

score. It is only at the end of the piece that the listener becomes aware that the phonemes are part of an understandable language. At that point the text is sung in its entirety. In the final analysis, when individual phonemes are used, the only way a listener would know if they come from a chosen text is if that text is sung in its original form. Otherwise, the ear hears the succession of phonemes as having no meaningful connection or interpretative purpose.

Example 7.2 indicates the continuation of a particular phoneme through a series of indeterminate pitches. The straight line between the phonetic "ah" (as in "father") and the phonetic "ih" (as in "hit") shows the singer when to change to the next phoneme. This is a clear and useful device for picturing vowel length and has become standard usage in contemporary compositions using phonemes. Two composers who used it are Ramon Zupko, in his extended work for mezzo-soprano and tape, called *Voices*, and Elizabeth Vercoe, in her *Nine Epigrams from Poor Richard* for voice and tape. Both are discussed in appendix B.

Example 7.3 shows a notation for *vowel morphing*, or graduated vowel change. Modern technology has allowed us to view the morphing of two faces on a screen or in a series of printed pictures. The first face shown gradually shifts its features little by little, picking up the features found in the second face until the second face appears in full. Vowel morphing is built on the same principle, but it is sonic rather than visual. The vowel printed under the first tone gradually changes to another vowel, printed under the fourth tone by way of two intermediate pitches and a wavy line designating the subtle shift in vowel sounds. This vocal technique may seem at odds with traditional singing, but it promotes a beautiful legato and a clear definition of vowel placement and projection. Its only unique aspect is that of gradually changing from one vowel to another through spatial manipulation inside the mouth. This vowel migration is a device more closely associated with speech than song.

George Crumb used nontextual sonic vocabularies in several works, including *Apparition* for soprano and piano (appendix B). He wrote three vocalises for this six-part work. Each uses a combination of vowels and consonants in a nontextual way. In the second section ("Vocalise 1: Sounds of a summer evening"), the voice makes numerous bird calls and cooing sounds devised through the combination of various vowels and consonants. At the end, Crumb asks for a "turtle-dove" effect: bending the pitch down while singing on an "oo" vowel. The three vocalise sections provide captivating vocal contrasts within a large work that uses the voice in a primarily traditional way and with an understandable, complete, poetic text.

What should it sound like?

Each individual vowel and consonant should be formed according to the IPA rules. If there is more than one vowel on a note, as in the final pitch of example 7.1, then each must be pronounced before moving to the next tone. If no specific tempo or pacing is indicated for the tones and vowel connections (as in all three examples), then the singer is free to experiment with the speed of the glide between vowels. If vowel morphing, as in example 7.3, is indicated, then the pacing of the subtle shift between vowels is extremely important. The voice gradually changes from one vowel to the next, never shifting quickly as in normal singing. The mouth space, tongue, and lips are all involved in the formation of vowels. Therefore, a measured and imperceptible shift must occur in all of these areas for the morphing process to occur smoothly. A resonant singing tone, with vibrato, should be employed unless otherwise indicated.

How do I do it?

The psychological effect of nontextual sonic vocabularies is of primary concern. Since a traditional text has been eliminated, the singer will need to develop a vocal interpretation in which the essence of sound itself is the primary goal. That idea is not foreign to singers, since we generally concentrate on the quality and focus of sound during vocal warm-ups and when practicing technical exercises designed for range development, breath control, resonance, and flexibility.

Thinking of the vocal line as a vocalise can be very helpful. In a vocalise, clarity of tone, precision of pitch, vowel formation and placement, and the use of vocal color are key issues. Those elements apply here, as well. Remember that communication through nonlanguage sonic vocabularies requires a deep sensitivity to the basic elements of vocal production: breath support, resonance, musical phrasing, coordination of vocal registers, and imaginative interpretation of the musical notation and expression markings. Similar standards would be found in the interpretation of music containing traditional text settings. The only difference here is that complete words or phrases are absent.

Practice plan

1. *Analyze the text setting*

Does it contain individually sung vowels connected to other vowels? Are there complete syllables (vowels and consonants)? Is there vowel morphing? Is the piece built on only one kind of sonic vocabulary or does it contain several applications of the IPA system?

2. *Prepare the score*

Use a highlighter to mark similar usages of the IPA throughout the work. For instance, all vowel-vowel connections might be marked in yellow, while the vowel morphing sections could be designated with blue. This quickly gives the eye a reference during rehearsals and performances, allaying distractions when the mind must be involved in other things.

3. *Do your research*

Verify all IPA vowels and consonants used in the work with a complete published chart of IPA symbols. Keep the chart available for reference during early rehearsals in case there is a question concerning one or more of the symbols. Write out the pronunciation of any IPA symbols with which you are unfamiliar.

If needed, choose a familiar word in which the sound occurs and write it in the score for quick recall of the sound.

4. *Rehearse*

One of the most difficult things to overcome is an ingrained error of any kind. This is especially true for unfamiliar notation. Rooting out mistakes in the first few rehearsals is very important. Divide the work into small sections and slowly mouth the sounds indicated. *Do not whisper.* Silently imprint the proper vowels and their connections to consonants or other vowels prior to a singing rehearsal. This will allow the voice to rest until the IPA usage is fully understood and habituated. Pay attention to the position of the tongue, lips, and jaw for all vowels, being careful not to use the jaw as an articulator. Notice the coordinated, smooth glide of all these elements when practicing vowel morphing. Remember that the tongue has various elevations for individual vowels and the lips are more rounded for some vowels. Consequently, allowing the tongue and lips to lie dormant during this process will result in an imprecise or extremely vague realization of the desired morphing combinations.

5. *Sing*

Learn all pitches on a neutral syllable first. Disregard rhythm at this point. Once pitches are secure, apply the printed IPA symbols to their designated pitches, thereby connecting pitch with vowel formation. Check to make sure that all IPA symbols are fully understood and formed correctly. Use a tape recorder to assist in decisions about vowel production. Sometimes we think we are making a certain vowel formation, but it may be slightly off. Hearing it on tape will relieve doubts about accuracy.

6. *Orient the declamation to the indicated pacing*

The next major rehearsal decision involves organizing the pace of the piece. Now that all IPA usages have been identified, vocally habituated, and intellectually understood, begin to rehearse them in their printed rhythmic forms. The piece may contain no meters or definitive tempo. It could be totally improvisational. The important issue is that you *know* what kind of freedom is allowable and place the syllables or vowels within those parameters.

7. *Follow directions*

Use all resources printed in the score for determining the interpretation.

- Read all performance directions and mark areas of the score where they apply.
- Notice and mark all points where you must coincide with other instrumental lines. This will allow for easier coordination with ensemble members when rehearsals begin.
- Identify all expression and dynamics markings. Rehearse them thoroughly until they have a natural flow.
- Vocalize the text, using a normal vibrato unless directed otherwise.

• Put it all together. Rehearse any elements other than singing, such as stage movement, playing instruments, and costume or prop coordination. Then connect these external requirements to the vocal line.

8. *Engage the imagination*

This kind of notation for sonic exploitation relies heavily on the performer's imagination. No two voices are alike, therefore no two vocal interpretations will be exactly alike. Accept and enjoy that fact. It means that you can use your innate vocal qualities to create your own special sonic interpretation. In texts of this kind, the IPA is used as a means of adding texture and color to the composition as a whole. So the singer's major goal must be to enhance the characteristics of the composer's color choices as much as possible.

Since no unusual vocal technique is required for production of the IPA, the singer can produce all vowels and pitches with a normal, legato, lyrical tone quality. Any vocally experimental variations that might be considered vocal effects will be marked in the score.

USE OF SYLLABIC REPETITION AND NONSENSE SYLLABLES

For singers, vocal articulation (the efficiency with which the tongue, lips, and breath function) is always a primary concern. These elements determine clarity, stability, length, and precision of any vocal utterances, whether they are traditional text settings or nontextual sonic vocabularies.

As we have seen, the voice can be used to express numerous simple and complex articulations of text and pitches. Sometimes a composer's desire to exclude verbal meaning or textual expression is a major factor in the compositional style of a piece. In other cases, textual improvisation is used to create a stylistic or coloristic effect. The latter can be seen in a technique found frequently in twentieth-century music that contains elements of improvisation: the insertion of nonsense syllables or simple syllabic repetition.

Examples 7.4 and 7.5 show two notations commonly seen for this kind of text manipulation.

What should it sound like?

Example 7.4 shows a vocal line built on the repetition of short, simple combinations of vowels and consonants. They are given specific pitches and rhythms, plus exact points of articulation within the phrase. The short dash used underneath pitches indicates a repetition of the original syllable appearing at the beginning of the pattern. Occasionally, composers will use this kind of articulation with the addition of IPA phonemes to designate an exact vowel shape. In the example, IPA symbols have been added and surrounded by brackets to clarify the desired form of the vowel printed in the nonsense syllable. If no IPA phonemes are present, the consonant-vowel nonsense syllables should be pronounced as they would normally be sung in the language of any words or complete text used in another part of the composition. If no complete words or text exist, there are

Example 7.4   Nonsense Text: Syllable Repetition

na – – – – – – ki to pa du ki – to –
[ɑ]   [ɔ]   [ɔ]

Example 7.5   Nonsense Text: Ad Lib Style

shoo bah dee bah_____ *(ad lib)*

no language indications in the score, and the entire piece is built on nonsense syllables, perform them as if they were taken from the composers native language.

It may require a bit of research to make a final decision concerning some questionable vowel sounds. Composers would be wise to indicate IPA symbols for all such nonsense syllables or to state the language source used to develop them (Stone 1980). A singer might easily assume that syllables written by a Spanish composer should be pronounced as in Spanish, however, the composer may have lived in America or England and have English in mind. Confusion must be eliminated, as much as possible, through an understanding of the composer's intent, language source, and necessity for precision of syllabic repetition. In some works, the casualness of its usage precludes precision, especially if the piece is improvisational or built on spontaneous outbursts of sound, requiring no particular vocal color or nuance. In that case, the singer becomes the creator and spins out the tones in any manner that seems appropriate to the overall structure of the work.

In Christina Kuzmych's *Shapes and Sounds IV* for soprano and saxophone (appendix B), the text by e. e. cummings is often dissected into individual syllables and repeated for dramatic effect. In the last movement of the work, called "Airy-Fluttering," several words, including *twilight*, *vast*, and *are*, become central figures for inventive design. Kuzmych takes the word *twilight* and repeats the first syllable ("twi") ten times at increasing volume levels until finally writing out the entire word. Occasionally she pulls out a letter from a word and emphasizes it. For instance, the word *air* is emphasized by singing the word as a whole and then repeating the r and trilling it for an extended time while making a crescendo. In another location, Kuzmych repeats the word *are* four times followed by three repetitions of just the *a* ("ah") in the word. All of these effects derived from the text are interspersed with nonsense syllables that *do not* appear in the text (repetitions of "tika" and "sh"). The overall result is a thrilling, mesmerizing flow of vocal nuances that gives the sense that the voice is somewhat otherworldly, not tied to traditional language or consecutive thought patterns.

Example 7.5 depicts a typical ad lib usage of nonsense syllables. In this case, specific pitches and rhythms are printed, with only an indication of what is required vocally. In some pieces, a few syllables may be written at the beginning of an improvised section with an ad lib direction following it. At other times, no syllables are given at all, with simply a verbal direction to ad lib using nonsense syllables.

This kind of syllabic usage is commonly seen in pieces incorporating nonspecific textual vocabularies, such as *scat singing*. Scat singing has its origins in jazz and can be heard in its finest, purest form on recordings of such great artists as Louis Armstrong, Ella Fitzgerald, Mel Tormé, and Diane Schuur. A singer who is new to this style will find it helpful and inspiring to listen to various artists who are facile with the production of scat.

Though it has become a normal mode of vocal improvisation for jazz performers, classically trained singers may be quite unfamiliar with the scat style of nonsense syllabic flow. When confronted with scat singing as used by twentieth-century classical composers, such as William Bolcom in "Amor" from *Cabaret Songs*, or *Scat 2* by Victoria Bond (appendix B), they may feel out of their element. These two composers approached the use and notation of scat in slightly different ways. In "Amor," Bolcom inserted a nine-bar section of scat into the middle of an otherwise normally sung, poetic text. He begins the section with an indication of several syllables that could be used ("da," "de," "da") followed by the word *scat* for the rest of the notes. It is up to the performer to develop a natural scat style and pattern from the pitches and rhythms given. For that reason, each performance will be different, relying on improvisation for the final realization. The scat section is used to demonstrate the speaker's unabashed glee at being noticed and admired by everyone she meets on a particular day. It gives the effect of suddenly kicking off one's shoes and skipping through the park. More important, it seems to say that "there are no words to express how this attention makes me feel." Thus, the use of scat, a nonlanguage exaltation of how one feels.

Bond's *Scat 2* presents a classical approach to the development of the scat style as it is used in traditional jazz improvisation. This piece falls easily into the category of vocal display. The composer gives no syllabic indications. Instead, she states, "The singer should sing nonsense syllables as a text which can be freely invented." This piece for voice and trumpet recalls "licks" reminiscent of traditional jazz improvisation. The two soloists traverse myriad creatively written, stylistically strong, rhythmically exciting passages that show off the technique of each performer. The notation is traditional, written out in every respect, and is not improvised, like normal jazz style. It is only the syllabic freedom given the voice that puts this work into the realm of improvisation and nontextual sonic vocabularies.

In most cases, all that is required of the singer to understand this vocal form is a desire to expand his or her knowledge of vocal styles. There is no precise pattern or combination of consonants and vowels inherent in the style, and no two jazz artists would produce it in exactly the same way, which is the essence of jazz improvisation. As with any musical genre, vocal jazz and scat singing have unique organizational and sound qualities and may suit some voices and personalities better than others.

There are distinctive rhythmic and melodic characteristics inherent in the scat style. They involve vocal inflections that create a style of phrasing unlike that of any other musical genre. Certain pitches are bent, held, attacked, accented, and altered in unique ways. The style makes extensive use of several expressive and rhythmic elements. Some of these include:

1. Open vowels and clear consonant attacks that emphasize rhythmic articulation (common syllables are "doo," "dah," "bee," "dot," "bop," "dwee," "doo'n," "sha," "ba")

2. Use of glissando at the end of a tone (an ascending or descending slide called a "smear" or "fall-off")

3. Forte/piano accents, followed by a crescendo (a note is hit full voice, immediately diminished to piano, and then suddenly blossomed into a full crescendo)

4. Tenuto and staccato (a fully held tone is followed by a short staccato tone)

5. Horizontal accents (the shifting of the normal accents, usually on beats one and three, to a beat that is not normally accented, thereby creating a syncopation)

For the singer who wishes to delve more deeply into scat, several sources are available. Two excellent sources for the production of vocal jazz are Kirby Shaw's *Vocal Jazz Style* and Doug Anderson's *Jazz and Show Choir Handbook II* (see bibliography). Each gives specific examples of vocal jazz idiosyncrasies, with exercises and explanations of the vocal concept.

The same spontaneous, elusive quality present in vocal jazz is preferred for classical compositions containing scat. By using scat, the composer has already given up control of the text. He or she is trying to draw out the singer's imagination through a knowledge and understanding of jazz styles. The composer is not necessarily trying to create jazz but is merely trying to momentarily incorporate some of its elements within a classical setting.

There are two major differences between scat in a classical setting and scat in improvised jazz. First, in the jazz context, there will probably be no written melodic or rhythmic outline for the singer. Instead, the singer explores rhythms and vocal sounds that mimic the phrasing of accompanying instrumentalists and creates melodies that coincide with the harmonic progressions being played. Anderson remarks (1978, p. 58), "As he 'takes a ride' on his horn, the scat singer 'takes a ride' on his voice. He is 'showing off.' The vocal sounds that are made are of free choice and expression by the singer but should imitate the sounds that an instrument would make if the solo were being played on a horn." In the classical setting, the notes and rhythms will likely be printed, as in the aforementioned Bolcom and Bond pieces. However, the vocal jazz style described earlier should be applied, using its innate concepts of rhythm, attacks, and articulation.

The second differing factor involves improvisation itself. In the jazz context, all performers are free to improvise, but in the classical context, instruments accompanying the voice may have no ad lib or improvisatory elements at all. The scat line, simply a reference to jazz, may be placed over an otherwise traditional accompaniment.

How do I do it?

1. *Analyze and prepare the score*
   a. Does it contain jazz elements? Is the vocal line similar in style to the accompanying parts? Are specific notes and rhythms written for the voice, or is it a suggested, graphic score intended to be performed with improvisation only?
   b. Identify all uses of nonsense syllables. Is the entire piece built on syllabic textual vocabularies, or is there just a momentary insertion of this element into an otherwise traditional context?
   c. Determine the form of the nonsense syllables. Mark any verbal instructions that apply to the formation of written syllables, such as IPA symbols, language sources, or ad lib indications. If the nonsense syllables are completely written out with specific vowels and consonants, do not improvise. Place them with the proper pitch notation and sing as printed. Improvise only if there is a verbal indication to do so, such as like "scat," ad lib, or improvise.

2. *Begin a practice routine*
   a. Become familiar with the vocal style required by the piece you are studying. Listen to several recorded examples of fine artists performing music of that type (especially from the jazz repertoire). Refer to written sources of information on the style (see bibliography).
   b. If the entire work is built on nonsense syllables, divide it into short sections for rehearsal purposes. Set the sections off with a color marker or another visible indication of where to stop and start.
   c. Casually speak all nonsense syllables in a normal speaking range, disregarding pitch or rhythm. Do this in a moderately slow tempo until they flow easily from one to the other. Gradually speed up the tempo and let the voice inflection move liltingly up and down, creating a carefree melodic shape. This will prepare the mind and muscles for the next step: following the printed score.
   d. Learn the printed melodic lines or abstract notational gestures and their designated rhythms prior to the application of any syllables attached to them. During this process, use only one syllable, such as "me" or "ma," for all pitches. Paring down the complexities in this fashion will elim-

inate confusion that might occur if all elements of the vocal line were being applied at the same time.

e. Apply the nonsense syllables to the composed rhythmic structure. At first, silently mouth the syllables until the pattern is habituated. Then speak them quietly several times, checking for any articulation difficulties. Make sure that you use only the lips and tongue for articulation, leaving the jaw loose and uninvolved in the articulation process.

f. Once the musical gestures have become secure in pitch and rhythm and the nonsense syllables can be articulated easily and independently, put it all together. Begin to sing short sections of the work with all elements intact. It would be helpful to record your practice at this point in order to check for any mispronounced or unclear syllables and incorrect pitches or rhythms.

g. Add all expression markings and verbal instructions for vocal colorations.

VOCAL CONSIDERATIONS

Though the use of nontextual sonic vocabularies may present some intellectual and perceptual challenges, they generally do not create physical tension for the vocal apparatus. Problems occur when the singer assumes that novel text settings, perhaps combined with strange-looking notations, connote some type of foreign vocalization or potential vocal abuse. Although it is possible to encounter vocally abusive requests in some scores, the vast majority do not contain anything that should damage the singing voice, if produced naturally and with a properly prepared breath support. Common sense is the singer's guide in all choices of repertoire, whether modern or traditional. If the composer asks for a sound that is totally unnatural to the voice and attempts to make that sound cause vocal distress, then simply don't do it! Find another piece that offers similar challenges but stays within the normal and natural production of vocal sound.

Psychological stress caused by the novelty of some of these techniques can sometimes translate into vocal tension. The singer may inadvertently tense muscles in the throat, chest, or other areas of the body due to the complexity of the work. The same can be said for traditional repertoire. Attention must always be paid to physical relaxation and an optimum practice routine when learning new music of any kind, so that physical tension can be eliminated before it becomes habitual. It is imperative to keep the voice technically fresh while rehearsing any type of music. But it is especially valuable when working on new kinds of vocalization, such as nontextual sonic vocabularies. Some ideas that will help to make this process flow more easily are:

1. Always warm up the voice quietly, slowly, carefully, and in a relaxing manner before rehearsing new kinds of vocal declamation. Concentrate on freedom and flexibility, using a variety of warm-ups: humming; legato connections (scales, five-tone patterns, triads, or octave slides); staccatos; flexibility exercises (light and fast); and messa di voce, or sustained tone exercises.

2. Divide a typical rehearsal period of perhaps an hour into shorter segments that use the voice in various ways. Exercising the voice with repertoire from contrasting musical styles and periods allows for more flexibility of declamation. A steady diet of anything becomes boring and is less likely to spark creative expression.

3. Remember that the ultimate goal of a rehearsal is to unify all elements of the vocal process and to facilitate an effective coordination of all its facets: respiration, phonation, registration, resonance, articulation, dramatic expression, and musical understanding. Every practice session should deal with each of these concepts in some way. Some rehearsals will necessarily need to emphasize one or two concepts more than others, but none should be neglected. Always keep in touch with the basics of good singing. Be aware of efficient use of the breath; coordination of vocal registers; projection of a clear, free tone; development of maximum vocal resonance; clear, concise articulation of vowels and consonants; and the communication of ideas, moods, actions, or special effects required by the music.

4. Use aids such as mirrors, tape recorders, and video equipment to lift your performance to a higher level. This is especially helpful when studying music containing new vocalization styles or directions for stage movement. Physical tension, inappropriate body movements (stances, posture, or gestures), and poor articulation habits can be caught and eliminated by these methods. Relying on the way one feels he or she is performing is rarely dependable. It is impossible to be aware of all aspects of singing during every moment of rehearsal, especially when working on something foreign to the mind, the muscles, and the voice. So use all the tools available to weed out poor vocalization.

5. Don't fall into the trap of believing that a rehearsal period must mean nonstop singing. A rehearsal can consist of many things other than singing, including:
   a. Listening to recorded examples of fine vocal artists performing works similar to the repertoire being prepared
   b. Translating foreign languages or writing in IPA symbols for unfamiliar words or syllables
   c. Silently mouthing unusual text applications or foreign words
   d. Clapping and/or speaking complicated rhythmic patterns
   e. Walking through stage movement cues while silently repeating the text or playing a rehearsal tape of the work
   f. Physically diagramming musical phrasing with arm movements or a whole-body, dancelike approach

6. Find reasons to expand the capabilities of your voice. Do not be satisfied with the status quo. Advancement in technical ability and increased vocal flexibility/versatility will allow for more adventuresome programming. It will also keep the mind more alert and responsive to new ideas.

You must do a thing many times in order to do it well. That definitely applies to singing contemporary repertoire. A few short tries at some of these techniques will not suffice. As in performing Handel with accuracy, fluidity, and agility, singing modern music requires more than a cursory reading of the musical material. It requires active, continued, well-planned, and well-researched rehearsals over a span of weeks or months. A concerted effort to research, practice, and appreciate the style is a process rather than a gift.

A STUDIO APPROACH

Numerous elements inherent to nontextual sonic vocabularies can be adapted for vocal warm-ups and technique development. A few suggestions are listed below. Always be mindful of vocal freedom, efficient tone production, and adequate breath support while working these exercises.

EXERCISE 7A (VOWEL MORPHING)

Choose a tone in the middle of the voice. Begin the tone on the vowel "ah." Over a period of eight beats (paced at medium speed, around a metronomic marking of 60) gradually change the vowel to "oo." Sing at a medium volume. Pay attention to the slow change in the shape of the tongue and lips. Keep the palate raised, the jaw loose and uninvolved in the change of vowels. At the end of eight counts, breathe. Do this exercise on various pitches in the middle range, varying the vowels and their combinations ("ah," "ay," "oh," "oo," "ee"). When this can be done smoothly on all vowels, begin to expand the pitch range. Practice on lower and higher notes in your normal singing range.

This exercise is useful for developing concentration, legato connection, pitch stability, and consistent breath support. When habituated, it does not have to be done at the piano keyboard. Simply find a pitch that is easily sung and practice it anywhere, anytime. Eventually, the more casual the approach, the better. There is less chance that tension will creep into the vocal production if the exercise can be done while you are engaged in slow physical movement, writing, reading, or some other activity that does not disrupt breath.

EXERCISE 7B (SYLLABIC REPETITION)

This exercise is meant to loosen the tongue and lips, making them pliable and easily manipulated for fast articulation of vowels and consonants. It concentrates on the free movement of the front and back of the tongue in coordination with a smooth and gentle rounding and relaxing of the lips.

1. Speak each of the following syllabic patterns eight times. Use a normal speaking range in a medium volume ("TikiTaka," "LoolooLaLa," "TikiTuta," "WeewahWohwah"). Each can be done as a separate exercise, or the four syllabic patterns can be strung out consecutively with a breath between each. When they can be spoken easily eight times at a medium pace, find a comfortable pitch in

the middle of the voice and repeat each pattern on that pitch with a legato connection. Do not let glottal attacks appear in the pattern at any point. When this phase of the exercise can be accomplished freely, practice on various pitches throughout your easily singable vocal range. Stay away from extremely high pitches when doing work of this kind. Vocal stress is more likely to occur at that pitch level.

2. After rehearsing on a sustained tone at various pitch levels, invent a short melodic contour to fit each nonsense syllable pattern. The melody could be a simple a triad, five-tone-scale, or a more abstract design with intervals of your own choosing. To gain benefit from this exercise, it need not be practiced in one particular way. The fact that the voice is being used in various patterns, no matter their shape, will ensure more mental and vocal flexibility.

3. The final step in this process is to mix up the four nonsense patterns, repeating them in tandem and in no particular order, first on sustained tones and then in melodic patterns. Be inventive. Create your own contemporary phonetic and melodic design. Once you have decided on a pattern, write it down so that it will become part of your normal warm-up routine. The pattern may evolve into something new as you master each version that you compose.

EXERCISE 7C (SYLLABIC TEXT DISSECTION)

Select a line from a poem that you enjoy. It could be taken from a composed song with which you are familiar. Write the words in a straight line and put all of the IPA symbols that coincide with the sounds of each letter underneath them.

Arbitrarily take several letters or syllables (portions of words) from among the possibilities in the text and write them on another line. Read through each selected phonetic sound slowly, making certain that you have the correct IPA symbol listed for each consonant and vowel.

Now rearrange them in any order that seems to flow easily. You may need to read through them several times to determine the optimum order. It will be only a feeling. There is no one order for which to search. Remember that whatever feels right to you, is right for you. That is the first rule for this kind of vocal improvisation. Trust your instincts.

Once the order has been decided upon, invent a simple melody to go with the syllables. It can be based on tonal, triadic harmony or be completely abstract. If you have trouble getting started, simply speak the syllables, letting the inflection of the voice lower and raise at will. Continue the process until you find a general pattern for the melody. Draw that pattern on paper. A simple line will suffice to show the direction of the melody as it rises and falls.

Use your arms and hands to draw the melody in midair as you speak. Be playful with this exercise. Move around the room as you choreograph the melodic line with your arms in a fluid movement. Do not jerk the arms or stop them at the end of each syllable. Try to keep a consistent flow of motion. Enjoy the freedom of making sounds and melodic shapes that have no restrictions except those determined by your own need for conformity. This exercise is effective for building independence and creativity of expression, developing skills for improvisation, and freeing the mind and voice for experimentation.

EXERCISE 7D (NONSENSE SYLLABIC TRANSFER)

Choose a familiar song, one whose melody is totally ingrained in your mind and voice. Discard the text and devise a text completely composed of nonsense syllables. They could be standard combinations used for classical vocal warm-ups ("ma," "me," "za," "whee," "la," "va," etc.) or derived from scat syllables ("dwee," "doo'n," "dot," "dow," "shoo," "bop," "ba," "du," "dot'n," "weet," etc.). It would be ideal if both could be gradually incorporated into the vocalization of the melody.

Allow the voice, psyche, and intuition to rule the formation of sounds you create for each tone. Think of this as a form of play. Switch back and forth at will between syllables, creating ever-changing vocal colors and a chameleonlike foreign language with no rules. This exercise can be used for any style of music. Just be certain that the music you choose is well within your normal singing range and creates no vocal tension.

This playful, casual exercise is a good introduction to scat singing and other forms of nontextual syllabic expression. It promotes freedom of expression and is a marvelous way to relax the mind and body while vocalizing. It allows for great experimentation without judgment, the element that prevents most singers from venturing into the realm of improvisation.

chapter 8

Vocal Effects

The use of the voice as an extended sonic source was a primary creative motivator for twentieth-century composers. They already knew that the voice was capable of various kinds of vocalism, artistry, and communication due to a rich history in the development of vocalization in Western music. Several hundred years of music history had brought forth five basic approaches to vocalization: bel canto (a lyrical, legato-smooth vocal line); coloratura (florid music that emphasizes agility and flexibility); declamatory (a style that stresses extreme ranges of dynamics, pitch, and vocal color); recitative (a declamatory style that focuses on the delivery of a text within a limited vocal range); and folk song styles (based on naturalness, clarity, and simplicity, with little or no use of vibrato).

With the addition of *sprechstimme* to this list of vocal possibilities at the beginning of the twentieth century, composers suspected that the voice could be manipulated in numerous ways to create phantasmagorical sound effects. The potential of such an idea was limitless and creatively challenging for those composers involved in experimentation with color and sound variations. In some instances, the new vocal sounds incorporated into the music were the germinal ideas for the piece as a whole. Without that bold departure from traditional singing, the music would have remained too predictable and not a source for compositional experimentation. In short, the vocal techniques themselves were the impetus for the musical outcome. So the incorporation of vocal effects became a natural expansion of the normal activities that the composer expected of the solo singer.

Composers such as Berio, Stockhausen, Boulez, Bussotti, and Ligeti were pioneers in the development of a spate of special sonic sources called "vocal effects." They, among others, set out to create a new musical language, one that had few roots in the past. Paul Griffiths (1978, p. 201) quotes Boulez, the founder of the

Institut de Recherche et de Coordination Acoustique/Musique in Paris in the mid-1970s as saying, "Our age . . . is one of persistent, relentless almost unbearable inquiry. In its exaltation it cuts off all retreats and bans all sanctuaries; its passion is contagious, its thirst for the unknown projects us forcefully, violently into the future." This statement epitomizes the zeal with which these innovators approached every aspect of musical composition, including the expansion of the role of vocal declamation and the exploitation of its many possibilities. Numerous composers have followed the lead of these pioneers since midcentury and continue to use some of the vocal gestures and effects created by their originators, while developing new possibilities and placing them within even more current musical/compositional styles.

The term *vocal effects* refers to any nonstandard use of the singing voice. It also implies a vocal facility that incorporates sound sources not usually found in traditional Western vocal music. These sound sources are generally derived from speech, nature, or artificially produced origins, or from multiethnic vocal sounds produced for ceremonial, tribal, or ritual purposes.

When one reviews the multiplicity and originality of works that are built on special effects, the sheer uniqueness can be intimidating. But when dissected, rehearsed, and allowed to become a natural part of everyday vocalization, these effects tend to expand the singer's vocal technique. Jane Manning states (1998, p. 1), "Avant-garde scores may appear strange at first, but if given the chance, are often relatively simple to perform. I am inclined to bristle when asked to explain 'extended vocal techniques', since these seem to me to be largely a matter of rationalizing, annotating, and co-ordinating a variety of everyday sounds, which would all be familiar in different contexts."

Most composers of the period tended to blend the newly created vocal palette with elements of various standard uses of the voice. Often, the voice was surrounded by experimentation of all kinds: new musical instruments or novel uses for familiar ones; abstract compositional forms; theatrical elements; or total freedom to improvise for all performers involved.

Some of the earliest creators of eccentric vocal effects, such as Luciano Berio, seemed to revel in the newness and liberating elements of this departure from the vocal norm, using the effects almost to the exclusion of traditional vocalization. Though Berio's compositions were full of vocal effects, there was a symbiotic relationship between the voice and the music that accompanied it. Berio wrote numerous compositions for his wife, Cathy Berberian, the virtuoso vocal artist who set a standard for the production of novel vocal effects. A stunning example of the multiple use of vocal effects can be seen in Berio's *Circles* (appendix B), where he "demonstrates how sung tone can merge into and imitate the sounds of instruments, producing musical equivalents for the word music and the syntactic disintegration in e. e. cummings's poetry" (Griffiths 1978, p. 185).

There is no conceivable limit to the number of effects or sonic resources of which the voice is capable. No two voices have the same flexibility, strength, stamina, or power. Nor do any two singers have the same imaginative approach to the realization of such vocal anomalies. Therefore, the sound quality of each effect will be different according to the singer's innate vocal characteristics and technical ability.

Composers have invented vocal effects for several purposes. They are quite useful for expressing significant textual subtleties or coloristic contrasts in non-textual contexts. Also, they provide energy, vitality, spirit, and atmosphere within a more traditional musical organization or style. Sometimes vocal effects could be considered mere antics or jokes, where the effect is absurd, grotesque, or even a little silly. Perhaps that is the composer's true desire for their use in a particular context, not as a serious purveyor of deep textual meaning. In some compositions by Babbitt, Berio, Morricone, and others they are the essence of the vocalization. In some cases, the vocal effects alone deliver the message. No other kind of vocalization would suffice or is required.

There has not been a universal codification of all notational devices developed for vocal effects. Risatti (1975) lists 143 different vocal effects notations by several composers. Fifty-nine are for timbre alone and encompass everything from *hollow sounds* to *weeping*. Most of the examples are nonstandard usages by only one or two composers. Therefore, begin the study of any contemporary work by reading all explanations printed in the score. In the absence of such information, look at other scores by the same composer for clues to realization, refer to historical sources on the development of notation, or contact the composer, whenever possible. Listening to recordings of the works may or may not be of use, since the composer may not have been involved in the production of the recording and the artists may be using their own imagination and knowledge to produce the sounds. The results might range from extremely accurate to totally inaccurate. An example of this is in the recordings of Schoenberg's *Pierrot Lunaire, Op. 21*. If one listens to recordings dating from the 1950s to the present, a great variety of realizations will be found for the *sprechstimme* employed throughout the work. Some singers merely recite the text on any pitch, while others try diligently to achieve the outlined melody written in the score. Some use a limited speaking voice range, while others use the entire singing voice range. Still others seem to approach the work from a purely ad lib point of view, adhering to little that is in the score. If it can be determined that a specific recording had the composer's approval and the performers were familiar with the composer's desires, then more credence could be given to the recorded example. In the final analysis, each performer must study and do his or her own research rather than rely only on previously recorded examples.

It is impossible to list all extravagant and unique vocal effects in this volume. The most commonly seen and most easily performed effects are outlined below. Some have more than one notational gesture to indicate a particular effect, while others have become somewhat standardized, using one familiar notation recognizable as having a certain vocal sound. Though some consider *sprechstimme*, recitation, and nontextual sonic vocabularies to be vocal effects, they have already been discussed at length in earlier chapters and are not included here since they are more complex entities than those included in this chapter.

Example 8.1a, 8.1b   Laughter

quasi laughing

LAUGHTER

Examples 8.1a and 8.1b show two common notations for laughter within a musical score. Example 8.1a is a more indicative notation. No specific or approximate pitches are given and no particular style of laugh is indicated. This notation is found both with and without the use of staff lines. In pieces that are improvisatory and abstract, the "laugh" sign often appears without any reference to a five-line staff. When other pitches surround the "laughing" indication, it is most often placed on the staff, as shown here.

What should it sound like?

Since no specific pitches are written, the laugh must be intuited as to vocal pitch and related to textual or musical material surrounding it. This type of indication leaves all decisions as to pitch, vocal color projection, and dramatic intent to the interpreter.

Example 8.1b shows approximate pitches and rhythms and includes verbal instructions, as well. In this second example, the singer should attempt to let the melodic flow of the laugh generally follow the outline of the approximated pitches and use the voice only within the notated pitch range. As with the previous example, the interpreter is generally allowed choices for vocal color and other aspects of the projection and vocalization of the laugh, though some composers may write adjectives to describe desired effects. Words such as *piercing*, *brittle*, or *delicate* occasionally appear above or below the notated laughs and further delineate the color desired.

In some scores, the composer might only give verbal instructions to laugh without any kind of accompanying notation. The point at which a laugh should occur will be indicated clearly by a space in the score and accompanied by a direction to laugh. The instructions to laugh may include adjectives to elicit a particular type of laughter, such as *twittery*, *shrill*, *sultry*, or *nervous*. In such cases, the composer is attempting to invoke a particular dramatic impression that fits either the mood of the text, if any, or that of the musical context.

The laughter could occur with or without accompanying music and should be fitted into the designated silence provided if performed unaccompanied so that there is a natural flow of musical material. If instruments have continuing notation underneath the laugh, the interpreter must carefully plan the length of the laugh and its character to fit with that accompanying material. Then the instruments will not need to accommodate for a laugh that lasts too long or short a time. If no approximate pitches are given, the singer should use his or her normal laugh, adapting it to the length of time given in the score for the effect. Generally, females can use the full vocal range for a laugh, allowing it to start well above the chest/head passaggio and then drifting down naturally to the middle of the voice. Given an indication such as *sultry*, one might engage the lower part of the voice more than normal, bringing a darker, lower timbre to the laughter. Male voices should use head and chest voice only, unless there is a specific indication to incorporate the falsetto. If there is such an indication, then the falsetto can be blended downward into the head voice, eliminating any obvious break between the two registers.

How do I do it?

1. Articulate a laugh with a clean attack, a definite or approximate pitch (depending on the score indication), and nonlegato.

2. Articulate with a light thrust of the diaphragm and breath, not by squeezing the tone out by artificially opening and closing the throat. If the musculature of the throat becomes overinvolved in laughing, the voice tires and becomes raspy. There should be no feeling of "grab" or "grip" in the throat during the laugh. The laugh merely floats on top of the air stream and is projected into the resonance cavities as in a normal singing tone.

3. Using an "h" to expel a little air on the attack will help to relax the throat, keep it open, and get the breath moving.

4. A laugh can be rehearsed on specific pitches devised from traditional vocalises built on triads, five-tone scales, or 1-3-5-8-scale degrees in each key, moving up or down by half steps. As you vocalise, keep the laugh lyrical, delicate, and staccatolike in style and vocal weight. Strive for a lilting, clear, easily produced sound that hangs from the soft palate. Begin the first tone in a laugh with a legato attack. As you articulate each pitch in a sequence, keep the tongue relaxed and the throat open as in normal singing.

5. A laugh can be rehearsed in a totally improvised manner by merely thinking of a purpose or meaning for the laugh and allowing it to find its natural pitch level, flow, and placement. If you require a specific mental trigger for your desired laugh, choose several descriptive words that refer to moods or attitudes in which a laugh could occur, such as haughty, sardonic, sensuous, or hesitant. Each of these connotes a totally different mental attitude. You can take this one step further, by choosing a poem that exemplifies the word *haughty*, for example. Read it aloud dramatically, followed by a laugh that seems to fit the mood projected in the poem. This poetic reference will be helpful in the discovery process and can be recalled later when needed in a piece of music. Most people do not think of laughter as having particular dramatic intent. But a laugh, delivered in a significant way, can speak volumes about its context.

6. The laugh should always be well focused and projected exactly as a singing tone might be unless the composer has given some other dramatic designation.

7. The chest voice should not be pushed up to abnormally high pitch levels in order to simulate a hearty laugh. If a gusty laugh is required, then either lower

the pitch level to within the normal chest voice range or use more marcato thrust of the diaphragm for each tonal attack, while staying completely in the head voice. You can also give the laugh a heartier sound by rounding the lips slightly. If the lips are left in a natural smile, then the laugh will sound brighter and cheerier. Rounding the lips (perhaps thinking an "oh" vowel) as one laughs has the effect of covering the tone, making it slightly darker, more serious, or older in sound.

WHISPERED TONES

Whispering is a very common vocal effect in numerous scores from the twentieth century. It has been used in all compositional trends of the century (even the most conservative) for setting off a section or just a few words of text with a contrasting vocal color.

In some scores, whispers may not be notated at all. Words to be whispered are printed with or without accompanying music and contain a designation to *whisper*. If no pitches or rhythms are given, the interpreter is responsible for matching the words to the musical space allotted. This will be a felt sense of time. There should be no attempt to place words with particular beats or notes being played. Instead, natural word inflection, textual mood, and overall pacing are the primary factors to consider. In whispered sections of this kind, the composer often indicates a number of seconds (proportional distances) into which the phrase must fit. Dynamic levels, crescendo and diminuendo signs, and dramatic intent (adjectives such as *furious, sweet, or sensuous*) may accompany the text. All of these markings are helpful to the interpreter in determining the intent of the whispered phrase and an effective manner in which to interpret it.

Example 8.2 depicts three frequently used notations for whispered tones. These notations and others invented by individual composers generally include an indication to whisper or a capital *W* written above or below the notation. Since the first two notations look similar to unpitched speaking, it is crucial that the composer indicate exactly what effect is desired. Otherwise, the performer must guess—an unfortunate situation.

Example 8.2c shows the preferred method of notation for whispers. It is less confusing due to the broken lines used for stems. Stone (1980) believes that whispers should be notated without a full staff since specific pitches are virtually impossible to achieve.

A whispered sound is unvoiced but can have designated duration, volume, and limited pitch. Composers such as George Crumb (*Ancient Voices of Children*),

Example 8.2   Whispers

Luciano Berio (Circles), Victoria Bond (Molly Manybloom), Mark Kilstofte (Lovelost), Kenneth Timm (Three Poems of e. e. cummings), and Elizabeth Vercoe (Herstory I) used whispering judiciously to enhance coloristic shadings of the text in their works (see appendix B).

Whispering can be quite ineffective if placed within a piece that has accompanying instruments that cover the whispered sounds. Also, projection of the whisper is difficult in an acoustically dead space, as is the case in many recently built concert halls that were designed for a multipurpose use. In either case, the production of a whisper will require heavy aspiration and fortissimo consonant projection and articulation. If only a word or two need to be whispered, it is fairly easy to manage under almost any circumstances. But if long sections of whispering must be projected over accompanying instruments, it becomes increasingly tiring for the voice and almost impossible to be understood by the listener.

Many composers who write extended whispered sections intend for the interpreter to use a microphone. The microphone naturally magnifies the sound and can be adjusted to a level that will allow the performer to whisper easily and rather quietly while still giving attention to any specific nuances indicated. The amplification provided by the microphone allows the singer to experiment with subtle color and pitch differences in the whisper that could not otherwise be discerned by the listener. If using a microphone, rehearse with it several times to find the proper volume level, the optimum distance from the mic to the mouth, and the thrust with which the whisper would be delivered. If the volume level of the amplification system is too high or if the whisperer stands too close to the microphone while speaking, distortion can occur.

What should it sound like and how do I do it?

1. Keep the throat open and relaxed as in normal singing or speaking.

2. Project the whispered sound into the front of the face. Avoid a guttural rasp across the back of the tongue as the air is propelled up from the throat. Whispering the words *why, whee, shoo,* and *thought* will pinpoint a forward placement and indicate the point at which the air should be felt in the mouth as one whispers. Feel the air crossing the hard palate behind the front teeth and flowing over the lips. If the whisper falls into the back of the mouth or throat, it may cause the tissues to dry out faster, make the throat feel gritty and parched, or initiate a cough. A poor production of the whisper may also cause the performer's voice to tire more easily.

The initial onset (or attack) of each word or syllable must be thought of exactly the same as in a normal legato attack for singing. Since it is unvocalized, air will escape faster and no natural resonance will be present in the sound. Whispered sounds cannot be sustained as long as sung tones because of this. Therefore, more frequent breaths will be needed for phrases of rather short duration compared to singing a line of the same length.

3. Allow the air to make a whispered effect by moving forward out of the throat with the ease of a sigh.

4. Concentrate on clean, clear projection of consonants, using the lips and tongue for propulsion of air and articulation of specific consonants. Keep the dynamics of the projected consonants at a mf or f level unless directed to murmur or mutter the words. With whispering, it is the consonants that clarify the syllabic stresses and provide meaning.

5. Breathe normally and diaphragmatically. Support the whispered sound as vigorously as a singing tone. If the diaphragm disengages altogether during whispering, then muscles in the upper chest and throat begin to constrict in an attempt to compensate for the lazy diaphragm. This may cause tension in the throat.

6. Rehearse whispered sections silently (mouth the words) until they are totally habituated as to dramatic intent, rhythms, and dynamic differences. Visualize (image) pacing, vocal pitch, and mood determination until the section is ingrained. When the voice is finally engaged to whisper, these expressive elements will have been dealt with empirically, saving much overt vocal usage and practice time.

SHOUTS

Most of us have shouted at some point in our lives, but we may never have considered doing so within a musical context. Example 8.3 shows three notations that indicate shouts: note stems with an x for a head, note stems with a pinpoint head or staccato above it, and traditional notation with a verbal indication to shout written above it. Each notation can appear with approximate pitch, indeterminate pitch, or exact pitch. The crucial element is the verbal instruction either printed above it or indicated elsewhere in the score. As with whispering, individual composers have created several other novel notations for shouting, but no matter the style of notation, the indication to shout should be written in the score for the sake of clarity.

Singers are sometimes dismayed to find markings of this type in a vocal composition and immediately discard the music for fear of doing damage to the voice. Indeed, it is possible to stress the voice beyond normal limits if required to engage in abusive shouting. Use common sense in determining whether a piece containing shouts is right for your voice. Certainly works such as Peter Maxwell Davies's *Eight Songs for a Mad King* (appendix B) demand too much force of sound for some voices. Also, some works continue in a shouting manner for long periods of time. But there are pieces like William Bolcom's song "He Tipped the Waiter" (appen-

Example 8.3   Shouts

dix B) in which only a few words are shouted and the effect can be achieved by even the lightest voice. So it is important to know one's own voice, stamina, and vocal flexibility when choosing material that includes shouts.

What should it sound like and how do I do it?

1. Analyze how the shouts are set within the musical context.
   a. Does the voice have to compete with instruments playing at a high volume level in order to be heard?
   b. Does the shouting continue for a lengthy period or must only a few words or syllables be shouted?
   c. Does the vocal notation indicate shouting outside of the normal speaking range of the voice type for which the piece was written?

2. Analyze the notational structure of the shouts.
   a. Do they depict specific rhythms or pitches?
   b. Are there verbal dramatic markings to be inflected while shouting?
   c. Are there verbal directions for volume or quality of sound, such as *harsh, tense, yelling,* or *guttural?*.

3. Devise a sensible practice routine.
   a. Learn and rehearse all notations for shouts at a medium, normal volume level. Do not attempt to shout until all vocal inflections, approximate pitch levels, and rhythmic values are completely decided and secure.
   b. *Never* take the chest voice up to a high pitch level in order to sustain a shout. This is especially stressful for female voices. Heartier male voices can generally handle this technique more easily without undue stress, but even they should be careful.
   c. If the notation indicates shouting at a pitch level above the normal speaking range, engage the head register and keep the tonal focus in the front of the face for maximum resonance.
   d. Always use a traditional diaphragmatic marcato attack for shouts, punctuating each word, syllable, or phrase with an outward thrust of the diaphragm. This gives maximum breath and muscular support at the bottom of the breath system and relieves the throat and chest muscles of added tension or a need to physically engage while shouting.
   e. Remember that light, lyric voices will probably tire sooner when faced with this technique, so only rehearse it for a few minutes, quickly returning to a more subtle, relaxed vocal production.
   f. Watch yourself in a mirror while practicing shouts. Look for any signs of physical stress. The shoulders, chest, and neck muscles need to remain quiet, with all activity occurring in the diaphragm. Keep the jaw loose and relaxed. There is a tendency to exaggerate the physical opening and closing of the jaw when shouting. If the jaw overextends in a forward direction, you may hear a popping noise in the temporomandibular joint. Exaggeration of that kind can cause this complex joint, used for

chewing, speaking, swallowing, and singing, to malfunction and can lead to serious problems with its synchronization. Approach shouting with a singer's mind-set, using all of the health-conscious vocal concepts available to you. Do nothing that could cause the voice to function in a peculiar, bizarre, or irregular way in order to produce a shout.

HEAVY BREATHING

Luciano Berio (*Sequenza III*), Roman Haubenstock-Ramati (*Credentials*), and Sylvano Bussotti (*Il Nudo*) are among the many composers who experimented with various applications of audible inhalation and exhalation as a means to affect the timbre of the voice. Examples 8.4a, 8.4b, and 8.4c show three different notations for audible breathing. The notation in examples 8.4b and 8.4c indicates length or duration of each exhalation and inhalation. Sometimes this effect is drawn out slowly over several seconds or beats and can be manipulated as to pacing and dramatic intent. The notations usually have accompanying dynamic markings or signs for crescendo or decrescendo.

Various verbal instructions are found for this effect and are normally written in the score somewhere near the notation: *heavy breathing, audibly inhale and exhale, thrusts of air, voiced breathing,* and *inhale and expel air violently.* Normally, singers try to achieve a quiet, silent breath when singing. This not only eliminates unwanted sounds from the vocal line, but it is also a more desirable technique for throat relaxation. Allowing air to continuously rasp through the throat and mouth for an extended period can dry out surfaces of the mouth and throat, tiring the voice and leading to muscle and vocal fatigue. So this vocal effect, called "audible" or "heavy breathing," is for short-term use only and should not be carried over into the singer's normal vocal production.

In many cases, audible breathing is used in works that amplify the voice with a microphone, as in *Voices,* Ramon Zupko's showpiece for mezzo and electronic tape. It is an effective device when amplified and is often used to bring an eerie, emotionally charged, or erotic quality to the music. It can also be found in

Example 8.4a   Heavy Breathing

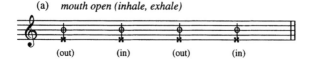

(a)   *mouth open (inhale, exhale)*

(out)   (in)   (out)   (in)

Example 8.4b, 8.4c   Heavy Breathing

(b)

inhale

exhale

(c)

⟵————————⊘ *inhale audibly*

⊘————————⟶ *exhale audibly*

unamplified works, but it is more difficult to perform and seems less successful since the audible breath has no natural resonance with which to project the sound into an auditorium. The acoustical performing space would have to be extremely "live" for this kind of vocalization to be meaningful or even detected at all by the listener.

What should it sound like and how do I do it?

Audible breathing can be likened to a heavy sigh without tone when exhaling. The air can be felt to blow across the soft palate and the back of the tongue as it is expelled. Think an "ah" vowel. This gives the sound a warm, relaxed quality. Variations can be achieved by rounding the lips into an "oo" or "oh" shape. The sound becomes darker and more ominous when covered in this way.

Another variation can be created by thinking an "ee" vowel and allowing the middle of the tongue to rise slightly toward the alveolar ridge (hard palate). This produces a more sinister, somewhat hissing exhalation. Other subtle colors can be achieved by slight manipulation of the lips and tongue. Experimentation is the best way to proceed here. If the score has verbal directions for dramatic nuance, then try out all of the formations suggested above. Record them to see which seems most appropriate for the context of the effect. If none seems quite right, use your imagination and combine different formations of the lips with various tongue positions to achieve a sound that fits. Remember, there is no absolute or right way to achieve an effect of this sort.

The same effect occurs in reverse on inhalation. The mouth is open, lips placed in the position of a particular vowel, tongue lying flat or arched slightly, and the air is drawn in with an audible sound; you should feel it pass across the back of the tongue and soft palate, and down into the throat.

When producing this effect, be mindful of negative tension factors. Never press the back of the tongue down in order to create a particular sound. Allow it to remain loose and flexible from front to back. Don't rehearse this technique for long periods of time due to the drying out effect it has on vocal tissues. Do most of the work mentally, with occasional bits of audible breathing. Drink plenty of water while rehearsing to keep the throat and mouth lubricated.

FALSETTO, WHITE TONE, OR HOLLOW TONE

In contemporary vocal music the term *falsetto* does not necessarily refer to the upper range of the male voice, as it does in traditional vocal music. Though women do not possess a falsetto range, the term is occasionally seen in twentieth-century music for female voice. In this case, it signifies a vocal color rather than a vocal range. Falsetto indications for females occur on pitches throughout the vocal range but are most often seen on tones located in the head voice, not the chest voice range. If the term and notation occur in works for male voice, then the falsetto range is generally the effect desired. However, a male singer may be given the *falsetto* direction for a pitch that is well out of normal falsetto range (much lower). In that case, it is meant as a color variation and not a registration indication.

Example 8.5   Falsetto, White Tone, Hollow Tone

Example 8.5 shows two contrasting vocal notations for falsetto. They are generally accompanied by a verbal description such as *falsetto, white tone,* or *hollow tone.* In some works, these verbal descriptions are printed above individual notes or sections of text using traditional notation. This effect can be found in works by George Rochberg (*Eleven Songs for Mezzo-Soprano*), Mauricio Kagel (*Anagrams*), Mel Powell (*Haiku Settings*), and many others.

What should it sound like and how do I do it?

The eeriness of this vocal effect is its major goal. An otherworldly, ghostlike, ethereal, sometimes spooky sound is desirable. A falsetto, white, or hollow tone has no vibrato and floats as if on a thin vapor of air. It is most effective when used in the upper octave of the female voice and should seem to hang as if suspended over a precipice.

Keep the soft palate raised. Never force, press, drive the tone, or allow it to blossom into a vibrato. It should glide easily as in the initial attack of a long vocalized glissando and be thought of as an open, free, plaintive sound devoid of emotion. It provides a convincing vehicle for vocal color contrast in a lyrical, nontaxing way. Modification of vowels to a round "oo" is helpful in the upper register of the voice and adds warmth to the tone, if required. When sustaining a falsetto, white, or hollow sound, be careful to support it with adequate breath. But don't overblow the delicate sound with too much thrust from the air stream. Allow the throat and tongue to relax as in normal singing. Let the sound float lightly on the air stream and rehearse this technique at a moderate volume. It should not tire the voice unless taken to extremes of range and volume. This is a simple, gently produced, relaxed technique, and it can be rehearsed and habituated quickly. Since it is generally used sparingly, for only a note or two, little effort is required to find a suitable and freely produced quality that fits the textual or musical context and in no way causes vocal distress.

Experiment with different vowel shapes, if no specific word or vowel is given, until you find one that seems to fit the mood and character of the vocal line. The goal is to set these notes apart from others being sung around them in a unique and mysterious way. This sound is effective in works using a microphone or those without amplification. However, an amplified falsetto or hollow tone is among the most effective of all coloristic subtleties.

TREMOLO MUTING

Example 8.6 shows the standard notation for tremolo muting (Stone 1980). This simple technique signifies moving the hand back and forth in front of the mouth to change the timbre of a tone as you close and open the sound. The quality of

Example 8.6   Tremolo Muting

the tones can be altered by fixing the lips in the position of a particular vowel. For instance, if the lips are rounded in an "oo" position, the tone will sound different than if the lips are relaxed in an "ah" position. The same concept applies to other variations of the vowel spectrum. There may also be a verbal instruction that accompanies it to designate the desired effect. If no specific vowel is indicated, the interpreter is free to decide which vowel will produce a sound to fit the musical context.

There are many other nonstandard notations for this effect. Risatti (1975) lists ten dissimilar ones that have been used by composers such as Erhard Karkoschka, Luciano Berio, and Bernard Rands. In cases of individualistic notation, look at the score's preface or other works by the composer for performance directions. In some cases, no description of the sound can be found and it is left to the performer to create a sound that seems appropriate.

What should it sound like and how do I do it?

1. Sustain the notated tone on the vowel indicated. If none is indicated, an open "ah" or "oh" will work nicely.

2. Damp the sound by lightly pressing the palm of your hand against your lips while continuing to sustain the tone. The "+" sign indicates a closed sound.

3. Keep sustaining the tone, but remove the hand from the lips about an inch or two to let the sound out. The "o" sign signifies an open sound.

4. Repeat the pattern according to the length of time or number of repetitions specified in the score.

5. This technique is similar to the sound achieved by jazz instrumentalists when they use a plunger over the bell of the horn, moving it back and forth to produce a "wah-wah" sound. In jazz this is also notated with a "+" for closed and an "o" for open.

GLISSANDO

The vocal glissando is the most familiar of all vocal effects mentioned in this volume. It has been used by composers for well over 100 years in both traditional and avant-garde music. Though Risatti (1975) prints fifty-four similar notations from works by modern composers such as Xenakis, Kagel, and Varése, three notations have become standardized for the glissando. Two are shown in Examples 8.7a and 8.7b. An earlier example in chapter 6 (example 6.5) shows the third: a curved or undulating glissando seen in indeterminate scores. In that case, the thin line traces the approximate course of the glissando. Each type of notation

Example 8.7a, 8.7b   Vocal Glissando

may be accompanied by verbal instructions, including *slide between pitches, connect pitches with exaggerated glissando,* or simply *glissando.*

The glissando should not be confused with the portamento. The portamento is an artistically controlled quick glide between two pitches; it is executed at the end of the duration of the first pitch, just prior to attacking the second pitch. In essence it is the concept of a supreme legato connection between tones. A glissando is a slower moving slide or slur between two tones with the intention of hitting all of the tones in between and may continue over several beats. Another major difference between the two in contemporary music concerns vibrato; the portamento uses it, while the glissando does not.

What should it sound like and how do I do it?

1. If a specific beginning and ending pitch is given, stay within those confines. If the glissando is indeterminate and merely indicates a general direction of pitch, then the singer is allowed great liberty of expression.

2. Glide or slide evenly between the two printed tones, touching on all tones in between as you move up or down in pitch. Do not stop and reattack the tone at any point until the destination pitch is reached. A continuous, uninterrupted vocalization is the goal.

3. Space the glissando evenly in tempo so that it gradually spans the desired rhythmic length given for the effect.

4. A glissando is a delicate, lyrical effect. Do not press or push the voice to extreme volumes. Even if a fortissimo is required, rely on natural resonance in the voice and do not go beyond a volume level that you would consider the peak for your voice during normal singing.

5. This effect is often used for vocal pedagogy purposes, being especially helpful for blending the vocal registers. A useful exercise for connecting the head and chest registers with a gliding glissando follows:

Start on a pitch well above the register change and clearly in the head voice. Sing on the syllable "ma" or "me" and slowly glide to the octave below, allowing the voice to loosen and lighten as it moves across the passaggio into the chest register. Float the tone and relax the throat as the voice descends. Allow the palate to remain naturally raised as you cross the passaggio. Keep the focus of the voice in the front of the face for low and medium to medium-high tones, allowing it to move up into the soft palate for higher pitches. Concentrate on a smooth vocal glide, a loose jaw and tongue, throat relaxation, and diaphragmatic support of

Example 8.8   Tongue Click or Cluck

the entire tonal range involved in the glissando. This exercise can be done moving up and down the scale by half steps. Once the initial syllables are secure, begin to use the other cardinal vowels ("oh," "ay," "oo") with various consonants in front of them.

TONGUE CLICK OR CLUCK

Example 8.8 shows three notations commonly used for both the *tongue click* and the *tongue cluck*. Scores do not always contain a clear indication of whether to click or cluck. Composers need to be as specific as possible concerning which sound is desired since there are various kinds of clicking sounds inside the mouth. A verbal indication should accompany the notation.

What should it sound like and how do I do it?

The *tongue click* is a popping sound made by sharply bringing the back of the tongue into contact with the velum or teeth at the back of the mouth, imitating a percussive, castenet-like sound. The sound can be varied in quality according to whether the click occurs in the center of the palate nearer the velum, where one would pronounce an *ng*, or on the hard surface of the gums just above the back teeth. The tongue click is a common sound used for other purposes (calling an animal, signaling another person, or showing a distinct appreciation for something or someone).

Though some have used the terms *tongue click* and *tongue cluck* interchangeably, the consensus is that a *tongue cluck* refers to a flip of the tip of the tongue against the alveolar ridge or upper dental ridge of the hard palate. This location is the same area used for producing the *d*, *t*, *l*, and *n*, plus the flipped *r* as in *merry* (meddy). After the tongue touches the dental ridge it falls quickly to the base of the lower teeth. The tongue cluck is less common in everyday use but can be heard in the sounds humans make when simulating the calls of turkeys or other wild animals.

Whether articulating a click or a cluck, the color of the sound can easily be changed by manipulating the shape of the lips into an "ee," an "oh," or an "oo." Each gives a unique quality to the sound. Experiment to decide which is easier to produce and most appropriate for a particular piece of music.

TONGUE TRILLS

Examples 8.9a and 8.9b give two standard notations for trilling with the tongue. This effect has also been called a "flutter tongue" (Stone 1980). Though tongue trills have been used as vocal effects in the twentieth century, they have been

Example 8.9a, 8.9b   Tongue Trills

around for hundreds of years as part of the normal pronunciation of some lan-
guages and as ritual sounds in several kinds of ethnic singing from Africa to Asia.
Classically trained singers learn to roll an r as part of the pronunciation of Italian,
French, and German. So in principle this technique is already quite familiar.

What should it sound like?

For singers, the major issue in the production of tongue trills in contemporary
music is how the tongue trill is characterized. A tone may be sustained for several
beats purely by means of the tongue trill. In some cases, an entire melodic line
may be outlined and vocalized by the tongue trill, as in Christina Kuzmych's
flamboyant display piece, *Shapes and Sounds IV* (appendix B) or Haubenstock-
Ramati's *Credentials*, where the voice moves through several pitches within a range
of an octave while trilling with the tongue.

How do I do it?

This effect is an exciting, energetic, and sometimes riveting sound that requires
a very flexible, loose tongue capable of consistent trills over a much longer time
frame than that of merely rolling an r. In this type of vigorous tongue trill, it is
important to adhere to any notated pitches and not to simply create an ad lib
melody line where none exists. If only one pitch is notated, then that pitch
continues for the length of time specified. If several pitches are printed that outline a vocal melody, then the trill continues through all pitches.

It is helpful to articulate a t at the beginning of a tongue trill to make contact
with the alveolar ridge on which the trill occurs. Giving a slight thrust of energy
from the breath will also propel the tongue and trill into action. A simple exercise
for developing the appropriate motion of the tongue trill is to repeat the phrase
"tuh, duh, rum," first slowly, then picking up speed until the sequence of syllables becomes an easy trill.

Tongue trills also have the capacity for a wide range of dynamics. In most
works, a dynamic marking is given for the tongue trill, but if not, project it
according to the dynamic level of other vocal or instrumental pitches being sung
or played around it. It should not become suddenly louder or draw attention to
itself as a vocal accentuation unless so marked in the score. When applying a
crescendo or diminuendo to a tongue trill, use normal singing as your guide.
The breath (increased air pressure) must be applied to increase volume. Allow
the tongue to remain free and relaxed as breath pressure is increased, supporting
well from the diaphragm. Be careful not to press the tongue hard into the dental

Example 8.10   Whistling

whistle

surfaces as you crescendo. This will cause the tongue to tense and interrupt the freedom of the trill.

Tongue trills are useful vocal warm-up tools and can be safely vocalized throughout a singer's range. As in other vocal effects, always adhere to normal singing vocal registration when applying the trills to warm-ups or musical scores. Never carry the chest voice higher than its comfortable range.

WHISTLING

Example 8.10 shows four notations that indicate whistling. In order to differentiate these notations from notations of the same kind used for other vocal effects, the composer must have a verbal instruction to accompany them. Generally, the word *whistle* is written below or above specific notes with a volume or style of whistle indicated.

Whistling is often used to create humor or a casual atmosphere, as Charles Ives did so marvelously in his song "Memories." But it has also been used to introduce an eerie, plaintive quality or starkness into the musical ambience, as Christina Kuzmych does in *Shapes and Sounds IV* (appendix B). She ends the work with a projected "sh," followed by a vibratoless whistle that gradually disappears into thin air.

What should it sound like and how do I do it?

1. One can whistle with puckered lips or through the teeth, whichever is more easily accomplished and fits the musical context.

2. Adhere to specific pitches and rhythms, if notated.

3. Use the diaphragm to support the whistle tone and propel the air stream into the front of the face.

4. Whistle with a clear tone unless otherwise marked.

5. Keep the neck and jaw relaxed and uninvolved in the articulation of pitches to be whistled. They should be initiated with the breath, as in a singing mode.

6. The use of vibrato or straight tone may be indicated. If not, it is an interpretative decision for the performer and a matter of technical ability. Some people have a difficult time accomplishing a whistle that has vibrato.

VOCAL MUTING

Vocal muting is a technique that involves the gradual opening or closing of the mouth. Example 8.11a shows the standard notation for this effect. Closed mouth

Example 8.11a   Vocal Muting

M_____ Ah   Ah_____M

Example 8.11b   Vocal Muting

Alternates

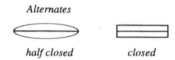

half closed   *closed*

is indicated by a "+" sign and open mouth by an "o." Verbal cues such as *bocca chiusa* (closed mouth) or *appena aperta* (mouth slightly open) may accompany the notation. The heavy, dark line between the open and closed notations shows a gradual change from one to the other. Two alternate indications for closed and half-closed mouth are shown in Example 8.11b.

This notation has been used by Lukas Foss, Haubenstock-Ramati, and others as an effective vocal colorization of vowel sounds. Vocal muting differs from vowel morphing (see chapter 7) in that the tone gradually moves from a closed, vocalized consonant, such as m, n, or ng, to an open vowel and vice versa. In vowel morphing the tone gradually changes from vowel to vowel.

What should it sound like and how do I do it?

This technique is directly opposite of vowel and consonant articulation used in normal, traditional vocal declamation of text. Ordinarily, vowels are sustained in an open, clear, consistent position through the length of a tone. Even when pronouncing diphthongs, the second vowel in the diphthong is enunciated only at the last possible microsecond before ending the tone. Also, consonants are normally enunciated quickly and precisely, with no attempt to graduate the sound.

In vocal muting the mouth is fully closed, lips together but not pinched at the notated closed sign. Then the lips and mouth open in small increments over the length of the heavy black line until fully open at the point of an open vowel notation. Keep the motion smooth, not jerky or spasmodic, with no holding of the jaw or tongue. An even, velvety, facile glide from one to the other is the desired effect. Depending upon the musical context, this effect may be sung with or without vibrato. Deleting the vibrato removes warmth from the tone and creates a nonemotional, stark sonority. In many contemporary pieces, this non-emotional approach is preferred.

This simple, timed exercise, added to a daily rehearsal routine, will be effective for preparing the singer when vocal muting appears in a musical context.

Choose a comfortable tone in the middle of the voice. Initiate the tone with an "m." Over a period of eight beats (at around 60, metronome) gradually open the mouth into a fully developed "ah" vowel. Breathe. Initiate the tone on the "ah" and gradually close the mouth to an "m" over eight beats. Keep the vibrato normal. Let the palate, tongue, and lips gradually move into the correct position for the "m" or "ah," with no sudden shifting of the articulators. When moving from "ah" to "m," use this visualization as you sing the exercise. (Pretend that you are watching a door as it is closing ever so slowly and without hesitation or interruption until it closes completely and soundlessly.) Visualize the reverse when moving from "m" to "ah."

Careful and knowledgeable selection of repertoire for any voice type is essential to a satisfactory vocal and interpretative outcome. When choosing repertoire from the twentieth century, one should consider overall vocal range and tessitura; text (appropriateness for the performance venue); dynamic and articulation requirements suitable to the singer's vocal/technical ability; pitch and rhythm complexities; scope of experimental vocal techniques present; ensemble difficulties (number of performers and rehearsals required); and additional equipment needed for realization (such as electronics, special lighting, or props).

This repertoire can be used to explore a variety of important vocal and performance concepts. Some of these include developing a sensitivity to various twentieth-century musical styles; establishing mood or character portrayal; eliciting audience response through humor; expanding one's ability to portray a variety of dramatic ideas and moods; improving the ability to hear complex intervalic movement within a melodic line; becoming more vocally flexible.

Those who are greatly involved with twentieth-century music may wish to program several contemporary works on the same concert to show the tremendous variance of musical organization and styles present in the period. It is an effective way to satisfy the need for contrasting declamation, mood, dramatic attitude, and pacing within a contemporary recital or concert setting. Theatrical elements can also be added to a conservative program by this organizational plan, bringing freshness and vitality to the traditional recital format.

The following sample programs for female and male voices are designed to enhance the performer's vocal flexibility and ability to engage an audience in the musical, emotional, dramatic, or theatrical elements presented by the various musical styles of the period. Each program contains at least one work that uses experimental techniques of some kind—extended vocal sounds, theatrics, or multimedia effects. *These pieces are designated with an asterisk (*) and discussed more fully in appendix B.* The remainder of works on each recital use the voice in a traditional manner while covering a wide range of musical and stylistic trends from the twentieth century.

Two suggested programs are shown for each voice type, with program 1 being less demanding than program 2. Since the twentieth century is now history, a recital of works from the period should include pieces that offer a variety of moods, vocal techniques, and varied instrumentation. Ideally, any such program will give the audience a taste of various twentieth-century musical trends by well-known and lesser-known composers, both male and female. Jane Manning's two books, *New Vocal Repertory: An Introduction* and *New Vocal Repertory 2*, are excellent sources for additional works from this period.

SAMPLE PROGRAMS

SUGGESTED RECITALS FOR SOPRANO

These two recital programs include twentieth-century music written in a traditional compositional style, as well as some extravagant, avant-garde show pieces. Each program contains at least one chamber work or a piece for voice and electronic tape. Each program's length is approximately one hour and fifteen minutes and requires a minimum of electronic or other specialized equipment.

Program 1 presents diverse stylistic contrast from the traditional, lyrical writing of Persichetti and Pasatieri through the more tonally experimental music of Lomon, Larsen, and Gideon. The Berberian and Crumb works provide novel colors and uses of the voice. The Berberian piece is the most avant-garde work of the recital and requires great imagination and acting ability to get a satisfying result.

Program 2 uses Laura Clayton's *Cree Songs to the Newborn* as its centerpiece. This atmospheric, memorable, extended work is built around the sounds of the Cree language. It is a creatively challenging work for a flexible voice. There is nothing else quite like it in the soprano repertoire. The remainder of the program offers a hauntingly beautiful cycle by Diemer, an uncommon vocalise by Cowell, several short, atmospheric pieces by Glanville-Hicks, a conversational and sentimental cycle by Hoiby, and an electronic and vocal showpiece by Bennett. Both programs are demanding in vocal technique and dramatic import. But individual works could be extracted for inclusion on a program requiring less technical advancement overall.

PROGRAM I FOR SOPRANO

Songs from Letters   Libby Larsen (1989)
    So Like Your Fathers (1880)
    He Never Misses (1880)
    A Man Can Love Two Women (1880)

A Working Woman (1882–1893)
All I Have (1902)
(App. 15 minutes)
Oxford University Press

Songs from a Requiem   Ruth Lomon (1977)
    Les Baux
    Interregnum
    The Mammoth Head
    Cancrizans
    Black Mesa
    Incantation
(App. 11 minutes)
Arsis Press

Madrigals, Book I (soprano, contrabass, vibraphone)   George Crumb* (1965)
(App. 10 minutes)
C. F. Peters Corporation

Stripsody   Cathy Berberian* (1966)
    (a sound effects piece for solo voice using a microphone)
(App. 6 minutes)
C. F. Peters Corporation

Four Epitaphs from Robert Burns   Miriam Gideon (1952)
    Epitaph for a Wag in Mauchline
    Epitaph on Wee Johnie
    Epitaph on the Author
    Monody on a Lady Famed for Her Caprice
(App. 10 minutes)
American Composers Alliance Edition

The Kiss (1976)   Thomas Pasatieri
The Harp That Once Through Tara's Halls (1975)
The Grass (1958)   Vincent Persichetti
Out of the Morning (1958)
(App. 12 minutes)
Pasatieri published by Belwin-Mills Publishing Co.
Persichetti published by Elkan-Vogel Publishing Co.

(*) experimental

PROGRAM 2 FOR SOPRANO

Four Chinese Love Poems   Emma Lou Diemer (1965)
    People Hide Their Love
    Wind and Rain
    By the Willows
    The Mulberry on the Lowland
(App. 10 minutes)
Seesaw Music Corp.

Vocalise (soprano, flute, piano)   Henry Cowell (1964)
                              (App. 8 minutes)
                              C. F. Peters

Thirteen Ways of Looking at a Blackbird   Peggy Glanville-Hicks (1951)
                              (App. 10 minutes)
                              Weintraub Music Co.

Cree Songs to the Newborn   Laura Clayton* (1978)
   (soprano and chamber ensemble)
                              (App. 15 minutes)
                              C. F. Peters

Three Ages of Woman, Op. 51   Lee Hoiby (1990)
   Manners
   Filling Station
   Insomnia
                              (App. 12 minutes)
                              Aquarius Music Co.

Nightpiece   Richard Rodney Bennett* (1972)
   (soprano and electronic tape)
                              (App. 10 minutes)
                              Universal Edition

(*) experimental

SUGGESTED RECITALS FOR MEZZO-SOPRANO

These two programs incorporate a wealth of variety in musical style and dramatic mood. Several of the works are already considered standard vocal repertoire, while others will be unfamiliar to many. Contemporary American and British composers, in particular, have written an abundance of music for mezzo-soprano. Some composers of the era stated that the color, range, and dramatic possibilities of the mezzo voice made it the most effective of all vocal categories for interpreting modern texts. Therefore, finding music for this voice type is more a matter of deciding between various options than trying to locate repertoire. A mezzo would have no trouble developing several significant recital programs using only works written since 1920. The music never lacks for quality, contrast in declamation, or dramatic interest.

Program 1 begins with four melodic songs by Mary Howe, essentially traditional in compositional style. The heart of the recital is the Argento cycle, an intense, dramatic piece that won the Pulitzer Prize in 1975. Terminus exploits vocal color changes in combination with the prepared tape of electronically produced sounds. The result is fascinating and otherworldly. Scat 2 is a showpiece built on the jazz idiom. The Ives and Vercoe songs furnish an intellectual comic relief from a rather intense first half.

Program 2 begins with Ned Rorem's Poems of Love and the Rain, a work that uniquely sets each poem twice with contrasting music. The Samuel and Crumb pieces involve vocal experimentation and combinations of instruments seldom heard in a concert setting. The Vehar and Barber cycles add humor, melodic beauty, and heart for a well-rounded, dramatically satisfying program.

PROGRAM I FOR MEZZO-SOPRANO

From "Seven Goethe Songs"   Mary Howe (1940)
   Zweifel
   Heute geh' ich
   Ich Denke Dein
   Die Jahre

(App. 15 minutes)
Galaxy Music Corp.

From the Diary of Virginia Woolf   Dominick Argento (1974)
   The Diary
   Anxiety
   Fancy
   Hardy's Funeral
   Rome
   War
   Parents
   Last Entry

(App. 25 minutes)
Boosey & Hawkes

Terminus   Jean Eichelberger Ivey* (1972)
   (mezzo and two-channel tape)

(App. 10 minutes)
Carl Fischer

Scat 2   Victoria Bond* (1984)
   (voice and trumpet)

(App. 5 minutes)
American Music Center or composer

There Is a Lane   Charles Ives (1921)
The Greatest Man
Memories
The Children's Hour

(App. 10 minutes)
Merion Music, Inc.

Irreveries from Sappho   Elizabeth Vercoe* (1983)
   Andromeda Rag
   Older Woman Blues
   Boogie for Leda

(App. 10 minutes)
Arsis Press

(*) experimental

PROGRAM 2 FOR MEZZO-SOPRANO

Poems of Love and the Rain   Ned Rorem (1963)
Prologue: from The Rain
Stop All the Clocks, Cut Off the Telephone
The Air Is the Only
Love's Stricken "Why"
The Apparition
Do I Love You
In the Rain
Song for Lying in Bed During a Night Rain
Interlude
Song for Lying in Bed During a Night Rain (conclusion)
In the Rain
Do I Love You (Part II)
The Apparition
Love's Stricken "Why"
The Air Is the Only
Stop All the Clocks, Cut Off the Telephone
Epilogue: from The Rain

(App. 30 minutes)
Boosey & Hawkes

In the Hall of Mirrors   Rhian Samuel* (1984)
(App. 10 minutes)

Night of the Four Moons   George Crumb* (1969)
(alto, alto flute-doubling piccolo, banjo, electric cello, and percussion)
(App. 16 minutes)
C. F. Peters

Three Songs, Op. 45   Samuel Barber (1974)
Now Have I Fed and Eaten Up the Rose
A Green Lowland of Pianos
O Boundless, Boundless Evening
(App. 10 minutes)
G. Schirmer

Women, Women   Persis Vehar* (1979)
A Fixture
Resisting Each Other
Survival

(App. 6 minutes)
Leyerle Publications

(*) experimental

SUGGESTED RECITALS FOR TENOR

Twentieth-century repertoire for tenor has much to offer. Some composers, such as Benjamin Britten, wrote numerous memorable works for tenor that are considered standards today. These two suggested programs would be most successfully performed by a lyric tenor who has a facile voice, an approximate vocal range of two octaves, and a keen sense of dramatic nuance.

Program 1 is less demanding vocally than program 2. The Argento, Barab, and Corigliano pieces are generally lyrical, while the Pasatieri offers intellectual, conversational, and melismatic diversity. There are two contrasting works with unique audience appeal. The *Canticle II* by Britten is a dialogue between Abraham and Isaac for tenor and mezzo-soprano with some sensitive and elegant duet sections. *A Maze with Grace* is a delicate "chance" piece for voice and an indeterminate number of instruments. The vocal score, built on the IPA, indicates that the IPA phonemes should be read left to right and the musical gestures read right to left. When all the players have completed their tour of the maze, the entire ensemble surprises the audience by performing the chorale, "Amazing Grace."

The serious mood of program 2 requires more weight and drama from the tenor voice, especially in the piece *Beata l'alma* by David Blake. It is a tour de force for the pianist and very demanding for the singer. There are numerous special effects and coloristic vocal changes, as well as a rather high tessitura with which to contend. The other experimental piece on the program is the Vercoe work for voice and electronic tape, a fanciful piece built on sonic vocabularies and numerous experimental vocal techniques.

The remainder of the program brings out possibilities for tenderness and serenity in the Birch and Copland works. Dramatic contrast is provided in the Walton, Kim, and Smith pieces. At times, they are intense, assuming the ability to achieve a wide dynamic and emotional range. Works from the two programs could easily be interchanged to accommodate the personality, vocal characteristics, and maturity of the performer.

PROGRAM I FOR TENOR

Six Elizabethan Songs   Dominick Argento (1970)
    Spring
    Sleep
    Winter
    Dirge
    Diaphenia
    Hymn

                (App. 15 minutes)
                Boosey & Hawkes

Three Irish Folksong Settings (voice and flute)   John Corigliano (1988)
    The Salley Gardens
    The Foggy Dew
    She Moved Through the Fair

                (App. 10 minutes)
                G. Schirmer

Canticle II (Abraham and Isaac)   Benjamin Britten (1952)
                        (App. 11 minutes)
                        Boosey & Hawkes

A Maze with Grace   Thomas Albert* (1975)
                        (Indeterminate length)
                    American Composer's Alliance

Three Married Songs (voice and cello)   Thomas Pasatieri (1970)
    Break of Day
    The First Fight: Out of Sight, Out of Mind
    Dear, If You Change
                        (App. 8 minutes)
                        Belwin-Mills

The Rivals   Seymour Barab (1971)
    The Daisies
    The Rose in the Wind
    The Hawk
    The Rivals
                        (App. 15 minutes)
                        Boosey & Hawkes

(*) experimental

PROGRAM 2 FOR TENOR

Beata l'alma   David Blake* (1966)
                        (App. 12 minutes)
                        Novello

I Long to See a Flower (1960)   Robert Fairfax Birch
If There Were Dreams (1956)
                        (App. 6 minutes)
                        Presser

Daphne   William Walton (1932)
Through Gilded Trellises
Old Sir Faulk
                        (App. 12 minutes)
                    Oxford University Press

Letters Found Near a Suicide   Earl Kim (1954)
                        (App. 5 minutes)
                    In New Vistas in Song
                    Marks Music Corp.

Poet's Song (1927)   Aaron Copland
Pastorale (1921)
                        (App. 7 minutes)
                        Boosey & Hawkes

Nine Epigrams from Poor Richard   Elizabeth Vercoe* (1986)
   (for voice and electronic tape)
                              (App. 8 minutes)
                         American Music Center

Time to the Old   William Schumann (1979)
   The Old Gray Couple
   Conway Burying Ground
   Dozing on the Lawn
                              (App. 11 minutes)
                              Merion Music, Inc.

Three Love Songs (high key)   Julia Smith (1954)
   I Will Sing the Song
   The Door That I Would Open
   The Love I Hold
                              (App. 10 minutes)
                              Theodore Presser

(*) experimental

SUGGESTED RECITALS FOR BARITONE

The baritone voice has been popular with contemporary composers. Works chosen
for these two suggested recitals include standards, less familiar pieces, single songs,
and song cycles. At least two pieces containing experimental ideas are on each program. Program 1 is best suited to a lyric baritone voice that can sustain a medium-
high tessitura. The recital begins with a challenging, exciting work by Castelnuovo-
Tedesco, a marvelous way to open a program. This is a conservative work,
compositionally and vocally, with only a few *quasi parlato* tones to simulate whispering.
The Bergsma cycle for voice, clarinet, bassoon, and piano provides a change in instrumentation. Three novel pieces by Gideon, Fontyn, and Cage also offer excellent,
short contrasts. The exotic and memorable Fontyn piece contains parlando, glissandos,
sprechstimme, and intoning. *Mixco* combines English and Spanish in an unusual, mesmerizing piece set to a text by Miguel Angel Asturias. *Forever and Sunsmell* sets a text by
e. e. cummings and asks the singer to "make any transposition that will give the high
notes an intense quality." A vibratoless tone is required throughout the piece. In
addition, a dancer and special lighting effects may be included in the performance.
The program ends with two familiar cycles by Bowles and Barber that rely on lovely,
long, legato phrases and a bit of humor.

Program 2 is much more dramatic in content and requires a voice with natural
power and a strong lower range. The Rorem cycle contains disjunct vocal lines, declamatory vocal writing that uses a dark text. It is a strong beginning for this recital.
Due to the work's wide intervalic leaps, an extreme dynamic range, and difficult-to-
hear pitches, the singer must have good tonal memory and an ability to sustain concentration. The other works on the program provide a variety of moods and vocal
usages. The two short pieces by Cage bring a bit of surprise to the concert hall. In *A
Flower* the singer uses no vibrato in alternation with a trembling vibrato sound. Trans-
pose the piece to any pitch that will keep the entire song low in the voice. The pianist

creates percussive effects with knuckles, fingers, and closed fists on the lid of the keyboard. In *Experiences 11* the voice sings an unaccompanied simple melody with no vibrato. Sections of sung text are alternated with humming. The two pieces work well together. The Carter, Ives (two contain whistling and recitation), and Duke groups contain a mixture of drama and humor and give the singer a chance to color the voice in myriad ways. The Bolcom songs draw upon the singer's acting skills and have several extended techniques, such as glissandos, shouts, speaking, and whispers.

PROGRAM I FOR BARITONE

Five Shakespeare Songs   Mario Castelnuovo-Tedesco* (1923)
  When daisies pied
  Tell me where is fancy bred
  It was a lover and his lass
  The poor soul sat sighing
  Hark! hark! the lark

(App. 18 minutes)
J. W. Chester, Ltd.

Ku Soto   Jacqueline Fontyn* (1990)

(App. 6 minutes)
POM

Four Songs (voice, clarinet, bassoon, piano)   William Bergsma (1981)
  This Is the Key to the Kingdom
  The Head from the Well of Life
  Frolic's Song
  Hokey, Pokey, Whiskey, Thum

(App. 12 minutes)
Galaxy Music Corp.

Mixco   Miriam Gideon (1957)

(App. 5 minutes)
American Composers Alliance

Forever and Sunsmell   John Cage* (1942)
  (voice and percussion)

(App. 5 minutes)
C. F. Peters

Despite and Still   Samuel Barber (1969)
  A Last Song
  My Lizard
  In the Wilderness
  Solitary Hotel
  Despite and Still

(App. 10 minutes)
G. Schirmer

Blue Mountain Ballads   Paul Bowles (1946)
  Heavenly Grass
  Lonesome Man
  Cabin
  Sugar in the Cane
                     (App. 10 minutes)
                      G. Schirmer

(*) experimental

PROGRAM 2 FOR BARITONE

War Scenes   Ned Rorem (1969)
  A Night Battle
  Specimen Case
  An Incident
  Inauguration Ball
  The Real War Will Never Get in the Books
                     (App. 20 minutes)
                     Boosey & Hawkes

A Flower (1950)   John Cage*
Experiences II (1948)
                     (App. 10 minutes)
                     C. F. Peters

Three Poems of Robert Frost   Elliot Carter (1942)
  Dust of Snow
  The Line-Gang
  The Rose Family
                     (App. 10 minutes)
             Associated Music Publishers

Memories (1897)   Charles Ives*
The Housatonic at Stockbridge (1921)
Slugging a Vampire (1902)
Charlie Rutlage (1920)
                     (App. 12 minutes)
                     Merion Music, Inc.

I Ride the Black Horses (1949)   John Duke
                     G. Schirmer

Luke Havergal (1948)
Richard Cory (1948)
Miniver Cheevy (1948)
                     Carl Fischer
          (App. 15 minutes for the group)

He Tipped the Waiter (1977)   William Bolcom*
Song of Black Max (1978)

> (App. 8 minutes)
> from *Cabaret Songs*
> Marks Music Co.

(*) experimental

SUGGESTED REPERTOIRE

Twentieth-century repertoire for the solo voice covers a wide stylistic range from traditional to experimental. Many fine composers of the period wrote numerous vocal works in a traditional style that are now considered standard repertoire. There are several good sources for that information. For the purpose of this listing, only those experimental pieces that use verbal vocal color indications, improvisation, novel notations, stage directions, multimedia effects, electronics, or extended vocal techniques were chosen. The list includes works that develop tonal memory and independence, works to develop humor and elicit audience response, and works that develop an ability to portray serious dramatic subjects.

This compilation by no means includes all twentieth-century works or composers who used extended vocal techniques, theatrics, or multimedia sources and other experimental ideas in their music. Rather, it offers a *starting point* for the investigation of such literature. It includes a cross section of musical trends, treatments, and uses of the voice; various instrumental and vocal combinations; and theatrical works requiring lighting, stage direction, and/or costumes. Incorporating a work or two from this list on an otherwise traditional recital would provide great vocal and dramatic contrast.

Works are listed in two categories: (1) repertoire for voice and one instrument; and (2) chamber works and monodramas. In some cases, pieces listed for one voice type or gender may also be sung by others, since some works are designated for *any voice type, high, medium, or low voice*. Those are indicated where appropriate. The compositions included as chamber works involve at least three performers and/or instruments. Any work described as a monodrama has been designated as such by the composer.

A level of difficulty has been assigned to each selection. It is a generalized, nonspecific ranking. However, several factors were taken into consideration when assigning a ranking for individual pieces: (1) the number and complexity of novel notational gestures present; (2) the compositional organization and its effect on the rehearsal process and ensemble coordination; (3) the intricacies of diction declamation, pitch relationships, rhythmic movement, and vocal interpretation; (4) the addition of multimedia or stage events and stage movement with or without props; (5) the requirement for the singer to play instruments or synchronize with electronically produced sounds; and (6) the presence of improvisatory elements or indeterminacy in the score.

The difficulty ratings of *moderately easy*, *moderately difficult*, *difficult*, and *very difficult* are meant to show in subjective and general terms how many of the items listed above are present in the score. Those scores using the fewest nontraditional concepts and the simplest, most straightforward vocal writing are ranked as *moderately easy*, while those with the largest number of unfamiliar concepts and numerous vocal/technical difficulties are ranked as *very difficult*, with numerous pieces ranked in between. No works are listed as *easy* due to the decision not to include works for beginning singers. All works have significant benefit for public performance. The easiest pieces are suggestive of repertoire for the serious student who has a good background in traditional repertoire and has achieved a moderately confident vocal technique. Other works are suggested for all levels of training, culminating with the professional performer. There is something for every level of vocal training except beginners.

The works are drawn from a variety of sources. Some pieces are published, and publishers are listed when available. Other works may be found by contacting the composer through one of the sources listed in appendix C. Some works may be available only from library sources if the composer is no longer living and the work is not published. Information concerning publication and availability can change rapidly. You may have to check several sources to find the status of each work. All works are for voice and piano unless otherwise designated.

REPERTOIRE FOR VOICE AND ONE INSTRUMENT: SONGS, SONG CYCLES, AND EXTENDED WORKS

James Aikman: "Spring Is Purple Jewelry." Anonymous text. Published by G. Schirmer as part of *The Art Song Collection, 1996 Edition*. A short, three-minute song that contains numerous glissando connections, numerous meter changes, verbal vocal coloration directions, and humming. A very effective, atmospheric song about spring. Its sparse and clean, angular vocal lines cover a wide vocal and dynamic range. Mezzo or soprano. *Moderately difficult*.

Violet Archer: *Epigrams* (1985). Text by David McCord. Available from Canadian Information Centre. An eight-minute, clever and charming cycle of six short songs that incorporate bitonality, a few extended techniques (shouts), and unaccompanied freely paced singing. Contains *ossia* at peaks in the phrase. Tenor or baritone. *Moderately easy*.

Dominick Argento: "War," song number six of *From the Diary of Virginia Woolf* (1975). Published by Boosey & Hawkes. This piece, based on vocal improvisation, is wide ranging in its vocal requirements. There are no extended techniques, but the voice must have tremendous control, moving quickly from staccato passages to long legato declamation while being suspended over a sparse accompaniment that depicts the austerity and devastation of war. The score contains numerous expressive and coloristic markings. Mezzo-soprano. *Very difficult*.

Milton Babbitt: *Phonemena* (1979). Published by C. F. Peters. A ten-minute piece for voice and piano. Built entirely on nontextual sonic vocabularies. The notation of vocal phonemes is diagrammed in the preface. A sparse piano part, angular voice line, intricate rhythms, wide vocal range, and nonsense syllables. This is a diction-and-rhythm workout for an advanced singer who has a great ear and loves to experiment. No extended vocal techniques. Soprano. *Very difficult.*

Milton Babbitt: "Sounds and Words." Published by Edward B. Marks Music Corporation in *New Vistas in Song.* A four-minute song built on vowels and consonants in various combinations. No complete words or traditional text. This is a wonderful exercise for diction. Phonetic symbols are given for vowel sounds used. The wide-ranging vocal line is quite angular and rhythmically difficult, with frequent meter changes and extreme contrasts in dynamics. A wonderful display piece for an advanced singer with an excellent sense of pitch. Soprano. *Difficult.*

Richard Rodney Bennett: *Nightpiece* (1972). Text by Charles Baudelaire. Published by Universal Edition. A hauntingly dramatic and coloristic piece for soprano and electronic tape. The tape was made by the composer and contains parts of the text, spoken and whispered. Exact synchronization with the events on the tape is not absolute except where arrows point to the voice part. This is a theatrical piece that uses whispering, *sprechstimme*, quasi parlando, glissandos, and a few shouts. Pitches are never exact but move through a very wide vocal range and require an enormous agility of voice, capable of great dynamic and dramatic contrasts. A wonderful piece for an advanced singer who loves to create an exotic atmosphere with the voice. Soprano or lyric mezzo. *Very difficult.*

Cathy Berberian: *Stripsody* (1966). Published by C. F. Peters. Musical graphics by Roberto Zamarin. A six-minute sound effects piece for solo voice. All notation is in the form of musical graphics. The humor of the graphics alone are enough to make this a one-of-a-kind piece. Short "scenes" contrast the basic material. It is a comical, improvisatory license to be a little "nuts." The singer uses a microphone and performs as if a radio soundman, without any props. Requires great acting ability, absolutely no inhibitions, and an ability to change the sound of the voice at will; there are no creative limits. Any voice type. *Moderately difficult.*

William Bergsma: *Six Songs* (1923). Texts by e. e. cummings. Published by Carl Fischer. Six diverse settings for high voice and piano. Mostly traditional vocal settings except for songs 3 and 5. These two songs contain some *sprechstimme*, unmetered sections, a bit of whispering, and one elaborate *wheeee* that slides up to the voice's highest note and ends on a trill. The music is at times rhythmically exciting and always sets off the text without distractions.) Tenor. *Moderately difficult.*

Luciano Berio: *Sequenza III* (1966). Text by Markus Kutter. Universal Edition. A nine-minute virtuosic display piece for unaccompanied solo voice. Written for Cathy Berberian. It explores the multitude of possibilities involved in singing, speaking, and everyday sounds from coughing and laughing to normal singing. A theatrical work built on several short dramatic cycles that tend to begin with tense muttering sounds and end on beautiful long tones. Very emotional and dramatically complex. Soprano or lyric mezzo. *Very difficult.*

Leonard Bernstein: *I Hate Music* (1943). Published by Warner Brothers Publications. A sophisticated, short group of "Five Kid Songs" containing numerous acting directions and verbal expression markings for vocal coloration and attitude. Numerous meter changes and some sections without meter, freely improvised. One short spoken section of text. Otherwise traditional in its use of the voice. Soprano or lyric mezzo. *Moderately difficult.*

David Blake: *Beata l'alma* (1966). Text by Herbert Read. Published by Novello. This twelve-minute work is a tour de force for the pianist and very demanding for the singer. Numerous special effects and coloristic vocal changes must be rehearsed prior to putting the voice and piano together. There is some free notation for the voice part. This twelve-tone composition contains two large poetic sections divided by a piano solo, as well as a few sections with a rather high tessitura for the voice. Tenor. *Very difficult.*

William Bolcom: "Amor," "Surprise," and "Toothbrush Time" from *Cabaret Songs* (1985). Texts by Arnold Weinstein. Published by Edward B. Marks Music Co. A cross between lounge singing and a concert approach. Develops projection of vivid characters and uses jazz, blues, and other popular styles, as well as some scat singing, speaking, *sprechstimme*, glissandos, and short vocal effects. Great acting pieces! Mezzo or soprano. *Moderately difficult.*

William Bolcom: "He Tipped the Waiter" and "Song of Black Max" from *Cabaret Songs*. Clever lyrics by Arnold Weinstein. Published by Edward B. Marks Music Co. Full of strong personality development and dramatic contrast. Contain glissandos, shouts, speaking, and whispers. To be sung in a somewhat spoken tone, not an operatic style. Baritone or tenor. *Moderately difficult.*

Victoria Bond: *Peter Quince at the Clavier* (1978). Text by Wallace Stevens. Published by Seesaw Music Corporation. The singer also plays wind chimes, triangle, tambourine, gong, and cymbal. A theatrical stage piece. Develops projection of dramatic ideas while creating atmospheric vocal sounds and ability to cope with a variety of stage events. Soprano or lyric mezzo. *Difficult.*

Victoria Bond: *Scat 2* (1984). Seesaw Music Corporation. An example of the merging of musical styles. This four-minute piece relies on characteristic rhythms and phrasing of jazz. It is a classically composed improvisation for trumpet and soprano. The vocalist sings in a scat style with freely invented nonsense syllables as a text. Rhythmically complex. No extended techniques for the voice or trumpet. A real audience pleaser and fun to sing. Soprano or lyric mezzo. *Moderately difficult.*

Elliot Borishansky: *Mother Goose and Co.* (1988). Available from composer. Five short, delightful songs of varying moods for voice and piano. Light, humorous, and full of whimsy, delicacy, and opportunities for acting with a guaranteed audience response. A variety of colors and moods. The work is a perfect study in pronunciation, enunciation, and articulation. Tonal music with a few *sprechstimme* tones, a bit of "sobbing," and a lot of "tongue-in-cheek". Mezzo or soprano. *Moderately easy.*

Benjamin Britten: *Cabaret Songs* (1937). Texts by W. H. Auden. Published by Faber Music Limited. A wonderful set of five songs built on blues, jazz, and other popular idioms. Approximately twenty minutes long. Primarily a traditional use of the voice with a few incidents of *sprechstimme*, exaggerated glissandos, and whistling and some quasi recitation. A wide vocal range with exceptional opportunities for a theatrical approach to art song. Lyric mezzo or soprano with good chest tones. *Moderately difficult.*

David Burge: *Life Begins at Forty* (1998). Text by composer. Available from composer. A twenty-minute cycle of five songs written for actress/singer Rolly Fanton. The texts, thoughtful and hilarious insights of a "mature woman," eloquently delve into the past and present choices of a woman who has seen and felt the gamut of life's experiences. Some songs are conversational and percussive, with rollicking rhythms, while others are poignant, beautiful, and personal. Mostly traditional song-style but contains jazz "licks," spoken phrases, sprechstimme, florid passages, and trills. For a singer who can emphasize the "chatty" feeling of much of this music. Soprano or lyric mezzo. *Moderately difficult.*

David Burge: *A Song of Sixpence* (1969). Text by composer. Tetra Music Corp, Alexander Broude, Inc. A five-minute song that includes a preset stage. The singer plays a small Chinese gong and an Indian sarna bell. The text is composed of nonsense syllables, English words interspersed with Italian and Japanese sounds. Extended techniques include sprechstimme and glissandi. Soprano or lyric mezzo. *Moderately difficult.*

John Cage: *Aria* (1958). Published by C. F. Peters. A musical improvisation of indeterminate length. Numerous extended techniques: tongue clucks, sprechstimme, throaty sound, wide vibrato, straight tone, nasality, vocal colorations. Can be sung in whole or in part with any instrument(s) included for the "black square" notation. Any voice type. *Moderately difficult.*

John Cage: "Experiences II: Solo" (1945–1948). Text by e. e. cummings. Published by Peters. A three-minute a cappella song that is part of a larger work. Can be transposed if done without part I of *Experiences.* Contains traditional singing, humming, straight tone. A good work for teaching ear training, independence, and a sense of inner pacing. Any voice type. *Moderately easy.*

John Cage: "A Flower" (1950). Published by C. F. Peters. A four-minute song for voice and closed piano. Built on sonic vocabularies, with no complete words, just vowels and consonants moving randomly between half steps and whole steps. Calls for straight tone and vocal sound effects, such as pigeon and duck sounds. Otherwise, a simple vocalise that can be transposed to any vocal range, but should be kept low in tessitura. The pianist plays no pitches, only percussive sounds on the outside of the piano. A good beginning piece for ear training and development of imagination. Any voice type. *Moderately easy.*

John Cage: *She Is Asleep II: Duet* (1943). Published by C. F. Peters. A five-minute vocalise for voice and prepared piano. Part of a larger work. To be sung without vibrato, except where indicated, and then exaggeratedly. Specific vowels are suggested for the vocalise. A good piece for the development of vocal flexibility and legato with minimal extended techniques. Any voice type. *Moderately easy.*

John Cage: "The Wonderful Widow of Eighteen Springs" (1961). Text by James Joyce. Published by C. F. Peters. A two-minute, lovely song for voice and closed piano using slow glissandos. Ideal for a young singer who wants to build steadiness and control. Can be transposed to any key but should be sung in a medium or low and comfortable range. Any female voice type. *Moderately easy.*

John Casken: *La Orana, Gauguin* (1978). Text by the composer. Published by Schott & Co., Ltd. A fourteen-minute song cycle for voice and piano. Covers a wide vocal range. Requires excellent musicianship and a good sense of pacing and dramatics. Many inventive notational devices that are now familiar to most who sing this kind of repertoire. Contains sections of flourishes and uncoordinated musical movement between voice and piano. Quarter tones, glissandos, sprechstimme, nonvibrato, and numerous coloristic markings are present in the vocal line. Soprano. *Difficult.*

Mario Castelnuovo-Tedesco: "The Poor Soul Sat Sighing" from *Five Shakespeare Songs, Set 1* (1923). Published by J. & W. Chester, Ltd. This is the only song in the set that contains any unusual vocal techniques. The four-minute piece is primarily developed through a lyrical singing style but incorporates two highly effective half-spoken, quasi-parlato sections that are notated with exact pitches. A very effective use of vocal declamation that brings out the question-and-answer aspects of the text. An excellent song for the development of vocal color contrast and acting out different characters within one song. Baritone or contralto. *Moderately difficult.*

Eric Chasalow: *The Furies* (1984). Text by Anne Sexton. Available from the Association for the Promotion of New Music (APNM). A thirteen-minute work for high voice and electronic tape. Extended techniques include whispering and speaking. Soprano or tenor. *Difficult.*

Barney Childs: *Lanterns and Candlelight* (1975). Published by Smith Publications. A five-minute piece for soprano or mezzo and marimba. The composer gives a diagram of the stage setup on the cover and suggests that the singer sit behind and stage left of the marimba. Vocal display and improvisation are foremost. The voice presents several contrasting qualities and moods, all built on the jazz idiom. Childs uses a quote from Orlando Gibbons's "The Cries of London" to open the piece. When syllables are sung, they should be blurred. Sometimes the voice hums, while at other times it sings quiet, bluesy, improvised syllables over approximated pitches. There are moments of quietude and virtuosic display for both musicians. Mezzo or soprano. *Moderately difficult.*

Lyell Cresswell: *Eight Shaker Songs* (1985). Nineteenth-century Shaker texts. Scottish Music Information Centre. A fifteen-minute song cycle of varying difficulty for voice and piano, some songs virtuosic and some quite simple in approach. Contains speaking, shouting, *sprechstimme*, glissandos, and a wide vocal and dynamic range. The singer should have a natural resonance and a full, strong voice throughout the range to avoid overexertion. Tenor or soprano. *Moderately difficult.*

George Crumb: *Apparition: Elegiac Songs and Vocalises for Soprano and Amplified Piano* (1979). Text by Walt Whitman. Published by C. F. Peters. A marvelously atmospheric piece for soprano and amplified piano, about twenty minutes long. A combination of vocalises using IPA phonemes, traditional texts, improvisation, approximate time values, a cappella singing, a few vocal effects, and vocal color markings. Requires an exceptional ear, great flexibility of voice and emotion, plus a willingness to improvise and feel almost total freedom when connecting with the pianist. Much of the work relies on approximate time valuation and nonsynchronization of piano and voice. Some vocal sections are unaccompanied. Each section is emotionally and vocally different. At times the voice sings beautiful languid phrases, while at others it is required to make quick birdlike sounds, dramatic outbursts, or fantastic roulades of tone from the lowest note to the highest in the voice. A highly dramatic, hypnotic work, unforgettable for performers and listeners. Crumb provides plenty of information both in the preface and within the score to enable both singer and pianist to realize his notation. Soprano or mezzo. *Very difficult.*

Tina Davidson: *Five Songs* (1975). Native Indian texts. Beyond Blue Horizon Music. Twelve minutes long. Beautiful, haunting songs with delicate textures created through a variety of vocal and instrumental extended techniques, as well as traditional playing and singing. Contains speaking, slow glissandos, straight tone, exaggerated vibrato, and whispering. Soprano or lyric mezzo. *Moderately difficult.*

Tina Davidson: *Shadow Grief* (1983). Text by Eva Davidson. Available from composer or Beyond Blue Horizon Music. A twelve-minute work for mezzo-soprano and two-channel prerecorded tape. The taped accompaniment is synchronized rhythmically with the voice and written in normal metrical notation. The voice part combines normal singing with nontextual sonic vocabularies, vowel morphing, occasional glissandos, and indications for the use of a wide vibrato. The text and music provide effective expressive contrasts. Mezzo-soprano. *Moderately difficult.*

Tina Davidson: *To Understand Weeping* (1980). Text by Giacomo Balla. Beyond Blue Horizon Music. An eight-minute piece written for soprano and tape. The singer makes a two-channel tape recording of Voice II and Voice III in the score. Voice I is to be performed live, with the other two voices coming from speakers located behind the audience on each side of the performing space, to create an illusion of three separate voices surrounding the audience. Sometimes the voice line contains a one-line staff, indicating the middle of the voice. All notes on this staff are approximate and within her singing range unless otherwise notated. Contains humming, normal singing, glissandos, *sprechstimme*, consonant repetitions, audible inhalation, speaking, whispering, and numerous directions for vocal inflection of the text. A very effective, unique piece. Soprano or mezzo-soprano. *Difficult.*

Violeta Dinescu: *Euraculos* (1980). Text by Ion Caraion. Published by Ricordi. A ten-minute piece for mezzo-soprano and B-flat clarinet. In Romanian with French and German translations. A display piece for both instruments. Quite experimental in concept. Nonmetered, freely interpreted music with novel notational devices. Some sections in proportional notation. The voice line is composed of many exotic sounds and techniques: notated *sprechstimme*, glissandos, indeterminate pitches, and numerous coloristic markings. The interpretation of the unusual notational devices is explained in the back of the score. A wonderful piece for an advanced singer who can maneuver well between registers and loves to experiment. Mezzo-soprano. *Difficult.*

Jacqueline Fontyn: *Ephémères* (1979). Poems by Robert Guiette. Published by POM. An eighteen-minute work in six parts. Comes in two versions: mezzo soprano and orchestra, and mezzo soprano and piano. Angular vocal lines, numerous meter changes, intricate rhythms, some novel notational devices that are explained in the preface. The vocal part contains normal singing, indeterminate pitches, glissandos, straight tone, and speaking in rhythm. Mezzo soprano or lyric soprano. *Difficult.*

Jacqueline Fontyn: *Ku Soko* (1990). Text by the composer in Swahili with collaboration of Doctor Ntihi Nyurwa M. Published by POM. A six-minute work in three versions. Independent vocal lines have been written so that it can be done by soprano, mezzo, or baritone. The singer also plays a few small percussion instruments. All novel notational gestures are explained thoroughly in the preface. Contains parlando, glissandos, exaggerated vibrato, approximate pitches, *sprechstimme*, and intoning. Baritone, mezzo, or soprano. *Difficult.*

Jacqueline Fontyn: *Pro and Antiverbes* (1984). Published by POM. A twelve-minute experimental piece for soprano and cello. Very colorful, hypnotic work in seven short sections, some quite serious, others humorous. Uses both English and French. The singer is required to play several small percussion instruments. Numerous vocal effects, extended techniques, and new notational devices in the score. Built on overall metric freedom and spontaneity and the use of seminal rhythmic patterns to hold the work together. Nontextual sonic vocabularies, glissandos, syllabic repetition, approximate pitches, improvisation, parlando, and *sprechstimme*. A fantastic display piece for two fine musicians. Soprano or lyric mezzo. *Very difficult.*

Don Freund: *Playthings of the Wind* (1975). Available from composer. Text taken from Carl Sandburg's "Four Preludes on Playthings of the Wind." An inventive, playful, ten-minute piece for soprano and piano. The voice is given numerous types of declamation and vocal effects: vowel morphing; humming derived from consonant sources; descriptive interpretative directions, such as *dry* and *mechanical*; unmetered movement; glissandos; extremely wide vocal range; syllabic and consonant repetition; indeterminacy; blues style; showy a cappella cadenzas; and beautiful legato cantabile singing. It has everything! Soprano or lyric mezzo. *Difficult*.

Jack Gottlieb: *Haiku Souvenirs* (1978). Text by Leonard Bernstein. Published by Boosey & Hawkes. Five short pieces for voice and piano. Delicate texture with some singing into the piano, a little *sprechstimme*. Memorable. Soprano or mezzo. *Moderately easy*.

Darrell Handel: *Lou and Ella's Pillow* (1987). Text by Marlyn Mainard. Available from composer. A delightful ten-minute cycle of three poems and a prologue for medium voice and piano. A good set for someone just embarking on the experimental process. Mostly traditional singing in a tonal context with a few extended techniques, such as slow glissandos, pitched *sprechstimme*, and some interesting possibilities for acting. Soprano, mezzo-soprano, tenor, or baritone. *Moderately easy*.

Darrell Handel: *Three Birdsongs* (1972). Text by Lyn Mainard Handel. Available from composer. A ten-minute set of three songs about birds for high voice and piano. A wind chime is also used to marvelous effect. It can be played by the singer or the page turner. This is an excellent set to use as an introduction to contemporary music. The musical concept is basically traditional, but modern elements give the pieces a freshness for both singer and pianist. The second song is entirely a cappella and free in tempo and dynamics, allowing the singer to experiment with pacing and dramatics. It uses only the wind chime as background. The vocal part progresses in a traditional manner with interpolations of parlando or intoning on a designated pitch, a few spoken words, and a quote from Charles Darwin that the singer reads at the end of the last song. Soprano or tenor. *Moderately easy*.

Charles Ives: "Charlie Rutlage" and "Like a Sick Eagle." From *114 Songs*. Published by Associated Music Publishers. "Charlie Rutlage" is a raucous, humorous, cowboy song using the spoken voice as well as normal patter singing and a little *sprechstimme*. "Like a Sick Eagle" is a short song to be sung in a weak and dragging way. Good for working on vocal color. Best for a medium female or male voice. *Moderately difficult*.

Charles Ives: "Memories." Published in *114 Songs*. A short, two-part song with differing sentiments for each. Contains whistling. Effective as part of a group or as an encore. Baritone, tenor, mezzo, or soprano. *Moderately Easy*.

Jean Eichelberger Ivey: *Terminus* (1970). Published by Carl Fischer, Inc. Text by Ralph Waldo Emerson. A nine-minute, forty-five second piece for mezzo-soprano and two-channel tape. Contains extensive vocal coloration markings, glissandos, humming, and short segments of *sprechstimme*. Requires a good ear, since there are few pitch references on the tape. The tape does not require stopping and starting during the performance. The score does a good job in pointing out tape cues so that synchronization is fairly easy. A very effective, atmospheric piece for contrast on an otherwise traditional program. Mezzo-soprano. *Moderately difficult*.

Ping Jin: *Shan gui (The Hill Wraith)* (1999). Traditional Chinese ghost story from *Anthology of Chinese Literature*. Available from composer. An eight-minute piece for voice and pipa—a traditional, ancient Chinese stringed instrument. The work is in Chinese and combines lyrical singing with sections of *sprechstimme* and traditional Chinese opera style of singing. Tenor, soprano, lyric mezzo, or lyric baritone. *Moderately difficult.*

Jack Johnston: *Diverse Voices of Herrick* (1986). Text by Robert Herrick. Published by Leyerle Publications. This seventeen-minute song cycle is one of a kind. The voice is treated traditionally throughout, except for a few exaggerated portamenti. The ten songs were conceived as a set of "character songs," but some could be sung individually. Each song is written to be sung with a different accent, such as North British, upper-class Oxonian, Standard British, London Cockney, Scots, and Irish. Each text is carefully written out in the IPA to give an idea of the correct pronunciation of words. This is a marvelous exercise in diction and all of its variations in the English language, as well as a gem for developing personality and character portrayal. Baritone or mezzo soprano. *Moderately difficult.*

Penka Kouneva: *". . . when time is grown . . ." (Five Songs of Edwin Muir)* (1992–1993). Available from composer. An eighteen-minute song cycle for mezzo-soprano or dramatic soprano and piano, setting four poems about aspects of love and other experiences. The composition assimilates various musical styles and traditions from melismatic Medieval vocal genres to Baroque "rage arias," minimalism, folk music, and pop music (such as vibratoless singing, pitch bending and various slides, voice shaking, grace notes, and vocalization on various vowels. An unusual and memorable piece. Mezzo-soprano or dramatic soprano. *Moderately difficult.*

Ernst Krenek: "The Flea." Text by John Donne. Published by Edward B. Marks Music Corporation in *New Vistas in Song.* A three-minute song ranging from the cynical to the frenetic. The piano part is spare and contains a few unusual techniques for sound production. The voice line has a wide range and is mostly traditional in concept with an occasional exaggerated glissando. The complicated rhythmic structure relies on a mathematical system of movement rather than traditional meters. Explanations of all symbols and rhythmic movement are given in the score. Tenor. *Difficult.*

Christina Kuzmych: *Shapes and Sounds IV* (1983). Text by e. e. cummings. Available from the composer. A ten-minute piece for soprano and alto saxophone built on numerous extended vocal techniques and improvisatory musical movement. There are five sections, each with a contrasting musical and textual character. Each uses the voice in a different way. This unmetered, improvisatory music requires a willingness to experiment. Contains jazz elements, huge dramatic and dynamic contrasts, and vocal effects such as whispering, whistling, improvised humming, glissandos, syllabic repetition, nontextual sonic vocabularies, and tongue trills. The voice and saxophone often imitate each other in sound and effects. This is a fabulous display piece for both instruments, great fun to perform, and a real audience pleaser! Soprano or lyric mezzo. *Difficult.*

Nicola LeFanu: *But Stars Remaining* (1970). Text by C. Day Lewis. Novello & Co. Ltd. An eight-minute a cappella piece with subtle voice shadings, quarter tones, whispers, speaking, echo effects, repeated syllables, breathy tones, and proportional notation. A very imaginative text setting. Female voice. *Difficult.*

Nicola LeFanu: *IL Cantico Dei Cantici II* (1968). The Song of Songs, Ch. Two. Published by Novello & Co. Ltd. A dramatic scena for female voice, unaccompanied. A work for an advanced singer who has a good sense of pitch and a secure vocal technique. Quasi-recitative throughout with some use of quarter tones, three-quarter tones, glissando, pitched *sprechstimme*, and quickly changing meters with contrasting dramatic accents. Soprano or mezzo-soprano. *Difficult.*

Ruth Lomon: *A Fantasy Journey into the Mind of a Machine* (1985). Available from composer. Text taken from "The Policeman's Beard Is Half Constructed," computer prose and poetry by Racter. An inventive, fantastical display piece for soprano and saxophone. The two performers must be quite adventurous, and accomplished and comfortable in their own technique, as well as compatible with each other. Excellent directions for notation realization and performance in the preface. The six songs may be sung in any order. Numerous vocal effects and extended techniques, including glissandos, sprechstimme, glottal stops, wide vibrato, sudden vocal cutoffs, quarter tones and trills, syllabic repetition, muttering, laughter, and directions for physical actions. Great fun! Soprano or lyric mezzo. Difficult.

Ruth Lomon: "Poème Macabre" from *Songs of Remembrance* (1996). Text by Francois Wetterwald. Available from composer. An eight-minute song from a longer cycle on poems of the Holocaust for four voices : soprano, mezzo, tenor, baritone. The voice is treated in a traditional manner except for this one song, a dramatic piece built on contrasts of tone quality and declamation. Contains normal singing as well as exaggerated portamento, shouts, and sprechstimme. A very effective piece in a most unusual and memorable song cycle. Baritone. *Moderately difficult.*

Chet Mais: *Songs from the Summer of Dust* (1998). Available from composer. Text by Malcom Glass. A ten-minute song cycle consisting of four contrasting songs that use the voice and piano in inventive ways. All vocal lines are traditional in concept, often angular, sometimes chantlike, and always interesting. Two of the songs are rhythmically exciting and difficult. There are sections of unnotated normal vocal speaking alone and over piano accompaniment. Soprano or lyric mezzo. *Moderately difficult.*

Daniel Manneke: *Five Songs on English Poems* (1974). Texts by Walter Savage Landor, Gerard Manley Hopkins, Sir Walter Raleigh, William Drummond of Hawthornden, and Thomas Hood. Published by Donemus. A fine addition to the song cycle repertoire for low voice and either harpsichord, piano, or organ. Use of proportional notation in some songs. The voice part is given clear indications of the use of glissando, senza vibrato, heavy vibrato, sprechstimme, parlando, and speaking. Each song is unique in its delivery of vocal sound. Baritone or mezzo-soprano. *Moderately difficult.*

Roger Marsh: *A Little Snow* (1994). Text by Nicanor Parra, translated by Miller Williams. Published by Maecenas Music. A six-minute avant-garde piece for unaccompanied voice. A theatrical work with numerous vocal effects: sprechstimme, intoning, glissando, indeterminate pitch, and quarter tones. Contains a clear explanation of vocal effects in the preface. Tessitura is left to the singer. Any voice type. *Moderately difficult.*

Donald Martino: *Two Rilke Songs* (1961). Published by Ione Press: E. C. Schirmer, Sole Selling Agent. Text by Rainer Maria Rilke. Two short songs in German with a good English translation. The first song, "Die Laute" (The Lute), covers a wide vocal range with large skips and contains pitches to be sung with the mouth almost closed and one glissando. The second song, "Aus einer Sturmnacht VIII" (On a Stormy Night VIII), is quite different. The voice is independent from the piano and contains staccatos, parlando, and murmuring sounds. Marvelous short pieces for developing a good ear, independence, and connection of vocal registers over a wide vocal range. Mezzo-soprano. *Moderately difficult.*

Edward McGuire: *Prelude 8* (1981). Text by composer. Available from Scottish Music Information Centre. A ten-minute piece full of acoustical and musical surprises. For tenor and tape delay. Most effective when performed in a large space that has hard surfaces, such as stone or brick. A technician will need to operate equipment during the performance. Tenor. *Moderately difficult.*

Neil McKay: *There Once Was* (1989). Published by Leyerle Publications. Introduction and five humorous limericks in approximately eight minutes. A delightful work for students interested in contemporary styles. Very rhythmic, short pieces with clean lines in a medium range. There are a few spoken tones, a few plucked strings inside the piano, and a section of rhythmic knuckle knocking on the wood at the right end of the keyboard. The text settings give the singer a marvelous diction workout. Baritone or tenor. *Moderately easy.*

Edward Miller: *A Lullaby for Ben* (1979). Poem by Kathleen Lombardo. Available from American Composer's Alliance. A short work for female voice and marimba. The poem is fragmented, delicate, and reminiscent of childhood's sing-song playfulness. Delicate musical setting, with the marimba player using very soft mallets throughout. Primarily a traditional use of the voice. Numerous large leaps and moderately difficult pitch realizations within a vocal line that shifts quickly between lyricism, *sprechstimme*, humming, staccato, and speaking or whispering. A lovely duet of carefree abandon, mostly displaying a gentleness and thoughtfulness rarely found in works of such spontaneity. Mezzo or lyric soprano. *Moderately difficult.*

Ennio Morricone: *Wow!* (1993). Published by Edizione Suvini Zerboni-Milano. Available through Elkin Music International, Inc. A short, approximately five-minute, a cappella display piece built on vowel sounds vocal flourishes, trills, glissandos, and staccati. A great vocalise for tonal memory and improvisation practice. Mezzo or soprano. *Moderately difficult.*

Dexter Morrill: *Six Dark Questions* (1979). Text by George Hudson. Chenango Valley Press. A fourteen-minute piece for voice and computer. The voice has a dialogue with the computer that produces vocal sounds and speaking that were prerecorded and combined with the computer-generated sounds. Requires some stage movement and acting. The voice imitates animal sounds. It uses sound effects and contains both lyrical singing and *sprechstimme*. Soprano. *Moderately difficult.*

Anthony Payne: *Evening Land* (1981). Text by W. H. Auden. Published by Chester Music. An eighteen-minute song cycle for voice and piano. Requires an excellent pianist who can cope with complexities of rhythm and score reading. The voice part is a combination of smooth, beautiful lines and an effective use of *sprechstimme*, both pitched and unpitched, a few voiced whispers, an occasional quarter tone, and spoken tones. Soprano or mezzo-soprano. *Moderately difficult.*

Mel Powell: *Haiku Settings* (1961). Haiku texts. Published by G. Schirmer. A delicate, imaginative, seven-minute experimental song cycle that calls for a "light" voice quality throughout. Contains difficult-to-find pitches, angular movement, and quick changes from normal singing to extended techniques that include *sprechstimme*, glissandos, whispers, quasi speech, and indeterminate pitch. Optional pitches given in sections where pitch stays in the low range. Soprano, mezzo, or baritone. *Difficult.*

Gwyn Pritchard: *Enitharmon* (1974, revised 1984/85).Text by William Blake. British Music Information Centre. A seven-minute piece for voice and piano. Excellent description of vocal effects and notational devices listed in the preface. Sparse piano part using many effects inside the piano. Contains numerous kinds of experimental vocal writing similar to that invented by Berio in the 1960s, such as phonetic and syllabic declamation, syllabic repetition, glissandos, pitched speech, vowel morphing, and inward gasps or vocalization on inhalation. Requires an experienced singer who is adventurous and loves to experiment. Technically demanding! Soprano. *Very difficult.*

Bernard Rands: *Ballad 2* (1970). Text by Gilbert Sorrentino. Published by European American Music Distributors Corp. A nine-minute theater piece for voice and piano. Written for Cathy Berberian. One of a series of ballads featuring a specific element of vocal technique and attitude. The composer uses quotes from works by Brahms, Wolf, Berio, Satie, and Cage. For a virtuoso actress and performer. Stage movement is indicated for both singer and pianist. The preface contains excellent notes for performance. The singer is required to improvise. The singer and pianist are totally independent of each other and should appear to be unaware of each other throughout. Numerous novel notational devices. Contains proportional notation, sighs, whispers, a muffled yawn, normal speech, nontextual sonic vocabularies, tense muttering, dental tremolo-requiring the jaw to wobble a bit, shouting, and other antics found in an aerobics class. Soprano or mezzo-soprano. *Very difficult.*

Ernest Richardson: *The Fall of a Man-made Star* (1983). Text about war by composer. Available from composer. A six-minute work for voice and viola. Contains glissandos and whispers. Soprano. *Moderately easy.*

George Rochberg: *Eleven Songs for Mezzo-Soprano* (1973). Published by Theodore Presser. A twenty-minute song cycle with magical, atmospheric texts by Rochberg's son Paul, who died in 1964 at age twenty. The poems are fragments with a sparseness the elder Rochberg likens to that of William Blake. Each piece is unique in the use of the voice and the setting of the text. Some pieces are metrical, while others are quite free and improvisational. Great use of color and dramatic variation within a generally dark mood. Contains quarter tones, *sprechstimme*, numerous vocal color effects such as breathy or white sounds, exaggerated portamenti and slides, novel notations for accelerando and ritard, and rhythmic and dramatic improvisation. Rochberg gives a detailed description in the preface of several notational gestures characteristic of his style. Mezzo soprano. *Difficult.*

George Rochberg: *Songs in Praise of Krishna* (1970). Texts translated from the Bengali, edited by Edward C. Dimock Jr. and Denise Levertov. Published by Theodore Presser Co. A thirty-five-minute song cycle of fourteen exotic songs that follows the love story of the captivating and beautiful girl Radha and the god Krishna of ancient Indian legend. The songs are short and the voice is always used beautifully and carefully, yet colorfully. The singer is given explicit directions for the use of half-sung dark and heavy tones, glissandos, very thin tone, nonvibrato, quarter tones, free rhythmic movement, and coloristic tone production. Soprano. *Moderately difficult.*

Patsy Rogers: "Breathing" from *Five Songs from "Sonja"* (1992). Text by Marian Owens Lokvam. Published by Casio Publishing Company. A four-and-a-half-minute song from a beautiful and poignant song cycle. The cycle presents a traditional approach to musical organization and to the use of the voice throughout, except in this song. Along with long, flowing vocal lines, it contains several spoken lines. The singer speaks in a normal voice, simply, not overdramatized above a sonorous, harmonic accompaniment. This is a good opportunity to work on vocal inflection and projection of the speaking voice within a dramatic context. Soprano. *Moderately easy.*

Rhian Samuel: *In the Hall of Mirrors* (1984). Text by James Merrill. Published by Stainer & Bell. Approximately ten minutes long. For medium voice and piano. Coloristic for both voice and piano. Fanciful treatment of the text with dramatic expression markings and numerous vocal effects, such as whispering on pitch and without pitch, *sprechstimme*, glissandos, staccatos, speech-cries, normal and unmeasured improvisation for both voice and piano. Delicate treatment of the voice in all respects. Mezzo or soprano. *Moderately difficult.*

Rhian Samuel: *The Hare in the Moon* (1978, rev. 1979). Text by Ryokan. Published by Stainer & Bell. A six-minute Japanese folk tale for soprano and piano. The composer calls this piece a "narrative." The work also exists in a version for soprano, vibraphone, marimba, and double bass. It is the telling of a fascinating tale about the friendship of a monkey, a hare, and a fox. Their friendship comes to the attention of the "god who lives in eternal heaven," who decides to test their loyalty. Unfortunately, all does not end well. The piece has a magical atmosphere through angular vocal lines that switch from singing to speaking. Includes *sprechstimme*, both pitched an unpitched vocal declamation, and a few sparingly used vocal effects, such as glissandos and sobbing. The audience will be mesmerized if the singer is totally immersed in telling the tale. Soprano. *Moderately difficult.*

Rhian Samuel: *Songs of Earth and Air* (1983). Texts by Laurie Lee, W. H. Davies, Jon Silkin, and Kenneth Leslie. Published by Stainer & Bell. A twenty-minute song cycle for voice and piano. The four songs are intended to be performed as a group, but they may be performed singly or in pairs, songs 1 and 2, songs 3 and 4. This is truly beautiful, exotic, picturesque music and very gentle to the voice. There are some unusual vocal techniques, as well as novel notational devices. The piano and voice create an exotic atmosphere through conventional and experimental rhythmic and color devices. There are ad lib sections, indeterminate pitches, proportional notation contained in boxes, numerous coloristic and expression markings, vocal glissandos, *sprechstimme*, intoned speaking, an occasional straight tone, a bit of whispering, and some very slow glides between pitches. All in all, it is a tonic for the voice with exquisite musical results. Mezzo-soprano, lyric soprano, or baritone. *Moderately difficult.*

A. M. Sauerwein: "Northwest Passage" from *Shadow March* (1997). Text by Robert Louis Stevenson. Available from composer on Web site. The third song from a cycle of five songs for soprano and piano. This song is the only one containing any extended vocal techniques, and they are placed within a traditional compositional style. Some *sprechstimme* and half whispers. A marvelous set of songs for a high soprano. Good pieces for building legato and line in the voice, as well as character and mood development. Soprano. *Moderately easy.*

Gunther Schuller: "Meditation" (1960). Text by Gertrude Stein. Published by Edward B. Marks Music Corporation in *New Vistas in Song*. Three-minute song with pitch references, but requires vocal independence. Contains only one spoken phrase. This is a very effective piece when its numerous coloristic and dynamics changes are achieved. Mezzo or soprano. *Moderately difficult.*

Clare Shore: "I'm Nobody" from *Four Dickinson Songs* (1981). Text by Emily Dickinson. Published by Arsis Press. The second song from a delightful cycle of four songs for soprano and piano. This song is the only one with any extended techniques. It contains semiwhispering, one pitched spoken phrase, and some exaggerated portamenti. A good piece for introduction into extended techniques within a musically interesting atmosphere. The entire cycle is a gem for soprano. Soprano. *Moderately easy.*

Karen Thomas: *Cowboy Songs* (1985). Poems by e. e. cummings. Available from the composer in low and high keys. A ten-minute cycle of six short songs that develop great flexibility of personality and voice. A real audience pleaser and fun to sing. Contains humor, satire, speaking, *sprechstimme*, swagger, and a great angularity of rhythmic motion. Soprano or mezzo-soprano. *Moderately difficult.*

Persis Vehar: *From Buk's Battered Heart* (2000). Texts by Charles Bukowski. Available from composer. Six songs for bass and piano that beautifully capture the ironic, clever, sometimes heart-breaking images of the poems. The voice is used traditionally throughout, except for short intermittent sections of rhythmically notated, unpitched speaking and a couple of shouts. An effective work for a dramatic voice with the ability to bring off a wide range of emotion. Bass or bass-baritone. *Moderately difficult.*

Persis Vehar: *Nine Silences for Song* (1993). Haiku text by Michael Ehrenreich. Available from composer. A riveting, nine-minute, dramatic moment in time. The Haiku are spoken dramatically rather than being sung. Due to the general timbre of the piece, a singer with a medium-range speaking voice, either male or female, would be more dramatically effective. The composer has indicated precisely where each phrase is to be spoken, but the overall dramatic interpretation is left to the imagination of the narrator. Sometimes the phrases are spoken unaccompanied, while at other times the voice begins a line to be joined by the piano or vice versa. This is an outstanding work for piano as well. It requires a good technician with an interest in using a few extended techniques for special effect. Medium speaking voice (male or female). *Moderately easy.*

Persis Vehar: "Second Butterfly" and "Final Butterfly" from *The Butterfly Songs* (1997). Poems by Arthur Axlerod. Available from composer. Two songs from a fifteen-minute, four song cycle that uses the voice in a rather traditional way. These two are the only songs that have any extended vocal techniques. They contain slow glissandos, a few spoken words, and whispering. The songs range from the intimacy and delicacy of "Second Butterfly" to the dramatic and broadly drawn lines of "Final Butterfly" with moods in between. Very singable, containing just enough vocal extensions for interest without creating stress for the uninitiated singer. Mezzo-soprano. *Moderately difficult.*

Persis Vehar: *Women, Women* (1979). Poems by May Swenson, Anne Waldman, and Barbara Greenberg. Leyerle Publications. Short cycle, around ten minutes, containing three songs using musical ideas and texts that readily bring to mind memorable female characters. Songs 1 and 3 show a subtle humor, while song 2 is contemplative. All contain inventive extended vocal techniques, such as speaking and some inventive applications of *sprechstimme*, creating a wide variety of vocal colorations. Mezzo or soprano. *Moderately difficult.*

Elizabeth Vercoe: *Irreveries from Sappho* (1982). Published by Arsis Press. A short song cycle of about ten minutes. Three intellectually humorous pieces built on popular musical idioms: ragtime, blues, and boogie. Wickedly satirical and full of musical jokes and parodies. Contains a few segments of *sprechstimme*, glissandos, and exaggerated portamenti. Marvelous for personality development and vocal flexibility. Soprano or mezzo. *Moderately difficult.*

Elizabeth Vercoe: *Nine Epigrams from Poor Richard* (1986). Available from composer or the American Music Center. A very inventive, fanciful, eight-minute piece for voice and electronic tape built entirely on sonic vocabularies. The tape is prepared by the singer and directions are given that involve a written-out series of repeated words and lines prepared by the composer. The sung vocal line contains vowel morphing, *sprechstimme*, exaggerated vibrato, glissandos, and numerous vocal effects, such as panting, whistles, and tongue clicks. Any voice type. *Moderately difficult.*

Elizabeth Vercoe: *The Varieties of Amorous Experience* (1994). Texts by Chaucer, Thomas Flatman, Shakespeare, and Coventry Patmore. Available from composer. A twelve-minute song cycle about love. The voice is used traditionally most of the time, with occasional adventures into varieties of vocal declamation. The second song, "An Appeal to Cats in the Business of Love," contains most of the extended techniques: quasi recitative, plaintive meows, and a long slow glissando at the end. A marvelous set of songs in a medium-high tessitura for a lyric voice with plenty of agility. Good for developing stage deportment, acting ability, and vocal color contrast. Soprano or lyric mezzo. *Difficult.*

Jeffrey Wood: *MCMXIV* ("1914") (1985). Available from composer. Six songs for tenor and piano on various texts about the First World War. Thirty minutes long. A major work for mature voice with capabilities of great dramatic import as well as subtle expression. The vocal writing is traditional, with no avant-garde techniques other than a few spoken words. Tenor. *Very difficult.*

Ramon Zupko: *Voices* (1972). Unpublished. American Music Center. A twelve-minute, multisound media piece for amplified soprano and four-channel magnetic tape. The preface gives concise descriptions of what to expect on the tape and realization of all notation for the soprano. There is also a diagram of the stage picture and a list of equipment required. The fascinating vocal part is built totally on nontextual sonic vocabularies. It includes vowel morphing, humming, IPA syllabic repetition, straight tones, indeterminate pitches, slightly breathy tones, quasi laughing, slow glissandos, pitched shouts, whispering, and heavy breathing into the microphone. One of the most effective electronic pieces in the repertoire. Mezzo-soprano. *Difficult.*

CHAMBER WORKS AND MONODRAMAS

Thomas Albert: *A Maze with Grace* (1975). American Music Center. A captivating chance piece for voice and indeterminate ensemble. The length can vary according to the number of repetitions of certain key elements within the work. The vocal part is based on the phonemes present in the text of "Amazing Grace, How Sweet the Sound." The score uses the IPA. The singer reads the phonemes from left to right, as usual, but reads the gestures they accompany from right to left. The musical gestures are also from the hymn tune. The work could involve as many players as desired. Each player must get through a maze, reaching the center. When all have reached the center, the tune "Amazing Grace" is played and sung. It is a total surprise to the audience. Any voice type. *Moderately easy.*

Elizabeth Alexander: *My Aunt Gives Me a Clarinet Lesson* (2001). Seafarer Press. Text by Gregory Djanikian. A twelve-minute scene for soprano, flute, clarinet, percussion, violin, cello, and piano. A humorous retelling of one's first clarinet lesson; replicates the menagerie of animal sounds that emanate from the instrument. The singer plays the part of a narrator, aunt and student, during which she uses some *sprechstimme* and plays a duck call. Soprano or lyric mezzo. *Moderately difficult.*

Elizabeth R. Austin: *Homage for Hildegard* (1997). Text from Antiphon No. 16, "Caritas Abundat," by Hildegard von Bingen. American Composer's Alliance. A nineteen-minute work in five movements for mezzo-soprano, baritone, flute, clarinet in B flat, percussion, and piano. Includes proportional notation for the entire ensemble.

The mezzo also participates in a visual and theatrical gesture, taking a large rainstick and rotating it slowly at the center of the ensemble. This occurs midway through the piece, as the work is proportionally designed on the basis of a star shape, quoting the central textual figure. Mezzo-soprano and baritone. *Moderately difficult.*

Ross Bauer: *Eskimo Songs* (1997). Native texts. Published by C. F. Peters. A ten-minute work for medium voice, flute, cello, and piano that includes whispering and speaking. Mezzo-soprano. *Moderately easy.*

Luciano Berio: *Circles* (1960). Text by e. e. cummings. Published by Universal Edition. An eighteen-minute theater piece for female voice, harp, and two percussionists. Instrumental lines reflect the phonetic sounds of the text and are grouped accordingly. The text setting develops an imperceptible transition from spoken to sung elements in a syllabic and vocalized close connection between music and speech. The score provides an intricate stage diagram for all instruments and voice. At the beginning, the singer stands alone, with instruments behind her, almost accompanying the voice. Then she gradually walks from one instrumental group to another and merges with their sounds and musical material. Finally, all comes full circle and the four performers become one. Everything in the piece is circular: use of text, sequence of effects, and sound sources. The vocal part moves in quick, delicate graces that contain normal singing, glissandi, indeterminate pitches and rhythms, humming, speaking, intoning, frame notation, improvisation, and sonic vocabularies built on consonants that have been dissected from words in the text. Pitch references are scarce. The percussionists also sing at the end of the piece. An extravagant, exotic piece with theatrical elements and a fantastical atmosphere. Soprano or lyric mezzo. *Very difficult.*

Luciano Berio: *O King* (1970). Published by Universal Edition. A five-minute work for soprano, flute, clarinet, violin, cello, and piano. The piece was written shortly after the death of Martin Luther King, and the entire text consists of "O, Martin Luther King." For most of the work, the soprano sings only the vowels of the text in what is primarily a unison line with the five instruments. The melodic line is varied by a constant changing of the combination of instruments that double the soprano and by variations in singing and playing techniques, such as tremolo from the soprano. Soprano or lyric mezzo. *Moderately difficult.*

Andrew Bishop: *The Soccer Fields of Sarajevo; Five Songs on Poems by Frank DeSanto* (1994). Available from University of Michigan Absolute Publications. A twenty-minute work for soprano, alto saxophone, and piano. Written for the Sotto Voce Trio—Dorothy Crum, Jean Lansing, and Sylvia Coats. Five pieces based on the ethnic conflicts that transformed the 1992 soccer field into a graveyard in former Yugoslavia. Uses *sprechstimme*, haunting melodies between the saxophone and voice, and minimal lighting effects. Soprano or lyric mezzo. *Difficult.*

Victoria Bond: *Mirror, Mirror* (1969). Poem by Michael Halprin based on Lewis Carroll's "Alice Through the Looking Glass." Published by Seesaw Music Corp. A two-and-a-half-minute piece for soprano, flute, and viola. A flight of fancy written in a delicate, lyrical, sparse texture. A wide vocal range incorporating normal singing with interspersed *sprechstimme*. Requires a good sense of rhythm and pitch. Soprano or lyric mezzo. *Moderately difficult.*

Victoria Bond: *Molly Manybloom* (1990). Published by Merion Music, Inc. Theodore Presser, Sole Representative. A major work, forty minutes long, for soprano and string quartet. Uses a dramatic, sometimes shocking text taken from James Joyce's

Ulysses. An intricately woven, intellectual work. The statements are at times bawdy, contemplative, humorous, feminist, and touchingly erotic. There is a prologue and sixteen sections using different combinations of instruments with the voice. The voice is treated in a traditional manner with short sections of glissandos, exaggerated portamentos, ad lib nonmetered recitative, numerous dramatic and coloristic directions, humming, whispering, and *sprechstimme.* Requires vocal stamina and solid technique. For an adventurous and bold singer. Soprano. *Very difficult.*

Pierre Boulez: *Le Marteau sans maitre* ("The hammer unmastered") (1952–1954). Text by René Char. Published by Universal Edition. A thirty-five-minute chamber work for contralto voice, flute, vibraphone, viola, guitar, marimba, and a battery of percussion instruments—one player. Built on serial techniques, the work is composed in nine movements, alternating purely instrumental pieces with songs, each featuring the unique sound of its own instrumental grouping. The voice appears in movements 3, 5, 6, and 9. Movements 3 and 6 use the voice in a traditional manner. There are a few *sprechstimme* tones and glissandos in movement 5. In movement 9 the voice is used in various singing styles. There are glissandos, long sections of *sprechstimme,* extensive humming, intoning on approximate pitches, and a direction to be *just one of the instruments,* not a soloist, but a collaborator of color design with the other instruments. The voice part lies in a medium-to-low tessitura throughout and is shimmering and luscious, though there are disjunct intervals. The mostly quiet, melismatic, and sustained vocal part contains sudden changes of register and frequent distortion of normal word inflection. The singer needs to have the ability to pick pitches from nowhere and to relate to ever-changing rhythmic and directional pulses and accents. The feeling of the piece is one of disconnection, as if being in limbo, in midair. It is extremely abstract with constantly changing meters. The work contains references to music of Bali and Africa and is built on contrasts of sound qualities with other elements: words, free and metric rhythms, silence, and instrumental qualities—sustaining and percussive diversities. Contralto, mezzo-soprano, or countertenor. *Very difficult.*

Benjamin Britten: *Canticle III (Still Falls the Rain), Op.* 55 (1954). Text by Edith Sitwell. Published by Boosey & Hawkes. A twelve-minute work for tenor, horn, and piano. The text is presented in the form of recitatives, culminating in a section of *sprechstimme* at the climactic point when the poet quotes a phrase from the end of Christopher Marlowe's play Doctor Faustus. The horn and piano play interludes between the recitatives. Tenor. *Difficult.*

John Cage: *Forever and Sunsmell* (1942). Text by e. e. cummings. Published by C. F. Peters. A five-minute piece for voice and percussion duo. Mostly traditional use of the voice. The singer may make any transposition that will give the written high E an intense quality. Use of straight tone and glissandos. A good piece for someone just beginning to experiment with this style. Any voice type. *Moderately easy.*

Laura Clayton: *Cree Songs to the Newborn* (1978). Published by C. F. Peters. A fifteen-minute chamber piece for soprano or mezzo and chamber ensemble consisting of two flutes, two violoncellos, contrabass, celeste, harp, and a battery of percussion instruments requiring two players. The voice sings in both Cree and English. The musical sounds created by the Cree language, an unwritten language, are fascinating. The language sounds are translated into phonetics in the preface. The look of the text is much like sonic vocabularies combined with English words and phrases. The voice is never overwhelmed by the ensemble and often sings alone, relying on the warm, humming quality of the language. Mostly traditional vocal part with only a few glissandos, grace notes, and staccatos. Numerous color references, at times mysterious, nasal, or frail. Some use of straight tone. An exciting, memorable work. Soprano or lyric mezzo. Difficult.

Michael Colgrass: *New People* (1969). Published by Carl Fischer, Inc. An eighteen-minute work for mezzo, viola, and piano. Contains nontextual sonic vocabularies, intoning, recitation. Disquieting atmosphere. Mezzo. Difficult.

Henry Cowell: *Vocalise* (1964). Published by C. F. Peters. An eight-minute vocalise for soprano, flute, and piano. The composer suggests using "ah" throughout. The six contrasting sections contain rhythmical freedom and rubato as well as more precise rhythmic flow. The vocal line is basically traditional with a few sections of modern notation for accents that emphasize certain metric beats. These accents must be stressed heavily by sudden thrusts of the diaphragm. The coordination is a bit tricky. The plaintive beauty of the piece is memorable. It is a wonderful vocalise to strengthen technique and equality of vocal registers. Soprano or lyric mezzo. Moderately difficult.

George Crumb: *Ancient Voices of Children* (1970). Texts by Federico García Lorca in Spanish. Published by C. F. Peters. A thirty-minute theatrical chamber work for soprano, boy soprano, oboe, mandolin, harp, electric piano, and percussion. The soprano sings a vocalise based purely on phonetic sounds. It is sung into an amplified piano, producing a marvelous echo effect. The piece uses the voice in a variety of singing and speaking styles, from virtuosic displays to intimately lyrical folklike melodies. Contains pitched speaking, tongue clucks, whispered tones, tongue trills, shouts, singing of indeterminate pitches and improvised pitches, and what the composer terms "half-sung, *sprechstimme*." Voice and instrumental parts are unmetered in the traditional sense. One must develop a natural flow within each musical section according to note length indications, physical spacing of vocal and instrumental parts, indications of breaks for several seconds, rests,and tempo markings. Soprano or mezzo. Difficult.

George Crumb: *Madrigals, Book I* (1965). Published by C. F. Peters. Texts by Federico García Lorca. A nine-minute work in three fragments for soprano, vibraphone, and contrabass. Unique combination of instruments, creating fascinating varieties of color. Extensive and well-explained performance notes on stage positioning, notation, and performance preferences. The vocal line contains many vocal effects, including *sprechstimme*, sonic vocabularies built on the IPA, rhythmic improvisation, unvoiced consonant sounds, speaking, whispering, and sighing. Soprano or lyric mezzo. Difficult.

George Crumb has three other books of madrigals with vocal characteristics similar to those in Book I. All use García Lorca texts. Each is distinctive in color and movement and could be sung by soprano or lyric mezzo.

> *Madrigals, Book II* (1965). Six and a half minutes long. For soprano, flute (also piccolo and alto flute), percussion (one player).
>
> *Madrigals, Book III* (1969). Seven and a half minutes long. For soprano, harp, percussion (one player).
>
> *Madrigals, Book IV* (1969). A nine-minute piece for soprano, flute (also piccolo and alto flute), harp, contrabass, percussion (one player).

George Crumb: *Night of the Four Moons* (1969). Published by C. F. Peters. A sixteen-minute piece for alto, alto flute-doubling piccolo, banjo, electric cello, and percussion. Text by Federico García Lorca in Spanish. In four contrasting movements, variously intense, languid, rhythmically exciting, sensual, dancelike, and frail. An intriguing, beautiful, and memorable piece. Includes a stage picture and movement diagrammed in the preface. Complete descriptions of notation and effects in the preface. The voice part has a low tessitura and contains vocal improvisation, whispering, glissandos, indeterminate pitches, numerous color and expressive changes, and normal legato singing. The singer also plays several small percussion instruments. Alto or mezzo-soprano. Difficult.

Tina Davidson: Unicorn/Tapestry (1982). Text by Maralyn Lois Polak. Available from composer or Beyond Blue Horizon Music. An extended work for soprano or mezzo-soprano, cello, and a prerecorded tape. This work may be performed two different ways. In the first version, the singer is directed to make a tape that contains voices 1 and 2. This tape consists of the poem being spoken or intoned in various manners directed by the score and then played at exact intervals during the live performance. The alternate version can be performed with live female voices of approximately the same voice quality instead of the tape. The vocal line combines some traditional singing with numerous extended techniques, such as nonvibrato, *sprechstimme*, wide vibrato, tongue clicks, speaking or intoning, bending pitches, and breathy sighlike tones. A flexible voice, able to move quickly through the registers, is required. The sequence of pitches written for the voice is quite complex and rarely aided by the cello. This is a wonderful piece for two virtuoso performers who enjoy experimenting with timbre and technique. Soprano or mezzo. Difficult.

Peter Maxwell Davies: Eight Songs for a Mad King (1969). Text by Randolph Stow. Published by Boosey & Hawkes. A thirty-three-minute theater piece for male reciter, flute, clarinet, keyboards, percussion, violin, and cello. The composer's first and most spectacular theater piece. The well-marked score is filled with visual and aural novelties. The vocalist's part is madness personified and directed toward the musicians who are in cages. The text is built on the wild ranting and madness of King George III and is a shocking, extreme use of the voice. The vocal part uses a five-octave range filled with a multitude of vocal effects: glissandos, whispering, speaking, screaming, shrieking, shouting, chording, recitation, bawling, normal singing, and wild ranting on indeterminate pitches. A riveting and memorable dramatic experience for all involved. Tenor. Extremely difficult.

Joel Feigin: Four Poems of Linda Pastan (1987). Unpublished. A fourteen-minute piece for soprano, flute, viola, piccolo, bass clarinet, and piano. There is some whispering and speaking in the voice part. Soprano. Moderately difficult.

Jacqueline Fontyn: Alba (1981). Text by Vincenzo Cardarelli. Published by POM. A fifteen-minute work in three parts for soprano, bass clarinet, cello, percussion or harp, and piano. A combination of traditional notation and free, approximated rhythm and pitch. Thorough explanation of novel notations and vocal requests in the preface. Exotic sound quality in the combination of instruments and voice. Soprano. Difficult.

Jacqueline Fontyn: Rosa, Rosae (1986). Text by Federico García Lorca. Published by POM. A thirteen-minute work for soprano, contralto, clarinet, violin, harp, and piano. All novel notations explained in the preface. Optional percussion instruments for the singers. Rhythmically intricate, angular vocal lines, parlando, slow glissandos, some ad lib vocal declamation. Soprano, contralto. Difficult.

Lukas Foss: *Time Cycle* (1960). Texts by W. H. Auden, A. E. Housman, Franz Kafka, and Friedrich Nietzsche. Published by Carl Fischer, Inc. A thirty-minute work for soprano, clarinet, cello, percussion, and piano-celesta. The four songs are not tied to each other by either a musical motive or a tone row, but they use individual serial devices. There is, however, a literary motive—that of *time*. Each poem refers to time, clocks, or bells. They contain angular vocal lines in metered notation and a few extended techniques: glissando, *sprechstimme*, intoning, and rhythmic unpitched speaking. A mesmerizing piece requiring a solid vocal technique and an outstanding sense of pitch and interval relationships. Soprano. *Difficult.*

Jennifer Fowler: *Letter from Haworth* (1984). Published by Universal Edition (Australia). A fifteen-minute piece for soprano (mezzo), clarinet, piano, and cello with words by Charlotte Brontë. The text comes from a letter that Brontë wrote to her friend and teacher, Monsieur Heger, in 1845. She had become friends with him and they corresponded for a time. The intensity of Brontë's replies put him in a difficult position, and his letters became more and more infrequent. This text is taken from her final letter to him. It is an outburst of grief at her realization that their relationship had ended. The vocal part is quite low in tessitura, and though the score states soprano as the preferred voice, a voice with considerable stamina in the low and middle ranges is required. The singer moves between normal speech, *sprechstimme*, and full voice singing at various times. An excellent description of notations used is in the preface. Even the instrumentalists are required to speak or chant, in a soft husky voice in rhythm with the music. Mixed meters, complex musical lines, and unique text make this a challenging but musically and dramatically satisfying work. Soprano or mezzo. *Moderately difficult.*

Jennifer Fowler: *Tell Out, My Soul* (rev. 1984). Published by Universal Edition (Australia). Listed as a Magnificat for soprano, cello, and piano. Approximately twenty minutes long and a tour de force for all involved. Contains some beautiful vocalises for the soprano that require flexibility and considerable control of dynamics. The wide-ranging vocal part is full of roulades, glissandos, approximate pitches, trills, vocal flourishes, and melismas. Extended solo sections for each musician contrast well with duet and trio sections. A very free display piece, improvisatory, with no meters, some use of modern notations for accelerando, ritard, glissando, approximate pitches, and spacing. Requires a good sense of pitch and great vocal flexibility. Soprano or lyric mezzo. *Very difficult.*

Don Freund: *Backyard Songs* (1990). Text by Gwendolyn Brooks. Published by MMB (ASCAP). A sixteen-minute jazz/blues style piece for soprano, flute, and harp. The voice part contains whispering and speaking. The flute and harp also join in speaking and singing in one section. Soprano. *Difficult.*

Kenneth Gaburo: *Two* (1963). Unpublished. Text by Virginia Hommel. A four minute song for mezzo-soprano, alto flute, and double bass showing great contrast in a short space of time. Sections based on proportional notation measured in seconds. The voice part requires an excellent ear, is rhythmically intricate, and contains a few extended techniques, such as whispers, breathy tones, a squeak, slow glissandos, a wide dynamic and vocal range, and what the composer calls "falsetto." Mezzo-soprano or lyric soprano with solid chest tones. *Difficult.*

Darrell Handel: *Mooncycle* (1980). Text by Paul Verlaine. Available from composer. A twelve-minute song cycle for soprano, viola, and piano. Primarily a tonal, metric work that uses the voice in a traditional manner. Melodic, cantabile vocal lines. Several long, slow glissandos cover a measure or more of music. Brief use of pitched *sprechstimme*. An excellent chamber work for a light, lyric soprano who wants to expand her standard vocal repertoire without too many difficulties in the score. Soprano. *Moderately easy*.

Mark Kilstofte: *Lovelost* (1993). Available from American Music Center. Text based on seven interior fragments of Walt Whitman's poem, "Out of the Cradle Endlessly Rocking." A fourteen-minute chamber work for baritone, flute, clarinet, horn, and a large battery of percussion instruments requiring two players, harp, piano, violin, and cello. The vocal part is mostly traditional. Contains some whispering, parlando, glissandos, and a few stage directions. Requires an excellent musical sense and a secure technique in the upper range. Baritone. *Difficult*.

Barbara Kolb: *Songs Before an Adieu* (1977–1979). Boosey & Hawkes. Texts by five twentieth-century poets: Robert Pinsky, e. e. cummings, Howard Stern, Vasko Popa, and Guillaume Apollinaire. An eighteen-minute cycle of five songs for soprano, flute (alto flute), and guitar. Five pieces that draw on the exquisite and diverse material found in the poems. Some are barren and whispering, one is a dialogue between the sung "soul" and the intoned insistence of our "collective-ness," and another shows off the lyrical qualities of both the flute and the voice. In one piece, the guitarist is asked to speak rather than play. The vocal part is wide ranging in emotion and pitch. It contains beautiful singing, as well as mod-ern nuances, such as speaking, proportional notation, ad lib, free rhythmic move-ment between parts, numerous coloristic designations, and white, empty, vibra-toless sounds. A wonderful atmospheric piece for advanced performers. Unique to this repertoire of music for voice, flute, and guitar. Soprano or lyric mezzo. *Difficult*.

Penka Kouneva: *Aeon* (1993). Available from composer. Texts taken from two Italian madrigals by Gesualdo di Venosa and Torquato Tasso and from a tenth-century sequentia from the codex "Las Huelgas" from Burgos, Spain. For two female voices, piano, percussion, and electric bass. A major addition to the duet repertoire for soprano and mezzo. This hypnotic, ten-minute composition reminds one of earlier historical periods with its melismatic, florid, and technically difficult vocal demands. Contains beautiful cantabile singing plus a large section of syllabic repetition built on the IPA. This work crosses several cultural barriers and allows the singers and listeners to experience a wide realm of colors and musical gestures, from art music to popular idioms. Soprano and mezzo-soprano duet. *Difficult*.

Meyer Kupferman: *Miro, Miro on the Wall* (1995). Soundspells Productions. A twenty-minute solo cantata for soprano, vibraphone, soprano saxophone, double bass, and piano. Jazzy, whimsical piece with glissandi, straight tone, extended range. Soprano. *Very difficult*.

Christina Kuzmych: *To Dust* (1985). Text by Oksana. Available from composer. A fifteen-minute dramatic work that uses glissandi, consonant clusters, tongue clucks, and other effects to be sung and played into the open piano. The text is printed in different size letters and the words are written in circles. The composer suggests, "This piece requires a lot of character acting . . . You are a woman/man who is dying or contemplating death." A wide array of feelings come through—disbelief, fear, rejection, acceptance. The saxophone is the personification of the grim reaper, and the piano personifies the tomb and eternity. Soprano or tenor. *Difficult*.

Marvin Lamb: *Lullaby on a Text by George Barker* (1975). Available from composer. A five-minute, sparsely textured piece for soprano, oboe, clarinet, and piano. Contains proportional notation built on seconds. There are few pitch references but some glissandos, *sprechstimme*, speaking, and whispering. Soprano. Difficult.

Thomas Oboe Lee: *I Never Saw a Butterfly* (1991). Text taken from children's poems from Terezin concentration camp (1942–1944). Available from composer. A twelve-minute work for voice, clarinet, and piano. Contains *sprechstimme*, spoken freely. Mezzo. Difficult.

Ruth Lomon: *Symbiosis (the intimate living together of two dissimilar organisms in a mutually beneficial relationship)* (1983). Available from the composer, the American Music Center, or the Library of George Washington University. An exotic, twelve-minute work for mezzo-soprano, piano, and percussion with texts taken from a variety of sources, including the Sermon on the Mount. The singer participates in creating some of the unusual sounds, such as bursting a balloon with a pin, singing through a paper towel roll, clicking the tongue on the hard palate, and playing a mouth organ. The voice part contains beautiful melodic lines, melismas, syllabic repetition, approximate pitches, and glissandos. It is suggested that the vocalist could enhance the drama by wearing a traditional ancient Babylonian costume, which might include draped shawls over a straight tunic, with fringe or tassels as decoration. Mezzo-soprano. Moderately difficult.

Ursula Mamlok: *Der Andreas Garten* (1987). Text by Gerard Mamlok. C. F. Peters Edition. A fifteen-minute piece in German for soprano, flute, and harp with whispering and speaking as well as normal singing. Soprano. Difficult.

Walter Mays: *Flowers of Silence* (1978). Available from composer at Wichita State University. Five songs on texts taken from poetry of the Bauls of India. A compelling, demanding, fourteen-minute piece for soprano and chamber ensemble: alto flute in G, piccolo, oboe, B-flat clarinet, bassoon, trumpet in C, trombone, two percussion, piano, celesta, harp, three violins, one viola, cello, one double bass. A combination of expressive melodies and extended techniques, including straight tone, breathy quality, glissandi, *sprechstimme*, intoning of text in upper register, and speaking. Soprano. Difficult.

Francesco Núñez: *Flores con luz de luna* (1982). Text by composer. Available from composer. A six-minute work for flute, piano, and medium voice with *sprechstimme*, indeterminate pitches, and singing into the piano. Soprano or lyric mezzo. Moderately difficult.

Rhian Samuel: *The Witch's Manuscript* (1985). Text by Carol Rumens. Published by Stainer & Bell. A brief work of fantasy and drama for female voice and brass quintet; piano reduction available. Primarily a traditional use of the voice with a wide vocal range, large leaps, great dramatic contrasts, and two sudden outbursts of pitched shouting that encompasses only the head voice range. Requires a voice capable of easily achieving enough vocal power to match the instruments. Soprano. Moderately difficult.

Murray Schafer: *Beauty and the Beast* (1979). Text by composer after the story by Madame Lepribce de Beaumont. Arcana Editions, Canada. A twenty-eight-minute mono-drama for soprano with string quartet. The voice part includes *sprechstimme* and speaking. The singer uses masks. Soprano or lyric mezzo. Moderately difficult.

Murray Schafer: *Patria II (Requiems for the Party Girl)* (1969). Available from Clark and Cruickshank, a division of Berandol Music Limited, Toronto. A dramatic, eighteen-minute piece for soprano, flute-piccolo, B-flat clarinet, horn, harp, piano, violin, viola, cello, and one percussionist. Extended techniques include wide vibrato, *sprech-stimme*, straight tone, whispering, glissandi, and vocal "scream." Soprano or lyric mezzo. Difficult.

Arnold Schoenberg: *Pierrot Lunaire, Op. 21* (1912). Text by Albert Giraud with German text by Otto Hartleben. Often performed in English. Published by Universal Edition or Kalmus. A twenty-five-minute setting of twenty-one poems for voice, piano, flute/piccolo, clarinet/bass clarinet, violin/viola, and cello. Schoenberg's final composition of his atonal period. Employs *sprechstimme* throughout with both rhythms and approximate pitches notated. Conventional singing appears in only seven of the twenty-one poems and usually applies to only a word or two. Most effective when performed in costume. Soprano or mezzo-soprano. *Very difficult.*

Thomas Schudel: *A.C.T.S.* (1986). Text by Anne Campbell. Available from composer or Canadian Music Centre. A fourteen-minute extended work for narrator, flute, oboe, clarinet, double bass, and percussion (one player). A musically conservative work, melodic and rhythmically inventive with shifting colors and moods throughout six short movements. The narrator is used in two ways. Sometimes the voice is given exact rhythms on which to speak; other sections are spoken freely over an instrumental accompaniment. A diction workout. The narrator should have a clear, well-placed, projected speaking voice in a medium range. Unique piece, good for someone beginning to explore new musical styles. Any voice type. *Moderately easy.*

Thomas Schudel: *Edging Out* (1987). Text by Anne Campbell. Available from composer or Canadian Music Centre. A gentle ten-minute piece for soprano, flute, oboe, and vibraphone. Melodic and tonal music. The voice part is mainly traditional with short bits of whispering and a few glissandos. A wonderful, lively, straightforward piece. Soprano or lyric mezzo. *Moderately easy.*

Thomas Schudel: *Queer Cornered Cap* (1982). Text by Anne Campbell. Available from composer or Canadian Music Centre. A fifteen-minute chamber-theater piece for mezzo-soprano, flute, and marimba. Includes stage directions that diagram specific positions for each musician during the performance of the work. The piece is divided into eleven sections of contrasting moods and instrumental combinations. The performers sometimes walk around the stage while they are playing or singing. The vocal part is a combination of traditional singing, speaking, glissandos, *sprechstimme*, whispering, and singing in a blues style. In one of the final sections all three musicians speak rhythmically, inflecting their voices so that different pitches occur. The inflected pitches of the instrumentalists' voices would naturally be different according to their sex and voice type, creating a totally different composite sound, characteristic of the makeup of the ensemble. Mezzo or soprano. *Moderately difficult.*

Ann Silsbee: *Only the Cold Bare Moon* (1970). Available from composer or American Composer's Alliance. A twenty-minute song cycle on eight Chinese prose poems for soprano, flute, and prepared piano. The preface gives explicit directions for the preparation of the piano and explanations for vocal and flute notation. The rhythm is proportionate, and durations are shown by horizontal lines to which the note stems are attached, measured against a space-time scale indicated at the beginning of each song. The realization of this piece depends on a felt sense of pacing and a symbiotic relationship among the three performers. The vocal part contains glissandos, *sprechstimme*, intoning, and speaking. A delicate, ethereal, and effective piece with contrasting, coloristic sounds from all performers alone and in combination. Soprano or lyric mezzo. *Moderately difficult.*

Steven Stucky: *Sappho Fragments* (1982). Text by Sappho. Theodore Presser Co. An emotionally expressive, twelve-minute piece for voice, flute, clarinet, violin, cello, piano and percussion that includes *sprechstimme* with normal singing. Soprano or lyric mezzo. *Moderately difficult.*

Karen A. Tarlow: *Renascence* (1981). Text by Cornell Lengyel. Published by Smith College New Valley Music Press. Three songs, approximately ten minutes long, for clarinet, piano, soprano. Primarily a traditional use of the voice with a few *sprechstimme* tones. Soprano. *Moderately difficult.*

Kenneth Timm: *Three Poems of e. e. cummings.* Available from composer. A ten-minute cycle of three songs for soprano, flute, percussion, and piano. Whimsical brilliantly set and depicted texts. The voice part is high and mostly traditional with some effects: portamenti, whispering, quirky-sounding *sprechstimme*, childlike tones, and indeterminate glissandos. Soprano. *Moderately difficult.*

Reza Vali: *Seven Persian Folk Songs (Set A)* (1989). Folk song texts. Published by MMB, St. Louis. An eighteen-minute piece for soprano, flute, clarinet, harp, piano, viola, cello, double bass, and vibraphone. In addition to *sprechstimme*, the voice also imitates the ornamentation and melismas idiomatic to Persian and Azerbaijani styles of folk singing. Soprano. *Difficult.*

Persis Vehar: *Three from Emily* (1984). A nine-minute song cycle to poems by Emily Dickinson. Leyerle Publications. Scored for high voice, cello, and piano. The three songs offer great contrast in mood from simplicity to playfulness and drama. Both singer and pianist add percussive effects by tapping on the piano or music stand with the fist. The vocal line is traditional with an occasional glissando and some speaking. Tenor or soprano. *Moderately easy.*

Elizabeth Vercoe: *A Dangerous Man* (1991). Text from various sources, including John Brown, Henry David Thoreau, the Kansas Slave Code, Jefferson Davis, and the *New York Herald*, among others. Available from composer. A thirty-five-minute monodrama for baritone and piano on the life of John Brown. A riveting, intense piece and a tour de force for both musicians. Very dramatic. Requires a good, resonant speaking voice and the capability to achieve great dramatic and dynamic contrasts in the singing voice. Stage lighting and a simple costume are required. Slides of Brown and his contemporaries and of Kansas and Harpers Ferry could be used to create a set. Contains unmetered sections, slow glissandos, recitation, dramatic speaking (both pitched and unpitched), rhythmically notated stage whispers, inflected shouts, and numerous descriptive and dramatic directions for voice declamation. Could work in a number of concert or operatic settings. Baritone. *Very difficult.*

Elizabeth Vercoe: *Herstory I* (1975). Texts by Anne Sexton, Adrienne Rich, Sylvia Plath, and Pam White. Published by Arsis Press or available from American Composer's Alliance. A twenty-minute song cycle for soprano, vibraphone, and piano. Exotic sound resources with creative use of the voice and instruments. Each of the seven songs is unique in sound quality, vocal declamation, and mood. The voice part is angular at times and requires an excellent sense of pitch and rhythm, a capability of achieving numerous subtle dynamic changes, and a wide vocal range. Extended techniques include *sprechstimme*, intoning, glissando, exaggerated portamento, novel notations for rhythms and spacing, free rhythmic movement, and a little whispering. Soprano. Difficult.

Elizabeth Vercoe: *Herstory II* (1979). Thirteen Japanese lyrics translated by Kenneth Rexroth. Published by Arsis Press. For soprano, piano, and percussion. Approximately twenty minutes long. A feast for the accomplished soprano who loves to show great variety of color, declamation, and effects in the voice. Requires great flexibility, a fluid technique, and a wide vocal range. Contains normal singing, *sprechstimme*, exaggerated portamento, pitched speaking, unpitched speaking, whispering, and numerous vocal color and dramatic declamation indications. A work with major dramatic impact. Soprano or lyric mezzo. Difficult.

Elizabeth Vercoe: *Herstory III: Jehanne de Lorraine* (1986). Published by Arsis Press. A twenty-five-minute monodrama for voice and piano about the life of Joan of Arc. Contains dramatic and contrasting musical styles and effects. The text is taken from several sources. Joan is seen through the words of Francois Villon, Mark Twain, William Shakespeare, Joseph Chenier, George Bernard Shaw, Christine de Pisan, and Regine Pernoud. Several small percussion instruments and mallets are needed since the pianist often creates extraordinary atmospheric sounds inside the piano. A large gong is also used and can be played by the pianist or the singer. Not intended as a concert piece, but rather as a dramatic performance; Joan of Arc should be in character throughout. The singer wears a simple pale costume. There could be a few props. Two microphones are required, one for the piano to amplify the interior effects and another for the singer to use backstage. The work is in twelve sections, three of which are extensive dramatic readings with no music underneath. The singing voice is used in several effective ways: normal cantabile, *sprechstimme*, whispering, and theatrical intoning. This extraordinary work would be a wonderful second half for any vocal recital and would require minimum time to set the stage at intermission. It could also be paired with another chamber opera for a more dramatic evening. Mezzo or soprano. Difficult.

Elizabeth Vercoe: *In the Storm* (1989). Texts by Ingeborg Bachmann. Available from composer. A ten-minute cycle of four songs for voice, clarinet, and piano. Full of undulating rhythms and changing timbres and colors. The piece utilizes vocal contrast and flexibility to the fullest. Contains some *sprechstimme* and glissandos and is useful for building dramatic imagination within a short time span.) Mezzo soprano or baritone. *Moderately difficult.*

James Vernon: *The Lost Path* (1992). Text by Elinor Wylie. Unpublished. An extended work in five movements for soprano, string ensemble, piano, and timpani. Mostly traditional singing with some *sprechstimme*, glissandos, ad lib rhythmic movement, and unpitched recitation. Soprano. Difficult.

Heitor Villa-Lobos: *Poêma da criança e sua mamã* (1929). Text by composer. Published by Max Eschig. A conversational, seven-minute work for voice, flute, clarinet, and cello with some indeterminate pitches. Soprano or lyric mezzo. *Moderately difficult.*

Carol Ann Weaver: *Five Voices of Earth* (1983). Canadian Music Centre. Text by Henry David Thoreau. A beautifully crafted, musically exotic fifteen-minute piece for tenor, mandolin, harmonium, grand piano, and electric piano. The tempo is fluid throughout. The vocal part is made up of traditional legato singing, as well as some vocal effects: whispering, glissandos, vowel morphing, half-spoken sounds, a few breathy tones, falsetto, and scat singing. This is an unusual work for tenor. It contains many vocal techniques rarely found in music for male voices. Medium tessitura with a few higher notes. Tenor. *Moderately difficult.*

Carol Ann Weaver: *Timbrel in Her Hand* (1987). Canadian Music Centre. Text by Judith Miller. Published by University of Waterloo Press. A forty-five-minute music drama that deals with the lives of a few Old Testament women. Weaver also included some of her own lyric poetry as a response to what she was seeing in the Old Testament lives. Scored for soprano, reader/dancer, keyboards, and mandolin. Contains many contrasting performance styles ranging from recitative to jazz, spoken poetry to rap, and lyrical singing to funk. The soprano voice is used in the following ways: bel canto/lyric; jazz waltz; hard swing/funky; senza-vibrato/declamatory, and recitative/chant. The reader can be male or female and may also serve as the dancer. He or she reads freely at times and otherwise intones in notated rhythms. The soprano voice is treated traditionally within several musical styles. There are a few whispered tones. A mesmerizing, futuristic crossover work. Could be performed in a traditional concert setting, in a religious context, or in a festival about women. Reader: male or female voice; soprano or lyric mezzo for singing role. *Moderately difficult.*

Judith Weir: *King Harald's Saga* (1979). Published by Novello. A ten-minute grand opera in three acts for unaccompanied solo soprano singing eight roles. Based on the saga "Heimskringla" by Snorri Sturleson, 1179–1241; describes the Norwegian invasion of England in 1066 led by King Harald. No set or staging is required. Traditional use of the voice, except that the soprano gives a short spoken introduction to each act to establish the staging. Soprano. *Very difficult.*

Richard Wernick: *A Prayer for Jerusalem* (1971, rev. 1975). Published by Theodore Presser Co. A ten-minute work for mezzo-soprano and percussion. The singer also plays chimes. Intricate rhythmic passages, angular vocal lines, wide vocal range, and mathematically determined time values. The vocal line is a phonetic setting in Hebrew of portions of Psalm 122. The score states, "It reflects the composer's own feelings, as distilled through a thousands of years old document, concerning the post-1967 status of the city of Jerusalem." The voice part requires great flexibility to maneuver between registers and make large leaps. Includes numerous grace notes extreme dynamic ranges, stage whispers, and unmetered phrases built on the phonemes in the Hebrew text. Mezzo-soprano. *Very difficult.*

James Willey: *The Death of Mozart* (1975, rev. 1980). Published by Leyerle Publications. A theater piece for soprano, narrator, and chamber ensemble of flute/piccolo, oboe/English horn, percussion (four timpani, tambourine, sand blocks, triangle, suspended cymbal, pair of cymbals, pedal cymbals, large cowbell, tam-tam, small gong, vibraphone, tubular bell, two wood blocks, xylophone, ratchet, three tom-toms, snare drum, small bass drum, large bass drum), and cello, plus technicians and a conductor. A skillfully crafted musical setting of the almost totally incorrect account of Mozart's death contained in Rev. D. H. Mansfield's *The American Vocalist*, published in 1849. The silliness of this fallacious account is captured wonderfully through beautiful, chameleon like color changes, vocal and instrumental absurdity, tour-de-force requirements, and incidental use of popular styles such as rock, march, soft-shoe, and waltz. Stage setup in preface. Elaborate stage directions for action and characterization. The narrator should be a man with a soothing voice quality who can also play Mozart. He always speaks with a microphone. His declamation is intoned with specific rhythms at times and free natural speech at others. The soprano sings traditionally throughout. A stunning addition to any concert or opera evening. Male voice and coloratura soprano. Difficult.

Chen Yi: *As in a Dream* (1988). Text by Li Qing-zhao. Theodore Presser Co. A seven-minute atmospheric piece for soprano, violin, and cello in Chinese. Contains glissandi, slides, and sprechstimme. Soprano. Difficult.

Judith Lang Zaimont: *From the Great Land* (1982). Text by Frank Buske. Available from composer. A cycle of seven songs for mezzo-soprano, clarinet, piano, and Eskimo drum. A diagram of the desired stage picture is given in the preface. Rather low tessitura, numerous interpretative descriptions, and meter changes. The voice sings primarily in a traditional manner, but there are short sections of rhythmic speaking, using native Eskimo words. The seven songs cover a wide range of emotional and theatrical expression, describing life in the cold north. Mezzo-soprano. *Moderately difficult.*

Ramon Zupko: *La Guerre* (1965). American Music Center. Text by e. e. cummings. An eighteen-minute piece for female voice, clarinet, piano, vibraphone, and percussion. Filled with unusual sound effects, as well as distinct vocal and instrumental colors. The voice part includes pitchless sounds—mostly consonants; approximate pitches, half-spoken, half-sung, quasi-parlando; speaking with the inflection indicated by a curve; glissandos; and IPA phonemic pronunciation. The vocal range and dynamic range is very wide. The numerous novel notational gestures are explained in the preface. A memorable vocal display piece. Soprano or lyric mezzo. *Very difficult.*

SOURCES FOR COMPOSER
AND SCORE LOCATION

The following sources will be helpful in finding contact information about living composers and published or unpublished scores and their location. Relevant contact information is included for each source, current at the time of this printing. Some sources are repositories of music and composer information, while others are organizations to which a composer may belong, thereby making the contact information available for interested performers and researchers. In the latter case, the source may be able to provide composer phone numbers and street or e-mail addresses.

Many organizations and repositories have Web sites. Information on these sites changes daily. The repository sites listed and many others can be accessed by typing in key words such as "contemporary American composers" or "contemporary Italian composers." Most sites list biographical notes, works by composers, and where to access the music. In addition, personal Web sites are becoming prominent avenues for composers to make their works available to performers, since publishing companies are printing fewer new scores and often letting standard pieces go out of print. An investigation of Internet possibilities should be done during any search for a composer and his or her music.

SOURCES

African American Art Song Alliance
  Dr. Darryl Taylor
  The University of Northern Iowa
  School of Music
  110 Russell Hall
  Cedar Falls, Iowa 50614-0246
  www.uni.edu/taylord/joinus.html

American Composer's Alliance
  73 Spring Street, Rm. 506
  New York, N.Y. 10012

(212) 362-8900 (voice)
(212) 941-9704 (fax)
E-mail: info@composers.com
webmaster@composer.com
www.composers.com

American Composers Forum
332 Minnesota Street, Suite E-145
Saint Paul, Minn. 55101–1300
(651) 228-1407 (voice)
(651) 291-7978 (fax)
E-mail: mail@composersforum.org
www.composersforum.org

American Music Center
30 West 26th Street, Suite 1001
New York, N.Y. 10010–2011
(212) 366-5260 (voice)
(212) 366-5265 (fax)
E-mail: center@amc.net
www.amc.net
www.NewMusicBox.org

American Society of Composers, Authors, and Publishers (ASCAP)
ASCAP Building
One Lincoln Plaza
New York, N.Y. 10023
(800) 95-ASCAP (voice)
(212) 595-3276 (fax)
www.ascap.org

Archiva della musica italiana contemporanea (AMIC)
AMIC
Ligo di Torre Argentina
11-00186 Roma
++39 06 68190650 (voice)
++39 06 68190651 (fax)
E-mail: amic@amic.it
www.amicitalia.net

British Music Information Centre
10 Stratford Place
London W1C 1BA
0207 499 8567 (voice)
0207 499 4795 (fax)
E-mail: info@bmic.co.uk
www.bmic.co.uk

Broadcast Music, Inc. (BMI)
320 W. 57th Street
New York, N.Y. 10019
(212) 586-2000

E-mail: nashville@bmi.com
newyork@bmi.com
losangeles@bmi.com
london@bmi.com
http://bmi.com

Cadenza (contemporary music and musicians, resources, and information)
+44 (0) 20 8840 1564
E-mail: webquery@cadenza.org
www.cadenza.org

The Canadian Music Center
Chalmers House
Bibliotheque Ettore Mazzoleni
20 St. Joseph Street
Toronto, ON M4Y 1 J9
(416) 961-6601 (voice)
(416) 961-7198 (fax)
E-mail: info@musiccentre
www.musiccentre.ca

Center for the Promotion of Contemporary Composers (CPCC)
P.O. Box 631043
Nacogdoches, Tex. 75963
E-mail: cpcc@under.org
www.under.org

Classical Composers Database: Links
http://utopia.knoware.nl~jsmeets/abc.htm

College Music Society
202 West Spruce Street
Missoula, Mont. 59802
(406) 721-9616 (voice)
(406) 721-9419 (fax)
E-mail: cms@music.org
www.music.org

Czech Music Information Project (CzechArt agency)
U dubu 401
252 31 Vsenory
Czech Republic
+420 603 832561 (voice)
+420 2 9919528 (fax)
E-mail: mail@czechart.cz
www.czechart.cz/about.html

Donne in musica (women composers)
Sedde di Fiuggi
Teatro Comunale, Piazza Trento e Trieste
03014-Fiuggi Fr
Italy
www.donneinmusica.org

Une Galerie de compositeurs (French composers)
    www.france.diplomatie.fr/culture/france/musique/composit

Gaylord Music Library Necrology file
    Gaylord Music Library
    Gaylord Hall
    6500 Forsyth Blvd.
    St. Louis, M. 63105
    (314) 935-5563 (voice)
    (314) 935-4263 (fax)
    E-mail: music@library.wustl.edu
    http://library.wustl.edu/units/music

Institut de Recherche et Coordination Acoustique/Musique (IRCAM)
    IRCAM Centre Pompidou
    1 Place Igor Stravinsky
    75004 Paris
    01 44 78 48 43 (voice)
    01 44 78 15 40 (fax)
    E-mail: Diane.Liote@ircam.fr
    www.ircam.fr

Latin American Music Center
    School of Music
    Indiana University
    Bloomington, Ind. 47405
    (812) 855-2991 (voice and fax)
    E-mail: lamc@indiana.edu
    www.music.indiana.edu/som/lamc

Living Music Foundation
    Dr. Charles Norman Mason
    900 Arkadelphia Road
    Box 549033
    Birmingham Southern College
    Birmingham, Ala. 35254
    E-mail: lmhome@orion.e-universe.com
    www.e-universe.com/lmhome/index.htm

International Alliance for Women in Music (IAWM)
    IAWM Administrative Office
    Department of Music
    422 S. 11th Street, Rm. 209
    Indiana University of Pennsylvania
    Indiana, Pa. 15705-1070
    (724) 357-7918 (voice)
    (724) 357-9570 (fax)
    http://music.acu.edu/www/iawm
    Queries to: Sally Reid, IAWM list owner
    E-mail: reid@acu.edu

Sigma Alpha Iota (Composers Bureau Online)
  E-mail: webmaster@sai-national.org
  www.sai-national.org/phil/composers/composer.html

Society of Composers, Inc. (SCI)
  170 West 74th Street
  New York, N.Y. 10023
  (646) 505-0207 (voice and fax)
  E-mail: secretary@societyofcomposers.org
  www.societyofcomposers.org

Southeastern Composers League
  www.runet.edu/~scl-web

Anderson, Doug. *Jazz and Show Choir Handbook*. Chapel Hill, N.C.: Hinshaw Music, 1978.

Anderson, Doug. *Jazz and Show Choir Handbook II*. Chapel Hill, N.C.: Hinshaw Music, 1993.

Austin, William. *Music in the 20th Century*. New York: W. W. Norton, 1966.

Balk, H. Wesley. *The Complete Singer-Actor: Training for Music Theater*. Minneapolis: University of Minnesota Press, 1978.

———. *The Radiant Performer: The Spiral Path to Performing Power*. Minneapolis: University of Minnesota Press, 1991.

Barlow, Wilfred. *The Alexander Technique: How to Use Your Body without Stress*. Rochester, Vt.: Healing Arts Press, 1990.

Borroff, Edith. *Three American Composers*. Lanham, Md.: University Press of America, 1986.

Caldwell, J. Timothy. *Expressive Singing: Dalcroze Eurhythmics for Voice*. Englewood Cliffs, N.J.: Prentice-Hall, 1995.

Cope, David. *New Music Notation*. Dubuque, Iowa: Kendall/Hunt Publishing Company, 1976.

———. *Techniques of the Contemporary Composers*. New York: Schirmer Books, 1997.

Cott, Jonathan. *Stockhausen: Conversations with the Composer*. New York: Simon and Schuster, 1973.

Dalmonte, Rossana, and Bálint András Varga. *Luciano Berio: Two Interviews*. New York: Marion Boyars, 1985.

Doscher, Barbara M. *The Functional Unity of the Singing Voice*. Metuchen, N.J.: The Scarecrow Press, 1994.

Dunsby, Jonathan. *Schoenberg, Pierrot Lunaire*. Cambridge: Cambridge University Press, 1992.

Emmons, Shirlee, and Stanley Sonntag. *The Art of the Song Recital*. New York: Schirmer Books, 1979.

Emmons, Shirlee, and Alma Thomas. *Power Performance for Singers: Transcending the Barriers*. New York: Oxford University Press, 1998.

Green, Barry. *The Inner Game of Music*. London: Pan Books, 1987.

Griffiths, Paul. *Cage*. New York: Oxford University Press, 1981.

———. *A Concise History of Avant-Garde Music from Debussy to Boulez*. New York: Oxford University Press, 1978.

———. *Peter Maxwell Davies*. London: Robson Books, Ltd., 1982.

Hall, William D. "Choral/Vocal Concepts." American Choral Directors National Convention, Chicago. Photocopy, 1999.

Hanson, Peter S. *An Introduction to Twentieth-Century Music*. Boston: Allyn and Bacon, 1967.

Harvey, Jonathan. *The Music of Stockhausen: An Introduction*. Berkeley: University of California Press, 1975.

Ives, Charles. *114 Songs*. Reprint, New York: Associated Music Publishers, 1975.

Kagen, Sergius. *On Studying Singing*. New York: Dover Publications, 1950.

Karkoschka, Erhard. *Notation in New Music*. New York: Praeger Publishers, 1972.

Koblyakov, Lev. *Pierre Boulez: A World of Harmony*. New York: Harwood Academic Publishers, 1990.

Leyerle, William D. *Vocal Development Through Organic Imagery*. New York: Leyerle Publications, 1987.

Mabry, Sharon. "Twelve Poems of Emily Dickinson by Aaron Copland: A Stylistic Analysis" and "Vocal Problems in the Performance of Schoenberg's *Pierrot Lunaire, Opus 21*." D.M.A. diss., George Peabody College for Teachers, 1977.

Maconie, Robin. *The Works of Karlheinz Stockhausen*. New York: Oxford University Press, 1990.

Manning, Jane. *New Vocal Repertory: An Introduction*. New York: Oxford University Press, 1994.

———. *New Vocal Repertory 2*. London: Oxford University Press, 1998.

McKinney, James C. *The Diagnosis and Correction of Vocal Faults*. Nashville: Genevox Music Group, 1994.

Miller, Richard. *The Structure of Singing*. New York: Schirmer Books, 1986.

Moriarty, John. *Diction*. Boston: E. C. Schirmer, 1975.

Nyman, Michael. *Experimental Music: Cage and Beyond*. New York: Schirmer Books, 1974.

Payne, Anthony. *Schoenberg*. London: Oxford University Press, 1968.

Peyser, Joan. *Boulez*. New York: Schirmer Books, 1976.

———. *The New Music*. New York: Delacorte Press, 1971.

Pooler, Frank. *New Choral Notation*. New York: Walton Music Corporation/Hal Leonard, 1973.

Proctor, Donald F. *Breathing, Speech, and Song*. Vienna: Springer-Verlag, 1980.

Read, Gardner. *Music Notation: A Manual of Modern Practice*. New York: Taplinger Publishing Company, 1979.

———. *Source Book of Proposed Music Notation Reforms*. New York: Greenwood Press, 1987.

Risatti, Howard. *New Music Vocabulary: A Guide to Notational Signs for Contemporary Music*. Urbana: University of Illinois Press, 1975.

Rockwell, John. *All American Music: Composition in the Late Twentieth Century*. New York: Da Capo Press, 1997.

Sataloff, Robert Thayer. *Vocal Health and Pedagogy*. San Diego: Singular Publishing Group, 1998.

Shaw, Kirby. *Vocal Jazz Style*. Milwaukee: Hal Leonard Publishing Corporation, 1998.

Stein, Erwin, ed. *Arnold Schoenberg Letters*. New York: St. Martin's Press, 1958.

Stone, Kurt. *Music Notation in the Twentieth Century: A Practical Guidebook*. New York: W. W. Norton, 1980.

Turek, Ralph. *The Elements of Music: Concepts and Applications*. New York: Alfred A. Knopf, 1988.

Wall, Joan, Robert Caldwell, Tracy Gavilanes, and Sheila Allen. *Diction for Singers*. Dallas: Pst., 1990.

Ware, Clifton. *Basics of Vocal Pedagogy: The Foundations and Process of Singing*. Boston: McGraw-Hill, 1998.

Wellesz, Egon. *Arnold Schoenberg Chamber Music*. Seattle: University of Washington Press, 1972.

accelerando, notation for, 66–67
ad lib, 31–33
Albert, Thomas, 21, 108
aleatoric (chance) music, 32, 61
"Amor" (Bolcom), 114
Anagrams (Kagel),133
Ancient Voices of Children (Crumb), 30, 97, 127
Anderson, Doug, 115
Anderson, Laurie, 23
Apparition (Crumb), 109
Ashley, Robert, 23
augenmusik, 62

Babbitt, Milton, 21, 108
Balk, Wesley, 20, 25, 90
Barber, Samuel, 21
Bennett, Richard Rodney, 23
Berberian, Cathy, 44, 123
Berio, Luciano, 21, 23, 123, 128, 131
Bolcom, William, 114, 129
Bond, Victoria, 23, 114, 128
Boulez, Pierre, 69, 122
Britten, Benjamin, 10
Bussotti, Sylvano, 75

Cabaret Songs (Bolcom), 114
Cage, John, 11, 21, 23, 45

Carpenter, John Alden, 10
chance music. *See* aleatoric music
Chanler, Theodore, 21
"Charlie Rutlage" (Ives), 92–93
Circles (Berio), 123, 128
composer collaboration, 19
concert venues, innovations, 6–8
Cope, David, 62, 74, 75
Copland, Aaron, 10, 45, 50
Cowboy Songs (Thomas), 89
Crawford Seeger, Ruth, 11
Credentials (Haubenstock-Ramati), 131, 137
Crumb, George, 21, 30, 97, 109, 127

Dallapiccola, Luigi, 11
Davies, Peter Maxwell, 107, 129
DeGaetani, Jan, 44, 80
Die glückliche Hand (Schoenberg), 78
Duke, John, 10

education of children, 6
Eight Songs for a Mad King (Davies), 129
electronic tape synchronization, 62
Eleven Songs for Mezzo-soprano (Rochberg), 39–40, 63, 74–75, 133
Emmons, Shirley, 41, 42, 80
Erwartung (Schoenberg), 78

ether-machine, 1
exercises
    to develop a flexible vibrato, 47
    for imagery practice, 50–51
    for nontextual sonic vocabularies, 119–121
    proportional notation, 71–73
    sprechstimme and recitation, 102–104
    unpitched rhythmically free speaking, 89–91
experimental declamation, 29
extended ranges, 29–31

Fach system, 29–30
Forever and Sunsmell (Cage), 45
frame notation, 67–71

Gaburo, Kenneth, 63
Glass, Philip, 21, 23
"Going to Heaven!" (Copland), 45
Griffes, Charles, 10
Griffiths, Paul, 122, 123

Haiku Settings (Powell), 133
Handel, Darrell, 100
Haubenstock-Ramati, Roman, 131, 137
Herstory 1 (Vercoe), 128
Herstory 111: Jehanne de Lorraine (Vercoe), 88
"He Tipped the Waiter" (Bolcom), 129
Humperdinck, Englebert, 77
Hundley, Richard, 21

Il Cantico Dei Cantici 11 (Le Fanu), 75
Il Nudo (Bussotti), 131
improvisation, 31–33
indeterminacy, 61–62
indicative notation, 60–61, 87
International Phonetic Alphabet (IPA), 107–110
interpretation, text analysis, 35–38
intoning. See recitation
Ives, Charles, 10, 18, 21, 92–93, 138
Ivey, Jean Eichelberger, 23

Johnston, Benjamin, 74

Kagel, Mauricio, 107, 133
Karkoschka, Erhard, 53, 54–55, 67–68
Kilstofte, Mark, 128
King's Singers, The, 44
Königskinder (Humperdinck), 77
Kuzmych, Christina, 113–114, 137, 138

LeFanu, Nicola, 75
"Look Down Fair Moon" (Rorem), 45
Lovelost (Kilstofte), 128

Madrigals, Books 1 and 11 (Crumb), 97
Manning, Jane, 123
Maze with Grace, A (Albert), 108
"Memories" (Ives), 138
mental imagery, 42, 48–51
microtones
    description of, 73–75
    how to perform, 75–76
mixed media, 23
Molly Manybloom (Bond), 128
Morricone, Ennio, 21
musical graphics, 62, 87
musical organization, unfamiliar, 10

Night of the Four Moons (Crumb), 97
Nine Epigrams from Poor Richard (Vercoe), 109
Nono, Luigi, 107
nontextual sonic vocabularies
    exercises for, 119–121
    how to do, 110
    and the IPA, 107–110
    nonsense syllables used in, 112–116
    practice plans for, 110–112, 116–117
    and scat singing, 114–116
    and use of vowel morphing, 109
    vocal considerations in, 117–119
    and the vocalise, 105–107
notation
    deciphering of, 56–57
    and experimentation, 53–55
    and improvisation, 60–62
    novel systems for, 55–56
    rhythm and spacing, 59–60

Oliveros, Pauline, 21

Pazmor, Radiana, 1
performance art, 23
performance personality, developing, 24–27
personality pieces, 18
perspective, historical, 1–3, 10–11
Pierrot Lunaire, Op. 21 (Schoenberg), 78–79, 124
pitch
    angularity and complexity, 33–34
    security, developing confidence, 34–35
Poulenc, Francis, 10
Powell, Mel, 133
proportional notation
    definition of, 61
    depicting space in, 64–65
    depicting speed in, 66–67
    and frames, 67–71
    how to do it, 64, 65–66, 69–71
    and structure, 63–73
    vocal exercises for, 71–73
    what it sounds like, 63, 65, 69–71
psychic freedom, 11

quarter tones, 74–75

Read, Gardner, 83, 93
recitation
    characteristics of, 88–89
    and composer usage, 87
    a definition of, 77
    with designated rhythms, 92–96
    exercises for, 89–91, 102–104
    how to do, 89, 93–96, 97–99, 100–102
    pitched or intoned, 96–102
    unpitched rhythmically free, 87–91
repertoire choices
    accessible versus inaccessible, 15
    for diction development, 17–18
    and performance considerations, 14
    uses for specific, 18–19
    and vocal considerations, 15–17
Risatti, Howard, 124, 134
ritardando, notation for, 66–67

Rochberg, George, 21, 39, 63, 74–75, 133
Rorem, Ned, 45

Samuel, Rhian, 69
Sataloff, Robert, 43
Scat 2 (Bond), 114
scat singing, 114–116
Schäffer, Boguslaw, 68
Schoenberg, Arnold, 11, 21, 78–79, 124
Schudel, Thomas, 23
Sequenza III (Berio), 131
Shapes and Sounds IV (Kuzmych), 113–114, 137, 138
Sonntag, Stanley, 80
"Sounds and Words" (Babbitt), 108
spatial notation, 65
sprechgesang, 77
sprechstimme
    exercises to develop, 102–104
    fixed pitch, 77–87
    notational intent of, 60
    a practice plan for, 83–87
    text inflection in, 81–82
    and Schoenberg, 78–79
    use of glissando in, 80–81
    and vibrato, 81
    and vocal registers, 82–83
Stockhausen, Karlheinz, 69
Stone, Kurt, 64, 74, 127, 136
Stravinsky, Igor, 11

Thomas, Alma, 41, 42
Thomas, Karen P., 89
Three Birdsongs (Handel), 100
Three Poems of e. e. cummings (Timm), 128
Timm, Kenneth, 128
Topofonica (Schäffer), 68
Turek, Ralph, 61
Two (Gaburo), 63

unaccompanied recitation, 87–89

verbal cues, 61
Vercoe, Elizabeth, 21, 23, 88, 109, 128
versatility, developing

versatility, developing (cont.)
   definition for, 19–20
   with experimental works, 23–24
   through mental imagery, 20–21
   while playing instruments, 21
   and spontaneity, 22–23
   through text declamation, 21–22
vibrato, deletion of, 43–47
vocal coloration
   and choice, 48–51
   and imagery, 48–51
   and mind-body coordination, 41–42
   and muscle coordination, 40–41
   singer or composer control of, 39–40
   skill development for, 42–43
   and vibrato, 43–47
   and visualization, 41
vocal effects
   and composer usage, 123–124
   definition of, 29, 123
   falsetto or hollow tone, 132–133
   glissando, 134–136

   heavy breathing, 131–132
   laughter, 125–127
   shouts, 129–131
   tongue click and cluck, 136
   tongue trills, 136–138
   tremolo muting, 133–134
   vocal muting, 138–140
   whispered tones, 127–129
   whistling, 138
vocal lines, nontraditional, 28–29
vocal registers, 16–17
vocal skills, development, 11–13
Voices (Zupko), 30, 109, 131
voice teacher, influence of, 9
vowel morphing, 109

Ware, Clifton, 16, 107
Webern, Anton, 11
"World Feels Dusty, The" (Copland),
   50

Zupko, Ramon, 21, 30, 109, 131